Meaningful METRICS

A 21st-Century Librarian's Guide to Bibliometrics, Altmetrics, and Research Impact

Robin Chin Roemer & Rachel Borchardt

Saginaw Chippewa Tribal College
2274 Enterprise Drive
Mt. Pleasant, MI 48858

Association of College and Research Libraries
A division of the American Library Association
Chicago, Illinois 2015

The paper used in this publication meets the minimum requirements of American National Standard for Information Sciences–Permanence of Paper for Printed Library Materials, ANSI Z39.48-1992. ∞

Library of Congress Cataloging-in-Publication Data

Meaningful metrics : a 21st century librarian's guide to bibliometrics, altmetrics, and research impact / edited by Robin Chin Roemer and Rachel Borchardt.
   pages cm
Includes bibliographical references and index.
   ISBN 978-0-8389-8755-1 (pbk. : alk. paper) -- ISBN 978-0-8389-8757-5 (epub) -- ISBN 978-0-8389-8756-8 (pdf) -- ISBN 978-0-8389-8758-2 (kindle) 1. Bibliometrics. 2. Bibliographical citations--Evaluation. 3. Scholarly publishing--Evaluation. 4. Research--Evaluation--Statistical methods. 5. Communication in learning and scholarship--Technological innovations. I. Roemer, Robin Chin, editor. II. Borchardt, Rachel, editor.
   Z669.8.M43 2015
   010.72'7--dc23
                2015006338

Copyright ©2015 by The Association of College & Research Libraries, a division of the American Library Association.

All rights reserved except those which may be granted by Sections 107 and 108 of the Copyright Revision Act of 1976.

Printed in the United States of America.
19 18 17 16 15   5 4 3 2 1

Table of Contents

Foreword v

PART 1. IMPACT
Chapter 1: Understanding Impact 3
Chapter 2: Impact in Practice 13

PART 2. BIBLIOMETRICS
Chapter 3: Understanding Bibliometrics 27
Chapter 4: Bibliometrics in Practice 71

PART 3. ALTMETRICS
Chapter 5: Understanding Altmetrics 99
Chapter 6: Altmetrics in Practice 155

PART 4. SPECIAL TOPICS
Chapter 7: Disciplinary Impact 181
Chapter 8: Impact and the Role of Librarians 209
Glossary 233
Acknowledgments 239
About the Authors 241

Foreword

A few days ago, we were speaking with an ecologist from Simon Fraser University here in Vancouver about an unsolicited job offer he'd recently received. The offer included an astonishing inducement: Anyone from his to-be-created lab who could wangle a first or corresponding authorship of a *Nature* paper would receive a bonus of $100,000.

Are we seriously this obsessed with a single journal? Who does this benefit? (Not to mention, one imagines the unfortunate *middle* authors of such a paper, trudging to a rainy bus stop as their endian-authoring colleagues roar by in jewel-encrusted Ferraris.) Although it's an extreme case, it's sadly not an isolated one. Across the world, a certain kind of administrator is doubling down on 20th-century, journal-centric metrics like the impact factor.

That's particularly bad timing because our research communication system is just beginning a transition to 21st-century communication tools and norms. We're increasingly moving *beyond* the homogeneous, journal-based system that defined 20th-century scholarship.

Today's scholars increasingly disseminate *web-native scholarship*. For instance, Jason's 2010 tweet coining the term "altmetrics" is now more cited than some of his peer-reviewed papers. Heather's openly published datasets have gone on to fuel new articles written by other researchers. And like a growing number of other researchers, we've published research code, slides, videos, blog posts, and figures that have been viewed, reused, and built upon by thousands all over the world. Where we do publish traditional journal papers, we increasingly care about broader impacts, like citation in *Wikipedia*, bookmarking in reference managers, press coverage, blog mentions, and more. You know what's not capturing any of this? The impact factor.

Many researchers and tenure committees are hungry for alternatives, for broader, more diverse, more nuanced metrics. Altmetrics are in high demand; we see examples at Impactstory (our altmetrics-focused nonprofit) all the time. Many faculty share how they are including downloads, views, and other alternative metrics in their tenure and promotion dossiers and how evaluators have enthused over these numbers. There's tremendous drive from researchers to support us as a nonprofit, from faculty offering to pay hundreds of extra dollars for profiles to a Senegalese postdoc refusing to accept a fee waiver. Other altmetrics startups like Plum Analytics and Altmetric can tell you similar stories.

At higher levels, forward-thinking policy makers and funders are also seeing the value of 21st-century impact metrics and are keen to realize their full potential. We've been asked to present on 21st-century metrics at the NIH, NSF, the White House, and more. It's not these folks who are driving the impact factor obsession; on the contrary, we find that many high-level policy-makers are deeply disappointed with 20th-century metrics as we've come to use them. They know there's a better way.

But many working scholars and university administrators are wary of the growing momentum behind next-generation metrics. Researchers and administrators off the cutting edge are ill-informed, uncertain, afraid. They worry new metrics represent Taylorism, a loss of rigor, a loss of meaning. This particularly true among the majority of faculty who are less comfortable with online and web-native environments and products. But even researchers who are excited about the emerging future of altmetrics and web-native scholarship have a lot of questions. It's a new world out there, and one that most researchers are not well trained to negotiate.

We believe librarians are uniquely qualified to help. Academic librarians know the lay of the land, they keep up-to-date with research, and they are experienced providing leadership to scholars and decision-makers on campus. That's why we're excited that Robin and Rachel have put this book together. To be most effective, librarians need to be familiar with the metrics research, which is currently advancing at breakneck speed. And they need to be familiar with the state of practice—not just now, but what's coming down the pike over the next few years. This book, with its focus on integrating research with practical tips, gives librarians the tools they need.

It's an intoxicating time to be involved in scholarly communication. We've begun to see the profound effect of the web here, but we're just at the beginning. Scholarship is on the brink of a Cambrian explosion, a breakneck flourishing of new scholarly products, norms, and audiences. In this new world, research metrics can be adaptive, subtle, multidimensional, responsible. We can leave the fatuous, ignorant use of impact factors and other misapplied metrics behind us. Forward-thinking librarians have an opportunity to help shape these changes, to take their place at the vanguard of the web-native scholarship revolution. We can make a better scholarship system, together. We think that's even better than that free Ferrari.

Jason Priem
Heather Piwowar
Cofounders of Impactstory

Section 1
IMPACT

Chapter One

Understanding Impact

Once upon a time, there was no such thing as bibliometrics. Like its conceptual predecessor, statistical bibliography, bibliometrics is a concept predicated on the widespread existence of printed material and the acceptance of a specific printed format (the journal article) as a fundamental means of communication between scholars and experts within a field. Within library and information science (LIS), we have seen many excellent books and articles published over the last 20 years, each telling its own version of the history of bibliometrics and predicting what lies in store for scholars and practitioners of bibliometrics with new advancements in technology, research methods, and general higher ed.

This is not one of those books. This is a book that tells stories—some of which are about bibliometrics, others of which are about altmetrics, but all of which are about impact and human beings' never-ending quest to measure, track, and compare their value.

At this point, let's take a moment to reflect on what we mean when we say the word *impact*, particularly in the context of an academic book. Impact is a word that we in the LIS field hear and use every day, yet it can be a surprisingly tricky word to define, at least without lots of additional context. For example, researchers in public health would certainly be disappointed by an English department's assessment about what it means for faculty to produce "impactful" scholarship. This is because impact is a word with a variety of subtle definitions, each changing over time and with different audiences, geographies, and local institutional philosophies. The result is a curious situation, often making it easier for academics to focus on personal techniques for measuring impact—citation counts, indices, journal rankings—than to engage in larger conversations about what impact means for and across their respective disciplines. This gap is unfortunate for both individual academics and their institutions alike in that it delays sharing new ideas and observations about what it means for scholars in a given field to engage meaningfully with one another or with their target audiences. We will discuss the various disciplinary definitions of impact in more detail later. For now, however, it is important for us to understand impact as a term that generally encompasses two important principles: first, *effect*, in the sense of a perceptible shift, change, or influence; and second, *force*, in the sense of the strength or degree of this effect. The two-part determination of where a work can be said to have an effect and to what extent the force of this effect can be quantified and benchmarked is what makes impact such a complex and potentially broad-reaching conversation that many stakeholders can offer valuable perspective.

This issue of stakeholders brings us back to the purpose of this book: to provide librarians and LIS researchers with a collection of stories on the subject of impact that they can use to build their own conversations and add their own contextualizing chapters to. Some of you, especially those of you who are not librarians or LIS students, may wonder why we have chosen to address this population as our primary audience rather than faculty or researchers in a specific academic field or discipline. The question is a good one and deserves a chapter of its own (see Chapter 8). However, for purposes of this introduction, we will simply point out that librarians are, and have been for many decades, crucial connectors between faculty, departments, and university administrators. They are used to telling stories to an academic audience, whether to faculty about the metrics administrators value for purposes of tenure and promotion or to administrators about the support that faculty need to apply for grants and perform essential research. LIS researchers are similarly well positioned because of the multi- and meta-disciplinary nature of their work with patterns of information.

That said, these stories can't translate into action without the understanding and help of enthusiastic faculty and innovative administrators, so this book will also explore their needs, challenges, and opportunities, particularly in partnership with libraries.

Now let us move on to three additional questions for understanding the premise and organization of this book, starting with the measurement of impact itself.

What Do We Get When We Measure?

The first thing to know when it comes to measuring impact is that it is, strictly speaking, totally impossible. As an abstract human concept—like *power* or *worth* or *cool*—impact is inherently immeasurable. Still, much like the "ultimate question of life, the universe, and everything" in Douglas Adams' *Hitchhiker's Guide to the Galaxy* trilogy, impact is stubbornly viewed in academia as a question that must be answered, whether that answer is *42* or *50 citations* or a *$1,000,000 research grant*.

To understand what we get when we measure impact, we must jump back to what we actually mean when we talk about particular impact metrics. When we say, for instance, that a journal has an impact factor of three, what we mean is that *in the last three years, this journal averaged three citations per published article*. Does this mean if we publish in this journal we will have achieved impact? Not really, but it does tell us something about citations, which historically have been viewed as the best available approximations of academic impact. Indeed, the entire field of bibliometrics is based around the acceptability of this sort of substitution. But what we get when we count citations or perform analysis on book and article bibliographies is just that: information about citation patterns. It is only when we start to tell stories with these numbers (e.g., "my average is higher than your average") that we get to a place where impact can thrive. It's a small distinction but an essential one, particularly as we tackle our preconceptions and prejudices about the "legitimacy" of different impact metrics. This brings us to the second fundamental question of this book, regarding the need to move beyond the limits of citation-based impact indicators.

Why Move Beyond Bibliometrics?

As we will discuss further in Part 2, the field of bibliometrics developed in a fundamentally different era of scholarship and culture, back when libraries were all about "the stacks" and university professors were predominantly tenured, white, and male. Since then, not only have technology and faculty demographics changed dramatically, but academic pressures to demonstrate impact have also significantly risen. At the same time, academia has seen faculty research shift along increasingly complex interdisciplinary and subdisciplinary lines—both of which frustrate efforts to standardize expectations for citation-based impact. Consequently, it is now more necessary than ever that the suite of metrics we use today is able to keep up with rapid developments in the landscape of academic knowledge. To say we must move beyond bibliometrics is, quite simply, to observe that bibliometrics can no longer represent the full spectrum of impact available to researchers in the 21st century. It is not that we must abandon bibliometrics entirely, far from it. However, by moving to embrace a fuller scope of metrics—one more in sync with the changes in practice and audience being seen in the current scholarly environment—we move significantly closer to fulfilling the needs of faculty across and within their areas of specialization.

This brings us to the third and arguably biggest question behind the premise of this book: the need to incorporate alternative web-based metrics into our scholarly portfolios and practices.

Why Do We Need Altmetrics?

Once we accept the idea that bibliometrics are not always sufficient to satisfy the impact-related needs of scholars, the next challenge is to understand the value of altmetrics, such as the specific advantages and disadvantages they offer in mapping the modern impact landscape. A common argument made against altmetrics, for instance, is their seeming lack of interest in distinguishing between points of engagement that happen within the scholarly sphere and those that occur in wider public forums, such as Twitter. However, if one recalls that the ultimate goal of collecting metrics is to accurately measure the impact of scholarship in general as well as within various key communities, we can see that altmetrics offer a means to collect metrics different from what we have used in the past and an opportunity to understand these new metrics in their emerging context. This is important for a number of reasons.

First, and perhaps most crucially, impact metrics are used by faculty in a variety of high-stakes evaluative situations, including applications for tenure, promotion, and research funding. For a career academic, it is essential that these metrics be understood accurately and in context by administrators and faculty members who may not be familiar with a given researcher's discipline or subdiscipline; otherwise, a lack of understanding may lead to unfair comparisons to highly disparate fields. As more academics enter the workforce, the competition and pressure to succeed in a tenure-track position increases. Consequently, many universities place an increasing importance on the ability of pre-tenure hires to demonstrate quantitative impact to ensure that departments retain only the best and most productive researchers. This shift places the burden of proof squarely on individuals, who are often unaware or untrained in how best to prove their worth in the fields and types of research they are pursuing. Thus, in the largest sense, altmetrics are needed for their power to change the course of academics' lives and for their ability to demonstrate the impact of research—particularly certain forms of publicly oriented research—in a dimension of scholarly communication that was not previously quantified or open for discussion.

A second factor in the present-day need for altmetrics is the sheer expansion of the amount of published research available to scholars via the Internet and other online or electronic resources. For more than 50 consecutive years, the US has seen a roughly 3% annual increase in the number of journal articles published.[1] The result of this growth is that academics are having a more difficult time than ever keeping up with and sorting through the journal articles and other published literature of their respective fields. One solution to this problem has been to use quantitative methods to judge the relative quality of research, including the impact that specific publications have had on similar scholarly communities. However, the simultaneous increase in interdisciplinary, multidisciplinary, and subdisciplinary research areas has created an environment that makes it difficult for individual researchers to determine what "similar" scholarly communities are, an obstacle that further frustrates attempts to measure the quality of published work. For instance, if a chemistry professor writes an article about the role that the media plays in influencing the adoption of chemical research findings in the context of daily life, how is he or she to know whether the resulting publication's impact metrics are best compared to those of articles from the fields of chemistry, communication, or public health? With different impact norms and expectations in each of these fields, the perceived impact of such an article would vary greatly depending on the context the article is presented in. With altmetrics, researchers have an opportunity not only to look for areas of influence outside of traditional disciplinary boundaries but to gather clues as to the scope of their influence outside of formal academic communities—information that may help balance citation-based metrics and broaden disciplinary expectations for researcher influence. In the third part of this book, we examine in depth how altmetrics offer a supplemental solution to the dual problems of information overload and impact silos and how it encourages scholars to broaden their definition of what it means to be part of a scholarly community. In part four, we return to the enormous challenge of satisfying the impact measurement needs of both disciplinary and interdisciplinary researchers as we identify special issues that continue to challenge and shape the future of both altmetrics and bibliometrics.

While quantitative pressures on tenure-track faculty and shifts in the boundaries of scholarly communication comprise the two of most common arguments in favor of altmetrics adoption, readers from within the LIS community will also recognize a third factor: the perpetual problem of university funding and subscription costs. For more than a decade, academic libraries have witnessed the double-edged sword of swiftly rising e-resource costs and decreasing collections budgets, to the point that many libraries have had to face cutting what in other years might have been considered core subscriptions. Sadly, this means that few institutions can afford to subscribe to more than one of the two major resources known for generating highly regarded bibliometric impact measurements—Web of Knowledge by Thomson Reuters and Scopus by Elsevier—and many more cannot afford to subscribe to either. For this reason, the new wave of free or low-cost web-based altmetrics tools have the potential to enhance, and perhaps even someday replace, expensive subscription-based bibliometric tools, particularly if they continue to work in complement to other free impact measuring resources, such as the downloadable program Publish or Perish or the increasingly popular Google Scholar Profiles tool. Once again, this is not to say that the big names in bibliometrics are on their way out anytime soon. Yet to deny that altmetrics are part of the future of impact measurement is to deny both the opportunities that altmetrics offer and the needs of researchers for updated resources and quantitative options related to 21st-century scholarship and impact. Thus, in the final chapter of this book, we discuss the responsibility that librarians have to follow trends in impact from bibliometrics to altmetrics and the various ways that librarians themselves can benefit from getting involved with such metrics today.

And so, at last, we come back to the book you hold in your hands and the stories it offers on impact and its various schools of measurement.

How to Use this Book

This book is divided into four thematic parts: impact, bibliometrics, altmetrics, and special topics. Each part is designed to take readers on a detailed and practical tour of the trends, topics, and tools currently at play within the theme at hand, while at the same time showing key points of overlap with other thematic areas. Any one of these parts may therefore be read on its own as an exploration of a limited piece within the greater puzzle of impact measurement. However, for readers new to metrics or looking to gain a greater understanding of the past and future directions of impact measurement, we encourage you to consider approaching the chapters sequentially.

Another organizational structure you will notice in this book is the inclusion of "in practice" chapters, which intersperse more information-driven "understanding" chapters within some thematic sections. Such chapters speak to the nature of this book as both an introductory text and a practical guide to the many ways that LIS professionals and researchers can engage with impact within the context of their daily lives. Additionally, many chapters include anecdotes, advice, and scenarios from current practitioners within the field, from academic librarians to the metric tool creators. These voices help tell alternative stories about the challenges and opportunities of engaging with impact measurement, and they can help interested readers identify further ideas for resources, discussions, and partnerships at their local or home institutions.

How Not to Use this Book

Like other areas of librarianship, including medical and legal librarianship, working in the field of impact measurement has the potential to result in profound effects on the users with whom we work. A librarian who has read the literature and followed up with the tools available is more than qualified to offer information to a faculty member or researcher on the options available for measuring impact. At the same time, however, the information a librarian offers should not be considered legally binding advice; the application of metrics to any situation is ultimately up to the individual user, for better or worse. This case applies equally in the application of information gathered in the course of reading this book: It is up to each of you, as individual readers, to determine the best and most responsible way to use the information you find in its pages. To treat this book as list of prescriptions for which approaches impact should be taking place at your campus, institution, or workplace is to misunderstand the complexity of the local academic climate and the diversity of needs that researchers have when it comes to measuring impact. For this reason, we ask again that you use this book as a presentation of stories and options, some of which may resonate with you and some of which may not. What you decide to do next is ultimately up to you—just as what your users do is ultimately up to them.

Additional Resources

National Science Foundation (NSF) Grant Proposal Guide
>An online guide to grant proposals provided by the NSF. Like many funding agencies, NSF requires applications to include a description of both the expected intellectual merit of each proposal and the broader impact of the related research. ***http://www.nsf.gov/pubs/ policydocs/ pappguide/nsf13001/gpg_2.jsp***

Harvard Medical School and School of Dental Medicine's Promotion Policies
An example of an academic unit's specialized promotion policies, in this case for Harvard's Medical School and School of Dental Medicine. Note that "demonstrated impact" is required of candidates at virtually every stage of promotion. This requirement is common to many faculty promotion policies. *http://www.fa.hms.harvard.edu/administratorresources/appointment-and-promotion/promotion-policies/*

University of Pennsylvania Wharton School's Social Impact Initiative
An online resource of the University of Pennsylvania's Wharton School of Business that makes clear the specific emphasis placed by the university on tracking the impact of the school in ways that transcend traditional scholarly definitions. Many professional schools are similarly rethinking their "impact stories" to include populations beyond the walls of academia, such as the public sphere. *http://socialimpact.wharton.upenn.edu/faculty-research/*

Association of American Colleges & Universities' (AACU) High-Impact Educational Practices
AACU's Liberal Education and America's Promise (LEAP) approaches higher education impact from another perspective beyond research: high-impact teaching, education, and practice. This online help page provides academic practitioners with plenty of practical tips and helpful guidance. *http://www.aacu.org/leap/hips*

Notes

1. Mark Ware and Michael Mabe, *The STM Report: An Overview of Scientific and Scholarly Journal Publishing* (The Hague, Netherlands: International Association of Scientific, Technical, and Medical Publishers, 2012), *http://www.stm-assoc.org/2012_12_11_STM_Report_2012.pdf*

Chapter Two

Impact in Practice

When broaching the topic of impact with someone, one of the biggest challenges is figuring out how to move away from the sweeping generalizations that the term can inspire to a more grounded territory of values, professional standards, and existing practices.

Within the internal context of academic libraries, for example, impact may at times be closely tied to university systems' mission statements and strategic plans and at other times be described in terms of national reputation, individual participation on external committees, or publication in peer-reviewed venues. This range of meaning only gets wider as we move to larger university populations, which inevitably lack a common vocabulary for describing their methods, venues, and approaches to producing output. Without the knowledge of common ground or language, how does one begin to talk with users about the pursuit of "impactful" activities? Or perhaps more usefully, what are librarians already doing to introduce curious faculty to the broader world of impact?

In this chapter, we briefly examine how to initiate and develop conversations about impact and how to translate these conversations into more specific considerations of how to measure impact appropriately and effectively.

Library Practices for Discussing Impact

Outside of questions of impact within the LIS profession, most public-facing librarians encounter impact for the first time as part of discussions with faculty or researchers who are preparing for a major evaluative event, such as a review for tenure or promotion. As mentioned in Chapter 1, researchers today face more pressure than ever to provide evidence of influence on their field of study or on surrounding areas of scholarship and practice. That such faculty choose to approach librarians with their questions and concerns is an encouraging sign of trust—yet it is also a precarious and stressful scenario for librarians who feel unprepared to answer such questions or who are unsure of how to introduce faculty to the options best suited to their current portfolio of work.

The following strategies represent two ways that librarians have frequently chosen to engage faculty on the general topic of impact. Furthermore, as we will find in subsequent In Practice chapters, they are also techniques that work for addressing the major subtopics of impact, altmetrics and bibliometrics.

One-on-One Consultations

One solution to this scenario is, of course, to focus first on ferreting out the specific needs and assets of the individual researcher—a classic reference interview approach, the strength of many librarians who spend regular hours on reference desks or in other modes of public consultation. Knowing some information about a researcher's area of specialty and the type of work he or she has produced (or are planning to produce) as part of his or her evaluation is incredibly helpful and can save both of you from pursuing options that are a poor match for the field and practices at hand. An up-to-date curriculum vitae, faculty website, or other professional profile can be a great starting tool for understanding a researcher's record and areas of self-articulated interest.

Another aspect of the impact conversation is to identify and analyze the set of external expectations and standards that have shaped the researcher's understanding of what it means to be impactful in his or her field. For instance, if working with a faculty member who will soon be going up for tenure or promotion, tailor the conversation according to the various guidelines for achieving a new rank that may already exist at both the departmental and university levels. This same common sense vetting applies to researchers who are fulfilling requirements of grant applications, project reports, or other initiatives that already include some guidelines on the subject of impact. Admittedly, in many of these cases, the guiding document's language will be vague, and thus open to a generous amount of researcher interpretation. However, it benefits no one to ignore the information that is already available in the context of the researcher's goal—acknowledge that because this information exists, it will help ground the researcher in the midst of other impact uncertainties. Additionally, in a few cases, departments or institutions may have very strict prescriptions for what it means to be impactful in the field, such as a specific list of "top" journals that faculty are strongly encouraged (or required) to publish in. Such cases do not necessarily mean that there is no value in helping the faculty member gather alternative and additional evidence of impact, but it certainly puts a high priority in meeting the expectations as they have been articulated.

> "Important elements in evaluating the scholarly ability and attainments of faculty members include the range and variety of their intellectual interests; the receipt of grants, awards, and fellowships; the professional and/or public impact of their work; and their success in directing productive work by advanced students and in training graduate and professional students in scholarly methods."
>
> —Sample language from the University of Washington Faculty Code and Governance[1]

A third consideration when discussing impact is the set of personal practices and beliefs that each researcher brings to the table—that is to say, how they go about identifying impactful literature within their area of specialization and what actions they already take to track and tout the impact of their work. This is a surprisingly sensitive area of discussion for some academics (including librarians) because our knowledge of what constitutes the "best" means of identifying quality information is, in practice, significantly different from how we actually gather information on a daily basis. A researcher, for example, may regularly read articles in the online open access journal *First Monday,* yet express concern during a conversation about the impact of publishing her work in any journal that does not appear in print. Likewise, a graduate student may mention to a librarian in passing that he actively uses Twitter at academic conferences to follow interesting sessions and interact with other attendees but has never thought to save the tweets generated by his own conference presentations in addition to noting session attendance. Listening carefully to where users gather and value information can help librarians further understand any unique tensions or cohesions in the relationship between standards and practices within the field's discussion of impact. This is not to say that revealing such dynamics will allow the librarian to go about "solving" them for the researcher—no more than a librarian can solve every research problem that she runs across in a traditional reference interaction. What it does accomplish, however, is the laying of groundwork for more specific advice and assistance, from delving into specific tools for gathering metrics related to the researcher's work, to a general discussion of the levels and types of impact metrics that may best move him or her forward in light of upcoming needs and roadblocks.

> According to a 2013 survey of 8,000 teaching faculty conducted by Babson Survey Research Group and Pearson, 55% of faculty reported using social media in a professional context ("any aspect of their profession outside of teaching").[2]

Proactive Outreach and Resources

Another approach to discussing impact that is becoming popular with libraries is the proactive creation of resources related to impact measurement. Guides and other library-curated research portals aimed at raising researcher awareness of impact can be readily found online (for examples see Additional Resources at the end of this chapter) and can be easily promoted to faculty, staff, and administrators at orientations, departmental meetings, and in e-mails to relevant listservs. Some librarians have also reported success in offering workshops on the general topic of impact to select departments and campus populations at large. However, the demand for such workshops will inevitably depend on the understanding that users already have about impact and the relevance of impact metrics to their unique academic goals. For this reason, librarians new to impact outreach may choose to begin on a more grassroots level by initiating meetings with researchers from relevant campus populations before deciding how next to invest their time.

Talking about Metrics in Terms of Levels

The concept of metrics levels may seem odd at first, given that so far we have only discussed impact as a single term, albeit with many potential definitions. Still, when introducing researchers to impact and its value to their work output, levels can be a useful way of organizing impact and preparing them for the overwhelming number of measurement options that are available. To explain that impact metrics can measure qualities at four different levels is less intimidating than to launch into a comprehensive list of metrics that a faculty member might want to access by signing up for service X or searching database Y. What's more, metric levels have the advantage of being a concept that can easily bridge the worlds of bibliometrics and altmetrics—a nice bonus for librarians who are trying to communicate the value of both approaches to a skeptical or uncertain user.

Let's now take a look at four levels that you can use to talk to academics about impact metrics. Later, in Parts 2 and 3 of this book, we will go into more detail about the bibliometrics and altmetrics that correspond to each of these levels and how to find, use, and calculate them effectively.

Level 1: Individual Scholarly Contributions

Individual scholarly contributions are the basic building blocks that all other impact measurements are based on. This level includes the block that most people think of when they talk about impact: journal articles. However, individual scholarly contributions include not only journal articles, but also books and book chapters; blogs and individual blog posts;

conference proceedings; posters and presentations; data sets; programming code; inventions and patents; poetry, fiction, essays, music scores, and other creative works; lesson plans; and so forth. Not surprisingly, given this range of individual contributions, the metrics on this level can vary wildly. Some metrics rely on specific and relatively objective moments of engagement like citations, mentions, views, and downloads of the contribution, while others rely on more nuanced and subjective engagements like audience size, evaluations, and formal or informal assessment feedback. Perhaps the important thing to keep in mind when dealing with this first level is that individual contribution metrics stem from the shift of the mere production of scholarship to the measurement of how a piece of scholarship was received and who it affected. From this perspective, it's no longer enough to say, "I presented at a conference!" Instead, researchers must use measurements like audience size, presentation feedback, and Twitter mentions to provide evidence that others found their presentation meaningful in some way.

You may note that some of the measurements mentioned on this level are qualitative—that's okay! The impact of an individual contribution can't always be measured in numbers, nor should it be. Sometimes, one published review or evaluation says more than a whole page of numbers does.

Level 2: Venues of Production

The second level of metrics is the first of the "macro" levels—those based on individual scholarly contributions aimed at a larger impact setting. In this case, the larger setting is comprised of venues that produce individual scholarly contributions and the quality that can be assigned to each venue based on its output, reputation, or exclusivity. Due to the journal article's dominance in many disciplines, the most well known of these venues by far is the academic journal—but venue could just as easily refer to a book publisher or editor, conference, or performance setting. You can compare the impact of this level to getting into an exclusive nightclub: How hard is it to get into the nightclub, and how well known is it? What is the average quality of the acts that perform in it, and what do they go on to do afterwards, career-wise? Some disciplines have very specific metrics to determine quality at the venue level, such as the well-known impact factor, while others have less-defined standards, such as a group of top-tier publishers commonly agreed on within the discipline. Other metrics that arise from this level include acceptance rate, number of subscribers, and affiliation of some sort with impactful peers.

Level 3: Individual Authors

Similar in certain ways to level two, the third level of metrics introduces even more meta-analysis as it considers the impact of an individual author over the course of his or her career. While interest has grown in the tracking of individual output over time, there are still only a few well-known individual-level metrics available, the most prominent being the calculation of impact as measured by average citations each year or average number of views, occasionally balanced by the number of trackable works that the individual has authored. The h-index, which we discuss in Part 2, is perhaps the best example of this supposedly balanced approach. However, it is worth mentioning that both early career academics and authors with a variety of types of scholarly contributions may have difficulty applying an author-level metric to measure their portfolio. Thus author-level metrics are typically best reserved for researchers who already have a substantial record of output, particularly those whose outputs favor formats that have been trackable via a consistent method (e.g., citations) for many years.

Level 4: Groups and Institutions

The fourth and final metric level is the newest, and it represents an interesting and important trend within both bibliometrics and altmetrics. As with the increase in pressure on individual researchers to quantify their scholarly impact, so too has pressure increased for departments, labs, schools, and even whole academic institutions to justify their impact relative to their peers. One big reason for this shift is the competition for funding support, both from the government at large and specific funding agencies. Offices that support research on college campuses have a keen and obvious desire to determine whether to invest funds in one research center over another as well as to know whether such funding is worth renewing given the center's subsequent record of impact. As such, funding bodies and institutions themselves are turning to this level of macro-level metrics, which target output and quality aggregated at the level of an academic group. As one might expect, these metrics require even more meta-analysis than the author-level ones in Level Three, restricting them (for now) to the analysis of group journal article output, and even then mostly within the sciences. That said, altmetrics toolmakers, such as Plum Analytics, have also begun to tackle the idea of institutionally aggregated metrics in earnest, and we can expect that more of these metrics will appear on researcher radars in the future.

Moving Forward

So far in this chapter we have looked at the ways librarians can successfully break down the concept of impact when meeting with researchers—but what about those of us still not comfortable initiating such conversations with researchers on our campuses? Broaching the topic of impact can indeed be an intimidating prospect for librarians, particularly those of us

> ### Off the Shelf: Scenarios for Discussion
> Review each scenario below and consider how you might respond to it as the librarian involved: *What information do you have, and what do you most need to know in order to proceed? What questions or concerns arise as you imagine what might come next?*
>
> ▼ A graduating PhD student sends you an e-mail asking which journals are the most impactful to his field in hopes of publishing his most recent article in the best venue.
>
> ▼ A researcher tells you that the funding agency for her grant is now asking for evidence of impact on the resulting research from the grant. The resulting research included several national and international conference presentations, journal publications, and write-ups of her research in blogs within her. She then asks you for suggestions on how to document that impact.
>
> ▼ A tenure-track faculty member who has published articles and monographs is going up for promotion in six months and wants to know what impact metrics he can include to supplement his file.

not used to thinking about impact as part of our professional outreach to faculty. Nevertheless, it's important to remember that impact is already an important part of researchers' lives, whether they consciously know it or not, and that bringing it up can be as simple as offering a conversation or pointing out a resource that's already folded into a library's collection. Talking about impact is arguably more about having confidence in one's own working knowledge of impact as it is about finding opportunities to speak with researchers on the subject. Thus, to conclude this chapter, let's take a look at some easy techniques that librarians and budding LIS professionals can use to prepare themselves to move forward on the subject of impact with confidence.

▼ **Develop your definition of impact.** One of the best ways to grow your confidence on the subject of impact is to practice defining impact in your own words, whether by saying it out loud or writing it down on a piece of paper. What are the words, terms, and artifacts that come to mind when you think about impact within higher education? Take time to reflect on these initial associations, and then work over time to refine them into a short, accurate statement of what impact means to you and your peers.

▼ **Prepare an elevator speech.** New librarians may be surprised to discover that opportunities to engage with students, researchers, and/or administrators on issues relating to metrics can happen at any time—not just at formal meetings or appointments. For this reason, preparing a very short speech or sequence of simple points that convey key messages about impact can help you take advantage of these opportunities whether they arise in an office or while walking across the street with a faculty member.

▼ **Plan key messages for different audiences.** Just as preparing a general elevator speech about impact can be an excellent step toward engaging with researchers about impact, the development of specialized speeches—targeted to the needs of different researcher populations—can help academic librarians think through the different ways that impact may be initially interpreted across their campuses. A graduate student, for instance, will be most receptive to statements about impact that apply to the building of a professional reputation, while a campus administrator will likely be most interested in statements that highlight institutional reach and reputation. For an excellent example of what real-world planning of messages for different audiences can look like, see Table 2.1, provided courtesy of Nazi Torabi at McGill University.

Table 2.1. Sample Key Messages Chart

Audience	Top Messages to Communicate	Rational for Why These Messages Should be Delivered	Suggested Mood of Delivery
• University administration • Research Unites • IT department	The need for a strategic plan for highlighting university's new publications in social media	Overall citation metrics may improve when new findings are disseminated via social media.	Library initiative by Dean of the library or the library administration
	Establish standards and policies in using platforms and tools for capturing research outputs.	Having standardized processes and tools in place for things like author identification and peer network dissemination will make it easier for the university and research units to gather and report university's research outputs.	
• Department deans • Promotion and Appointment committees	Shortcomings and strengths of all bibliometrics and altmetrics tools in evaluating research outputs and research impacts	In order to have a fair and equitable process during promotion, tenure, and hiring.	Formal training/workshop sessions should be offered to faculty
• Faculty • Research fellows	• How to calculate their h-index • How to set up their profile		Face-to-face/word of mouth or informal training sessions
• Novice researchers • Graduate students	Be aware of author's name variations. Make sure you always publish under same name.		Orientation session/Face-to-face/word of mouth or informal training sessions

▼ **Start looking at other library's research guides.** Browsing other research guides can not only prepare you to create your own guide but can also give you a feel for how other librarians organize metrics issues into key topics, which areas they've chosen to emphasize, and how the information is delivered. A Google search for "bibliometrics or metrics or altmetrics (library or libguides or research) site:.edu" will bring up plenty of examples. We also suggest looking closely at guides from libraries on campuses with similar faculty, student, and program demographics to your own.

▼ **Browse a local faculty manual.** Faculty manuals are extensive documents that help guide the activities, goals, and priorities of researchers at an academic institution, particularly around evaluation hurdles like tenure and promotion. When getting ready to talk seriously about impact with a faculty population, we suggest that you look at your institution's faculty manual (if available), specifically at any language related to the expectations for scholarship and research. Knowing how faculty are expected to perform in terms of research and scholarship can help librarians better anticipate the hopes, fears, questions, and ambitions that researchers bring to discussions of impact. Additionally, as many faculty departments have their own unique sets of scholarly evaluation guidelines, which may include suggestions about use of metrics, you will also want to see if copies of these documents can be obtained and reviewed. Taking these extra steps can provide librarians with early insight into the "citation culture" of their departments or institutions.

▼ **Talk informally with researchers.** Last but not least, a great way to become more comfortable talking about impact with researchers is simply to begin doing so on a casual or informal basis. Early career researchers, for instance, may welcome the opportunity to talk with people outside their departments about the ways scholars in their field are expected to prove their impact or about areas of confusion in the path to tenure. Likewise, more experienced researchers are often happy to talk about how they advise new researchers to plan their impact or to share personal stories of how they've succeeded in becoming impactful. The key in either case is to build on existing informal relationships with faculty and to preserve a sense of trust and confidentiality as befits any casual encounter between colleagues.

Additional Resources

"Research Impact," Yale University Library

This guide provides an excellent example of an online introduction to the topic of impact, including a mix of resources representing both bibliometrics and altmetrics. Note that the authors have chosen to add a Creative Commons license to the "Getting Started" homepage. *http://guides.library.yale.edu/impact*

"Research Impacts Using Citation Metrics," University of California Irvine Libraries

While focused primarily on citation-based definitions of impact, this guide, originally created by LIS student Laine Thielstrom in 2012, presents a robust introduction to the various levels of impact metrics available to researchers, including article impact, author impact, journal/ source impact, and institutional impact. *http://libguides.lib.uci.edu/researchimpact-metrics*

"Scholarly Impact Tools," Georgia State University Library

Another impact-focused research guide, this resource by Georgia State University librarian Brenna Helmstutler includes links to external resources on the use of impact metrics on a CV as well as information about upcoming workshops related to scholarly impact for faculty and graduate students. *http://research.library.gsu.edu/si*

Notes

1. "Faculty Code and Governance: Section 24–32 B; Scholarly and Professional Qualifications of Faculty Members," University of Washington, accessed January 6, 2015, *http://www.washington.edu/admin/rules/policies/FCG/FCCH24.html#2432*.
2. "New Survey: College Faculty Increasingly Use Social Media for Teaching and in Professional, Personal Lives," Faculty Focus, October 18, 2013, *http://www.facultyfocus.com/articles/edtech-news-and-trends/new-survey-college-faculty-increasingly-use-social-media-for-teaching-and-in-professional-personal-lives/*.

Section 2
BIBLIOMETRICS

Chapter Three

Understanding Bibliometrics

> "Like nuclear energy, the impact factor is a mixed blessing. I expected it to be used constructively while recognizing that in the wrong hands it might be abused."[1]
>
> —Eugene Garfield, "Journal Impact Factor: A Brief Review"

For many researchers looking to show their impact to a traditional audience of faculty and administrators, bibliometrics are an inevitable part of the conversation—a goal they must strive for or a hurdle they must leap over. But what are bibliometrics exactly, and how did they come to dominate our modern sense of what makes "impactful" research? In this chapter, we take a look at the 20th-century origins of bibliometrics before continuing on to a more detailed discussion of the present day state of the field, including major categories of metrics, popular bibliometric tools, and the bibliometric practices of 21st-century researchers and librarians.

The Definition of Bibliometrics

The first thing to know about the field of bibliometrics is that its origins lie squarely in the world of print. While coined as a term in the late 1960s by Alan Pritchard as "the application of mathematics and statistical methods to books and other media of communication,"[2] the idea of bibliometrics goes back decades further to at least the 1940s and the time of S. R. Ranganathan, whom students of library and information science will remember (some more fondly than others) as the father of information science and a fervent lover of all things bibliographic and statistical.

Bibliometrics was therefore born not only at a time when books and journals monopolized scholarly communication, but also in an academic era that had yet to see the rise of personal computers, let alone word processing, the Internet, or mobile devices. Its early champions were also almost exclusively scientists and science-oriented librarians, whose mutual interest in scientometrics—another mid-century "-ometrics" field that focused, as one might guess, on measuring science scholarship—set the disciplinary tone for bibliometric research for decades to come.

Today, bibliometrics has evolved into a significantly broader field of study—but its focus on print-based methods of communication and analysis has continued more or less unchanged. For purposes of this book, we will define bibliometrics as a set of quantitative methods used to measure, track, and analyze print-based scholarly literature.

> "Although recognizably bibliometric techniques have been applied for at least a century, the emergence of bibliometrics as a scientific field was triggered (in the 1960s) by the development of the Institute for Scientific Information (ISI) Science Citation Index (SCI) by Eugene Garfield, as a logical continuation of his drive to support scientific literature searching."[3]
>
> —Mike Thewall, "Bibliometrics to Webometrics"

The Practical History of Bibliometrics
Eugene Garfield and the Origins of Bibliometrics

Of all the people who contributed to the 20th-century development of bibliometrics research, the most well known by far is Eugene Garfield, a prolific US scholar of citation-based impact measurement who is also known as one of the fathers of scientometrics.

Born in 1925 in New York, Garfield earned his PhD in structural linguistics at the University of Pennsylvania in the early 1960s—but not before earning degrees in both chemistry and library science from Columbia University, both of which would later influence his interest in citation analysis and scientific information. In 1961, Garfield founded the Institute for Science Information (ISI), a groundbreaking research center that created the Science Citation Index (SCI) and invented the calculation for journal impact factor, which remains over half a century later the "gold standard" for measuring impact across the sciences.

Oddly enough, both of these staggeringly influential ideas grew out of a single 1955 *Science* article, "Citation Indexes for Science: A New Dimension in Documentation through Association of Ideas," authored by Garfield in his early doctoral days.[4] The article is only three pages long and still worth reading for the light it sheds on the logical origins of the journal impact factor as well as the mid-century roots of bibliometrics in general. The majority of the article is dedicated to the potential of a citation-based index of scientific literature to reduce "uncritical citation," the undesirable practice of engaging with published literature without first knowing if and how it had been lauded or declaimed by experts in the field. Such an index, Garfield argued, would allow scientists to trace "papers that have cited or criticized [other] papers"—thus filtering out less well-regarded or less influential articles while at the same time allowing article authors a chance more easily to trace the academic discussion of their work.[5]

The implied idea that journal citations are the only practical means of tracing what scholars are saying and thinking about the work of their peers is both familiar and yet strangely dated when judged by today's bifurcated academic standards. For 1950s-era Garfield, who would have considered punch card technology state of the art, the assumption is probably a fair one. However, for today's scientists who regard online tools like Google an old hat, the argument is considerably weaker. Nevertheless, the idea that citations are the best means of tracing engagement between researchers has continued well into the early 21st century. The incongruence of this assumption is at the heart of this book, and we will return to it frequently as we move into later chapters.

ISI and the Rise of Citation Analysis

The 1960s saw a distinct increase in the development of bibliometrics with the launch of major citation-mapping resources like the SCI in 1963 via Garfield's ISI. In the early 1970s, with the advent of breakthroughs in computing technology, ISI was able to produce not only a sequel to SCI—the appropriately named "Social Science Citation Index" (1973)—but also the first edition of Journal Citation Reports (JCR, 1975), a macroanalysis tool that was originally part of the SCI. JCR introduced scholars in the sciences to the notion of an objectively calculated journal rankings metric, which could be used to compare large, well-known journals to smaller, more obscure journals that nevertheless cover important areas of specialized research.[6]

Gradually, innovations such as JCR began to garner attention beyond elite research circles, increasing the discussion about the practical value of impact metrics in research universities across the US and Europe. Scholars under both the newly coined "bibliometrics" and "scientometrics" umbrellas began to publish studies rooted in the use of citation analysis tools, leading to the founding of the new peer-reviewed journal *Scientometrics* (1979) as well as the addition of some types of citable material beyond journal articles to ISI's indexes (1977). By the late 1980s, individual academics from across the sciences and social sciences were demanding access to bibliometric resources for purposes of research, strategic publication, and individual impact planning.

Bibliometrics, the Internet, and Thomson Reuters

The 1990s saw the entrance of two new key players into the bibliometrics realm: librarians and the Internet.[7] Of course, librarians had been part of the bibliometrics conversation since its beginning. As experts on the compilation and use of indexes, among other key resources for organizing and identifying published literature, librarians had long followed (and participated in) the rise of citation-based tools like those envisioned by Garfield and ISI. However, the importance of librarians to the development of bibliometrics took on new dimensions as they began to consider demand for access to such resources at their local institutions. In the 1980s, when ISI began to offer electronic versions of its various citation indexes

Bibliometrics Milestones by Year

▼ 1961: Eugene Garfield founds the Institute for Science Information (ISI).
▼ 1963: ISI releases the Science Citation Index (SCI).
▼ 1973: ISI releases the Social Science Citation Index.
▼ 1975: ISI releases SCI Journal Citation Reports with impact factor calculations.
▼ 1977: ISI adds new types of citable non-article materials to the Science Citation Index.
▼ 1978: ISI releases the Arts & Humanities Citation Index.
▼ 1979: The new journal *Scientometrics* is first published.
▼ 1988: ISI releases the SCI on CD-ROM.
▼ 1992: Thomson Scientific & Healthcare acquires ISI and becomes Thomson ISI.
▼ 1997: Thomson ISI's new Web of Science Core Collection launches online.
▼ 2002: Web of Knowledge launches as a consolidated research platform.
▼ 2004: Elsevier launches Scopus as a competitor to Web of Science.
▼ 2005: ISI is dropped from Thomson ISI and becomes Thomson Scientific.
▼ 2005: Jorge E. Hirsch invents the h-index for quantifying scientific research output.
▼ 2007: Thomson Corporation acquires the Reuters Group to become Thomson Reuters.
▼ 2007: Ann-Wil Harzing releases the first version of the program Publish or Perish.
▼ 2008: The new h-index metric is added to Web of Knowledge.
▼ 2008: Thomson Reuters adds citation mapping tool to Web of Science.
▼ 2011: Thomson Reuters launches the Book Citation Index.
▼ 2011: Google announces the new Google Scholar Citations feature.
▼ 2012: Thomson Reuters launches the Data Citation Index.
▼ 2013: Thomson Reuters launches the Scientific Electronic Library Online Citation Index.
▼ 2014: Thomson Reuters launches the second generation of InCites, including Essential Science Indicators and Journal Citation Reports in one platform.

on CD-ROM, many libraries decided to invest in the products as an extension of their print reference collections. This decision led librarians to take on new roles as educators and gatekeepers with regard to bibliometric content—a role that most of us continue today, unofficially or officially.

The birth of the Internet in the mid-1990s marked another milestone in the history of bibliometrics as researchers began to recognize and enjoy the convenience of accessing information via the World Wide Web. ISI (renamed Thomson ISI when it was bought by Thomas Scientific & Healthcare, and then it became Thomson Reuters when Reuters Group was acquired in 2007) responded swiftly to this expansion in digital technology by developing a new web interface for its various citation indexes, which they launched in 1997 as the tool Web of Science. Covering nearly 9000 journals and allowing users to search across the expanded SCI and the Social Science and Arts & Humanities Indexes, the Web of Science online citation portal quickly became one of the most popular and well-known multidisciplinary library resources for supporting research and higher education.[8] The dominance of Web of Science, furthered by the efforts of libraries and librarians, helped assert the validity of impact factor and citation-based bibliometrics as the standard measures for capturing and comparing scholarly impact across the academy for the rest of the 1990s and into the early 21st century. Today, over 7,000 universities, governments, and research institutions provide users with access to Web of Science and JCR through Thomson Reuters' Web of Knowledge consolidated research platform.[9] This number is over double that of Web of Knowledge's closest competitor in the bibliometrics tool market, Elsevier's Scopus database, which claims to have approximately 3,000 academic, government, and corporate institutional subscribers, although many of these almost certainly overlap with Thomson Reuters' client base.

The Categories of Bibliometrics

As introduced in Chapter 2, most impact metrics can be grouped into four levels, which distinguish between the items different metrics choose to focus on rather than the methods they produce their results by. These levels are as follows:

▼ **Level 1:** Metrics focused on individual scholarly contribution.
▼ **Level 2:** Metrics focused on the venues that produce individual scholarly contributions.
▼ **Level 3:** Metrics focused on author output over time.
▼ **Level 4:** Metrics focused on group and institutional output over time.

Within the sphere of bibliometrics, we will touch on all four of these metric levels to some degree. However, we will soon discover that the historical development of bibliometrics has meant that the most refined bibliometrics are overwhelmingly concentrated in the first two of these levels, particularly those associated with the impact of journal articles and journals. Keeping this in mind, let's start by taking a look at some of the most well-known bibliometrics associated with each level. Or as '90s pop group En Vogue would say, "Now it's time for a breakdown."

Level 1: Individual Contribution Level Metrics
Times Cited
Technically, this section only has a single metric in it, but it's a big one: the number of times an article has been cited. The central premise behind times cited is that an item—by default, a journal article—can be considered to have impacted someone else's work if another scholar cites that item in his or her subsequent publication. Many article databases offer a "times cited" link within the records of individual articles for this reason, which when clicked reveals other sources within the database that list the original article as a reference.

Currently, three online sources are considered to be the most authoritative and comprehensive for discovering citation-based connections between scholarly articles: Web of Science, Scopus, and Google Scholar. Studies have shown that the overlap between these sources varies depending on the discipline. For example, a 2013 study comparing coverage of nine South African scientific journals found an overall content overlap between the three sources to be 81.6%.[10] Therefore, for the majority of article authors, it is still worthwhile to check as many sources as possible for times cited figures. Authors can then use these figures to create a master list of "cited by" works along with a final metric for times cited that combines the various online sources that were consulted.

As the simplest and most straightforward of the citation-based metrics, the number of times an article has been cited is the basis for virtually all bibliometric measures, which have become significantly more sophisticated since the invention of advanced computing modeling, as we'll see in the following sections. (For more detail on extracting times cited data from Web of Science, Scopus, and Google Scholar, see Chapter 4, where we walk step by step through the practical use of each of these tools.) In the meantime, the most important thing to realize about this foundational metric is that a true times cited value is nearly impossible to calculate—not the least of which because scholars have yet to agree about what the phrase "true value" even means in this context. Consider, for example, the characteristics of a citable scholarly item. A citation can generate from or refer to other journal articles, books, conference presentations, posters, blog posts, reference texts, web pages, and so on. Web of Science and Scopus largely still confine their results to citations by or of journal articles, despite the specific addition of other forms of citable material to Web of Science in the late 1970s. Google Scholar, by contrast, encapsulates a wider variety of sources like unpublished works, theses, patents, and dissertations—but it too is inevitably confined in scope by the fact that its citation network is based on a limited index, like the names of people listed in the city phone book as opposed to the names of all the people living in the city. To truly discover how many times an item such as an article has been cited, one would need access to the references of all works of scholarship, including those that have never been indexed, have not been digitized, or are not electronically accessible. As librarians, we understand that this type of access isn't possible and would likely result in definitional disagreement even if it were possible. Thus, we find ourselves with no perfect agreement on what should or should not be considered valid when calculating an item's times cited—and yet we can see that our decisions about times cited can have a big impact on an item's acceptance as having or not having significant impact.

> "Journal performance is a complex, multidimensional concept that cannot be fully captured in one single metric."[11]
>
> —Henk F. Moed et al., "Citation-Based Metrics Are Appropriate Tools in Journal Assessment Provided That They Are Accurate and Used in an Informed Way"

Level 2: Venue-Level Metrics

Just as the journal article is the traditional type of individual scholarly contribution in the context of bibliometrics, scholarly journals are by far the most popular venue of production to be quantitatively addressed by the field. From a researcher perspective, the quality of a journal is an important factor in deciding which articles to read (e.g., Does this journal generally publish material that ends up being impactful?) and where to submit their own articles for publication (e.g., Will my article have a better chance of being impactful because it appears in this journal?). Obviously this does not discount the possibility that highly respected journals will at least occasionally publish less-than-impactful material and that marginal journals will at least occasionally publish highly impactful material. Still, for researchers looking to approximate the impact of their individual contributions or project the future impact of recent publications, journal-level bibliometrics are often the best they can use outside of the foundational metric of times cited. In other words, if times cited is the most frequent bibliometric that researchers use to answer the question "How good is this paper?," it follows that journal-level bibliometrics are the most popular responses to the question "How good is this publication?"

We can now take a look at some of the major bibliometrics that focus on journal-level impact.

Impact Factor

As mentioned earlier in this chapter, Garfield's impact factor metric pioneered journal-level metrics and is still the most widely used and understood journal-level metric. Developed in conjunction with the 1975 launch of ISI's JCR, impact factor is in essence a ratio: an average of the number of citations generated by each citable item within a journal as calculated over a limited length of time. Because of the time it takes for citations to begin to populate within the academic community, the standard length of time for calculating impact factor is three years from the date of publication. However, JCR also offers a five-year calculation of impact factor. This alternative calculation is meant to reflect the longer rates of maturity in some academic fields as well as the interest from some scholars in the

---

Calculating Journal Impact Factor[12]

To understand impact factor, we begin with an imaginary journal called *Journal of Bibliometrics*. In the two previous years, 2012–2013, *Journal of Bibliometrics* published a total of 1000 citable items in its issues. Citable items are defined by Web of Knowledge and include all items of scholarly substance, from peer-reviewed articles to reviews.

A = Total citable items published by the journal in the two previous years

A = 1000

Next we do a comprehensive search of the references of all the scholarly items indexed within Web of Science this year, 2014. In doing this, we discover that these 1000 citable items published by *Journal of Bibliometrics* between 2012 and 2013 were collectively cited a total of 3000 times—again, just in the year 2014.

B = Total number of times that the items in A were cited in the current year

B = 3000

To arrive at the impact factor for *Journal of Bibliometrics*, we simply divide the total number of collective citations from this year by the number of citable items published by the journal in the previous two years. The result is an average of three citations per citable item, when examined 1–3 years after publication, which we call an impact factor of 3.0.

Impact factor = B/A

3000 total citations (2014) / 1000 citable items (2012–2013) = **3.0**

longer-term relevance of articles after they become available. Still, unless otherwise indicated, one can assume that impact factor has been calculated based on the standard three-year time period.

As with the times cited metric that underlies impact factor, it's important to remember that no single source can provide 100% complete data about journal citation patterns. In fact, since the classic impact factor is only calculated for sources indexed in Web of Science (see the Proprietary Article Databases section in this chapter for more about Web of Science's sources), many smaller academic journals and journals outside the STEM disciplines simply don't have an impact factor, even though they have strong reputations within their areas of specialization. Many faculty are surprised to discover this gap when searching Web of Science or JCR for the first time and can feel flustered or discouraged by the lack of a particular journal's inclusion. For these faculty, it may be worth informing them about alternatives to Web of Science's suite of journal metrics. We will discuss some of these alternatives later in this chapter.

Immediacy Index
Immediacy index is another journal-level metric developed by Thomson Reuters and published as part of JCR. It operates similarly to both, except immediacy index focuses only on the citation patterns and publications of a single calendar year whereas impact factor and five-year impact factor metrics look to balance article citations generated within a single year with citable items published by a journal in the previous three or five years (respectively). For instance, if a journal has a 2013 immediacy index of 0.250, that would indicate that in 2013, each citable item published by the journal generated an average of 0.250 citations *within the same year it was published*. Because many articles take more than a year to start generating citations by other scholarly works, immediacy indices for journals tend to be quite low, with few reaching higher than a value of 1.000. Again, however, this is not the case for every specialization, and certain journals may choose to specialize in publishing cutting-edge research. Users within a given discipline may be interested in JCR's alternative "aggregate" immediacy index—essentially an average of the immediacy indices for all journals within a JCR-defined subject area.

Cited Half-Life

Cited half-life, another metric published via Web of Science's JCR, refers to the median age of the items cited in the current JCR year. For example, if a journal has a cited half-life of ten years, that means half of the citations generated by the journal in the current year come from items the journal published in the last ten years. As an impact metric, cited half-life therefore indicates in theory about how long articles published by the journal continue to be considered impactful, although as JCR is quick to point out, "a higher or lower cited half-life does not imply any particular value for a journal."[13] This caveat is partly a nod to the fact that different disciplines and different types of publications have different expectations for currency and usefulness when it comes to their citations. A journal that publishes primary research would presumably have a longer cited half-life than one publishing reviews or secondary research on a quickly evolving topic like educational technology. On a related note, some librarians have found the cited half-life metric useful for purposes of collection weeding (e.g., binding or archiving only those journals with relatively high cited half-lives).

Eigenfactor and Article Influence Score

Eigenfactor and Article Influence Score are interesting examples of metrics based on the same citation data as Thomson Reuters' JCR but developed independently by a team of researchers at the University of Washington, led by cofounders Jevin West and Carl Bergstrom. Based on algorithms that combine advances in network analysis with information theory, both Eigenfactor and Article Influence Score use citations to measure the impact of scholarly journals according to the broad dissemination of their articles, such as the frequency with which researchers might encounter concepts that stem from articles published by that journal. Both calculations begin with five years' worth of citation data—almost double the number of years examined by traditional impact factor—and proceed by following a journal's published articles as they are cited by various papers. The resulting Eigenfactor metric is thus purportedly "an estimate of the percentage of time that library users spend with that journal," which researchers behind the project equate to "that journal's importance within network of academic citations."[14] By taking this approach to impact, Eigenfactor sets its strengths in the identification of both large and high prestige of certain journals (both of whose articles would likely be cited both more frequently than small or specialized journals) and in the differentiation of citation patterns in different disciplines (as subjects with smaller citation practices would result in higher influence values per article cited within that network node). The Article Influence Score metric supplements this spatial perspective on journal impact by providing a measure of a journal's average influence per article over the five-year citation period, or the Eigenfactor equivalent of five-year impact factor. Article Influence Score can therefore be very useful to JCR users who are looking for an alternative calculation to impact factor for the average per article impact of a journal that they have published in or are considering publishing in.[15] For more information about how to interpret Eigenfactor and Article Influence Score, see the FAQ page on the Eigenfactor website (*http://www.eigenfactor.org/faq.php*).

SCImago Journal Rankings
Affiliated with both the SCImago Lab group and Elsevier's Scopus database, SCImago Journal Rankings (SJR) is a relatively new but increasingly popular metric for journal-level impact. Like its competitor, Web of Science, Scopus works by indexing citations from academic journal articles across a range of publications, dates, and disciplines. However, unlike Web of Science, which grew its own bibliometric formulas out of the ISI in the 1970s, Scopus's bibliometrics are provided by an outside group called SCImago, and then subsequently displayed within Scopus's journal-level records.[16] As for the value of SJR, it provides the major alternative to Web of Science's impact factor as it is similarly aimed at measuring the level of impact a journal has on its field or discipline. However, ScImago has developed its ranking based on a more complex method than ISI. According to researchers, SJR is based on Google's PageRank algorithm—an approach to impact that uses elements of probability as well as actual cases of use (i.e., citation).[17] More information about the formula and rationality for the SJR algorithm can be found in a white paper titled, "The SJR Indicator: A New Indicator of Journals' Scientific Prestige."[18]

Source Normalized Impact per Paper

Source Normalized Impact per Paper, known more commonly as SNIP, is a metric calculated by the Center for Science and Technology Studies (CWTS) at Leiden University. It is closely related to but independently calculated and maintained from SCImago's SJR. SNIP is based on another metric called Raw Impact per Paper (RIP), which is comparable to both impact factor and SJR. As an impact metric, SNIP is unique because it attempts to correct for varying sizes and citation rates across different scientific fields to allow for a fairer comparison of metrics across each discipline.[19] Realistically, the result is a virtual flattening of the normal distribution curve you could plot with SJR metrics for indexed scientific journals in Scopus. Thus, journals with higher SJR numbers will sometimes see their SNIP metrics decrease, and journals with lower SJR numbers will occasionally see increases in their SNIPs. It is also important to note that while SNIP was created by CWTS to compare scientific discipline journals only, every journal in Scopus is given a SNIP value alongside its SJR value. Our unofficial observation has been that SNIP values for nonscience journals don't adequately equate to SNIP values within science disciplines, so that the "flattening" effect can't be observed across all journals. Still, SNIP represents a laudable step in the development of metrics that can be directly compared across the disciplines—a necessity for any administrator or outsider looking to understand the meaning of a journal's bibliometrics without already possessing a deep familiarity with the field it targets.

As a side note on the future of SNIP, to provide a better understanding and long-term context for SNIP values, CWTS now calculates a stability interval to show how SNIP values for a single journal may have changed from year to year. The stability interval, shown in Figure 3.1, can help show whether SNIP values for a particular year are likely to be a representative of a journal's longer term value or whether the journal's impact tends to change erratically (indicating that a journal's articles may vary in quality more than other journals).

H5-Index and H5-Median

As variations on the h-index—an author-level bibliometric described later in this chapter in the Level 3 section—h5-index and its corollary h5-median

Figure 3.1. Journal Stability Interval Indicators, retrieved from www.journalindicators.com

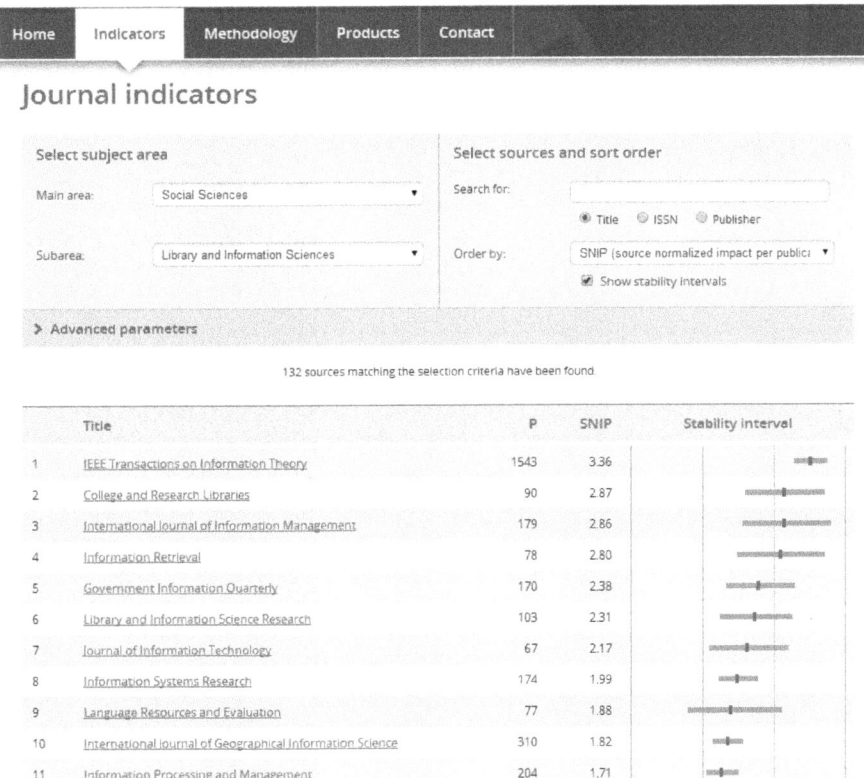

are journal-level impact metrics that are becoming increasingly popular due to their inclusion in Google Scholar Metrics. Many readers may already be aware that Google Scholar tracks times cited for individual author contributions. However, fewer readers are aware that Google Scholar Metrics maintains metrics at the journal level, just like Web of Science and Scopus. Its metrics, the h5-index and h5-median, are based on citations collected from the last five years of a journal's publication history. The h5-index seeks to determine how many of those articles (a number we'll call h) have been cited at least h times during the five-year period. Consequently, an h5-index metric of 200 means that the journal has published 200 articles in the past five years that have been cited at least 200 times each. As of 2013, the highest h5-index was 349 for the journal *Nature*. As one might expect, the h5-median takes the journal articles included in the h5-index and returns the median number of citations they have generated.[20] This second metric gives users a feel for the citation counts actually represented by the set of articles identified in the h5-index.

> ## "Fuzzy" Metrics: Non Citation-Based Bibliometrics
>
> While interest in the impact of journals and journal articles have historically driven advances the field of bibliometrics, other forms of citable print-based scholarship, from books to conference proceedings to data sets, have gradually made their way into the makeup of the field, thus changing the approach of some toolmakers to indexing and bibliometric calculation and putting pressure on individual researchers to identify quantitative measures of impact and quality that go beyond simple article-to-article practices of citation. The difficulty of this, of course, is that bibliometrics is a field by definition reliant on both quantitative methods and the world of print. This means that any print-based item that defies quantitative analysis must occasionally be shoehorned into a bibliometric perspective with highly variable results. (We will talk about some of the failures and successes that have stemmed from these efforts in this chapter's Categories of Bibliometrics Tools section.) In the meantime, however, it is worthwhile to briefly introduce some of the non citation-based "fuzzy" metrics that have already found acceptance in most academic circles, especially in close combination with journal-level bibliometrics. As you will see, many of these metrics are simply statistical translations of qualitative practices pulled directly from the publishing and library worlds—hence why they are not typically recognized as actual bibliometrics—yet they still can have tremendous value to researchers who work with a variety of printed outputs or are just seeking to tell a more robust story about their recent accomplishments within a field. Such metrics may also hold inspiration for researchers whose work extend into nonprinted outputs, such as performances, exhibitions, and conference presentations.
>
> ### *Acceptance Rate*
> An item's acceptance rate indicates the percentage of items submitted to a venue that are ultimately accepted for publication or production. In the context of scholarly venues, a lower acceptance rate is traditionally indicative of a more prestigious, selective venue (similar to the acceptance rate

for a college or university). Some venues, such as many academic journals, will display their acceptance rates on their websites. Others may be collected and tracked by an outside source, such as Cabell's Publishing Opportunities subscription database.[21] For researchers interested in finding out more about a specific publisher or producer's acceptance rate, we recommend a simple phone call or e-mail to the venue's appropriate contact.

Subscription and Circulation

Subscription and circulation metrics are numbers that indicate the size of the audience for a particular venue or, in some cases, specific scholarly contribution. In the context of journals, for example, circulation is understood to mean the number of journal issues that circulate both to libraries and individual subscribers on a regular basis due to previous agreements or payments. The idea here is that journals with a higher impact will be more widely circulated or have more regular subscribers than journals that are less impactful. Again, this information is sometimes made available to researchers via a venue's website. In other circumstances, however, it may be obtained via a call to a subscription or public relations office.

Library Holdings

As a metric of impact, library holdings is remarkably similar to circulation data, although it holds a different appeal to some researchers (and administrators) for the connection it implies with institutions of learning. Defined as the number of libraries that count an item within its holdings, this metric can especially demonstrate impact for authors of scholarly monographs, whose major audience is almost always academic libraries. At present, the best way to obtain library holdings data is to search the online resource WorldCat, familiar to most librarians and LIS students as the "world's largest library catalog."[22] Personal experience shows that WorldCat results are not entirely accurate reflections of actual holdings of libraries, particularly for electronic journal subscriptions, because cataloging practices inevitably vary from institution to institution. Nevertheless, WorldCat can give researchers a general approximation of how many libraries (and which libraries) have added an item to their collections. To maximize the effect of this metric, we advise researchers to compare holdings for similar items in WorldCat, as this can help produce a relative sense of the numbers meaning and provide a check on the probable accuracy of WorldCat's results for the type of item in question.

> "For the few scientists who earn a Nobel Prize, the impact and relevance of their research is unquestionable. Among the rest of us, how does one quantify the cumulative impact and relevance of an individual's scientific research output?"[23]
>
> —Jorge E. Hirsch, "An Index to Quantify an Individual's Scientific Research Output"

Level 3: Author-Level Metrics

Author-level bibliometrics—those aimed at quantifying the impact of a specific researcher over the course of his or her career—have become a bit of a hot topic within bibliometrics circles since the end of the 20th century. On one hand, individual researchers have been tracking their impact via metrics such as times cited and acceptance into journals with high impact metrics since they first became available in the 1960s. On the other hand, the idea that a scholar's body of work can be quantified and compared in the same way as a journal has offended certain academics who see it as a flawed approach to scholarly assessment. "It is one thing to use impact factors to compare journals and quite another to use them to compare authors," begins Garfield in a 1999 editorial on the modern use of impact factor. "Journal impact factors generally involve relatively large populations of articles and citations. Individual authors, on average, produce much smaller numbers of articles."[24] Still, the invention of new author-level bibliometrics in the last ten years has given new fuel to the argument in favor of the trend and has been reinforced by the explosion in profile tools for researchers like Google Scholar Citations. In this section, we highlight two of the fastest-growing bibliometrics, the h-index and i10-index, for quantifying and comparing the impacts of individual researchers.

H-Index

First suggested by Jorge E. Hirsch in 2005 as part of a paper on the relative quality of theoretical physicists, the Hirsch-index, or h-index, has fast become one of the best-known bibliometrics for comparing the impact of different authors over time. H-index is calculated by using the number of articles an author has published to date (*h*) to determine a citation count threshold, which the author's articles must meet or pass over (also *h*) to be included as part of the index. Thus, if a theoretical physicist has published 100 articles over the course of her career, and if 30 of those papers have been cited 30+ times, her h-index would be 30. If any of the other 70 papers with less than 30 citations receive 31 or more citations in the future, the h-index will correspondingly increase. The more prolific the author, the higher the potential for the final index value. This index cap can be frustrating for early career researchers, whose h-indexes may appear very low, despite having authored one or more articles that have generated a very high number of citations. Likewise, h-index does not account for works other than articles or citations that appear outside of articles. The debate over the advantages and disadvantages of h-index as a measure of impact has been active for years and has helped spawn the creation of numerous variation metrics, such as g-index, a-index, h2-index, h5-index (see the previous section, Level 2: Journal-Level Metrics), and countless others.[25] Nevertheless, h-index continues to be the most visible author-level metric and can be found in many author-level profiles tools.

Figure 3.2. Visual Demonstration of an H-index Calculation

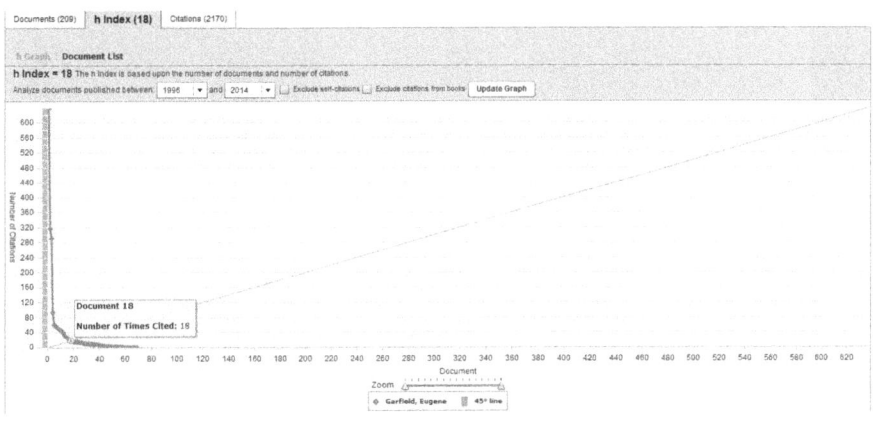

I10-Index

Arguably less well known in scientific circles, the i10-index for measuring author-level impact has gained new levels of distinction since appearing as part of the launch of Google Scholar Citations in 2011. The index is calculated by taking the number of articles that an author has published to date (i), and then identifying how many of those articles have generated at least ten citations. Simplicity is one of the major appeals of i10-index, particularly for researchers in fields where a citation count of greater than ten is a more reasonable shorthand for achieving impact on a case-by-case article basis. However, just as h-index does not identify the extent to which an article exceeds the ten citation threshold, i10-index does not necessarily tell a compelling story about the specific shape of an author's impact on his or her field. For this reason, Google Scholar displays i10-index alongside authors' total citation counts as well as their h-index values.

> "Concentration of research can be considered from two viewpoints: internal and external. The first compares the publication output of a university in a particular field to the same institution's output in other fields, and to its total output; the second compares it to the number of articles published by other institutions in the same subject field."[26]
>
> —Henk F. Moed et al., "Is Concentration of University Research Associated with Better Research Performance?"

Level 4: Institution-Level Metrics

Institutions and bibliometrics have an interesting history because of the natural competition that exists between higher education units, everything from student enrollments to donor funding to who won last year's volleyball tournament. Indeed, just as pressure exists for researchers to produce quantitative evidence of their impact on the field, administrators and other leadership figures also feel pressure from internal and external populations to measure and assess their institution's achievements. From an institutional viewpoint, there are inevitably multiple ways to approach the question of impact. Most approaches involve considerably more information than just the data related to researcher output—which is why there has yet to be a boom in bibliometrics that target group-levels of impact. Instead, what we commonly see is the hacking of journal- and author-level metrics (Levels 2 and 3) to fit the needs of an institution with hundreds of authors and potentially thousands of citable publications. This in turn has opened up a market for tools that do at least some of the work of aggregating and merging bibliometrics for institutions or even come up with formulas that combine bibliometrics with new quantitative values, like "the percentage of an institution's output [in which a member of the institution is listed as a] main contributor."[27]

In this section, we highlight the work of two recently developed tools and an initiative that represent the deployment of institution-focused bibliometrics.

Essential Science Indicators Rankings

Originally launched by Thomson Reuters as a standalone tool for bibliometric assessment, Essential Science Indicators (ESI) provides users with the ability to rank institutions based on performance statistics within the sciences and top scientists, countries, and journals by fields of research. Like its sister tool for identifying impact JCR, ESI uses citation counts, averages, and set time periods to create its rankings and benchmarks. Institutional rankings are calculated based on both the aggregated institutional output (e.g., items attributable to affiliated researchers) and the aggregated citations generated by this output over a ten-year period.[28] In 2014, Thomson Reuters integrated ESI into the updated InCites platform (see the Categories of Bibliometrics Tools section later in this chapter).

SCImago Institutions Rankings

From the same lab behind the journal-level impact metric SJR, SCImago Institutions Rankings (SIR) is a free online resource that ranks research entities around the world based on three areas of achievement: research, innovation, and web visibility. In the sub-ranking category of research, SIR uses data from Scopus to create metrics for seven indicators: output, scientific talent pool, excellence, leadership, international collaboration, normalized impact, and specialization. These indicators are balanced to form overall rankings, although users can sort results by specific indicators; institutional sector (e.g., government, health, higher education, private, or others); country; and publication year (within the last five years). The final scores for each indicator are normalized on a scale of 0 to 100, which limits their practical use for peer comparison and benchmarking.[29] A full explanation of each indicator as well as criteria for inclusion in the rankings can be found on the ScImagoIR website, along with an extensive bibliography of related work published by the ScImago Lab (***http://www.scimagoir.com/***).

Snowball Metrics
Unlike the other resources highlighted in this level, Snowball Metrics is not a tool but an initiative, born out of a partnership between eight UK universities and Elsevier. Inspired by a 2010 report on research information management, the initiative's goal is to create an agreed-upon set of methodologies for institutional benchmarking, one sufficient for covering a wide spectrum of research while staying both "data source- and system-agnostic" (i.e., free for any institution to use around the world).[30] In 2014, Elsevier published an online "recipe book" on behalf of the program, which defines the Snowball Metrics approach to measuring impact while mapping out its various outcome metrics, such as citation count, citations per output, h-index, and collaboration. It's useful to note that altmetrics are also explicitly mentioned in the Snowball Metrics recipe, a sign of the blurring line between these two primary schools of impact measurement, which we will further discuss in Chapter 5.

The Categories of Bibliometrics Tools

Categories of tools can be hard to define in bibliometrics, in part because of the natural desire on the part of toolmakers to create resources that address multiple levels of impact at once or in different portions of the same overall dashboard. Even tools that clearly address one purpose or level of impact today can easily change to address a different (or additional) level tomorrow—a story of change we have seen played out many times as the market has expanded for new types of academic analysis. Still, when being introduced to a myriad of options, a set of loose categories can be helpful for highlighting points of overlap and potential competition. Accordingly, in this section, we introduce three categories of major bibliometrics tools, each of which has served to shape the field for practitioners.

> "Any aggregator of citations could create its own bibliometric measures if they are willing to invest the time and expense."[31]
>
> —Robin Kear and Danielle Colbert-Lewis, "Citation Searching and Bibliometric Measures: Resources for Ranking and Tracking"

Proprietary Article Databases

These tools, often the best-known sources of bibliometrics, are typically made available to researchers through institutional subscriptions, such as those managed by the library. Their impact calculations are based on data from within their article indexes, which are by necessity large and interdisciplinary.

Web of Science

Web of Science is more or less synonymous with the term bibliometrics; it was the first database to track the web of citations created when scholars cite others' works, the method by which we can create bibliometrics. Though other tools now exist, Web of Science is still considered by many to be the premier source for bibliometrics, and it is certainly the most well known. Web of Science is comprised of multiple indexes and complementary resources. The majority of Web of Science's citations are drawn from the Science Citation Index, Social Science Citation Index, and Arts & Humanities Citation Index. Today, these indices, along with additional resources with specialized citations, such as chemical reactions and conference proceedings, are combined to form the Web of Science Core Collection.[32] Together these form the basis for Web of Science's citation coverage.

Coverage is one of the most important considerations when using any journal database, even more so when extracting bibliometric data. Therefore, it's important to understand more about what is and what is not included in Web of Science because all calculated metrics are derived based on the available sources within the database. Thomson Reuters considers many factors when choosing journals for inclusion in Web of Science (see a full description of the process and factors at Web of Science's "The Thomson Reuters Journal Selection Process:" *http://wokinfo.com/essays/journal-selection-process/)*. In practice, Web of Science has the strongest coverage in STEM disciplines and favors journals with English language, peer review, and a longer publication history. These strengths harken back to the history of the database and its strong background in the sciences, which it was first built around.

Web of Science indices go back as far as 1900, which may be necessary when researching authors with a longer publication history. Additionally, it's good to know that Web of Science has one great author feature that at least partially avoids any coverage limitations: the Distinct Author Records Set (DARS). Individuals' publications can be grouped together, relying on information supplied by ResearcherID.[33] When using DARS, the entire set of publications within the citation indices are counted, thus giving a more accurate count of publications. However, only publications within your subscription will be displayed. For the many institutions unable to afford the complete backfile of online coverage, print indices or calling upon the friendly services of another library may be necessary to get the most comprehensive publication information (necessary for bibliometric analysis) for an author.

> "Never underestimate the power of a good network graph when teaching research impact, especially name disambiguation, to constituents. You can easily make comparisons between pre- and post-correction citation data to showcase why attribution inconsistency is a problem."
>
> —Kayleigh Ayn Bohémier, Science Research Support Librarian, Yale's Center for Science and Social Science Information

Journal Citation Reports

Journal Citation Reports (JCR) is another product in the Thomson Reuters suite of tools. Since all of these products (including JCR and Web of Science) are built based on the same set of citations from the Web of Science Core Collection, they can all be considered to be databases that arise from the same set of citation data. But while Web of Science is primarily concerned with tracing the web of citations and times cited, JCR steps up one level from the individual article level (Level 1) to consider metrics at the journal level (Level 2).

JCR contains a few journal-level metrics but is most well known as the only place to get journal impact factor. JCR was very recently revamped, so the screenshots may not look familiar to longtime JCR users, but we like the changes; the revision is a more intuitive navigation experience, with the left-hand navigation bar taking the place of several drop-downs and removing the previous clunky welcome page. Thomson Reuters has also added some exciting new metrics to the 2013 edition of JCR (the latest available during the writing of this book)—including Aggregate Impact Factor, which nicely complements the older metrics—and has also added the ability to compare multiple disciplines at a glance in addition to rankings within one discipline.[34]

Figure 3.3. The Updated JCR Interface

At the individual journal level, impact factor back more than 15 years is available at a glance, which is very useful for researchers looking for a publication's impact factor from the year of publication or for anyone looking to get a sense of the impact factor "trend" for a journal. One final much-needed upgrade to JCR is the ability to easily download any page with a click of a button.

Figure 3.4. JCR Journal Profile

Year ▼	Total Cites Graph	Journal Impact Factor Graph	Impact Factor Without Journal Self Cites Graph	5 Year Impact Factor Graph	Immediacy Index Graph	Citable Items Graph	Cited Half-Life Graph	Citing Half-Life Graph	Eigenfactor Score Graph	Article Influence Score Graph
2013	16,130	162.500	162.182	107.740	27.760	25	3.1	5.4	0.06027	34.642
2012	13,722	153.459	153.081	88.550	27.040	25	3.3	5.8	0.05136	29.408
2011	10,976	101.780	101.488	87.410	21.263	19	3.8	5.6	0.04502	24.502
2010	9,804	94.333	93.833	70.245	8.667	18	3.8	5.6	0.04893	24.729

Scopus

In 2004, Elsevier announced the arrival of Scopus, the first competitor to Thomson Reuters' monopoly on citation indexing. Scopus continues to serve an important role in diversifying options for those seeking metrics while giving Thomson Reuters healthy competition, which has ultimately resulted in better products competing for valuable library funds.

On paper, Scopus and Web of Science have similar coverage; both tout journals in the sciences, social sciences, and arts and humanities. However, experience shows that Scopus has a stronger emphasis within the nonscience disciplines. (A look at the subject categories in Chapter 4 helps demonstrate this difference.) Another large difference is in the main years of coverage. Scopus indexes citations and their bibliographies back through 1996 compared to 1900 in Web of Science. Both contain older citations from these bibliographies, but coverage is limited. One big philosophical difference between the two relates to the level of control that each maintains over its products. Scopus has a demonstrable history of working with outside partners to deliver metrics and information based on Scopus's citation database while Web of Science develops the majority of its information in-house.[35] As a tool, Scopus features article-level, journal-level, and author-level metrics.

> "The use of Scopus and GS [Google Scholar], in addition to WoS [Web of Science], helps reveal a more accurate and comprehensive picture of the scholarly impact of authors."[36]
>
> —Lokman I. Meho and Kiduk Yang, "Impact of Data Sources on Citation Counts and Rankings of LIS Faculty: Web of Science Versus Scopus and Google Scholar"

Free Online Ranking Resources

Tools in this category stand in contrast to the high-cost, institutionally aimed tools of the previous category, even as there is a growing relationship between the two on the level of data sources and displays of data.

SCImago Journal and Country Rank

SCImago is a research group from the University of Grenada that focuses on the visualization, analysis, and retrieval of information. Its main metric, SJR, can be found in Scopus, but not everyone knows that this same metric information is freely available at its website (**www.scimagojr.com**). As mentioned in the journal-level metrics section, some analyses can only be performed on this website such as journal rankings within disciplines. SCImago also offers country rankings of research impact (primarily sorted by a countrywide h-index), which can be filtered by discipline and subdiscipline. This tool enhances large-scale metric comparisons, particularly for countries with smaller research budgets or fewer resources.

Google Scholar Citations, Profiles, and Rankings

Google Scholar quietly entered into the metrics field with the addition of Google Scholar Citations in 2004. On the surface, Google Scholar operates similarly to Web of Science and Scopus, indexing journals and providing citation counts to scholarly literature. However, the scope of what is considered for indexing in Google Scholar is, in practice, much broader than either proprietary database, drawing on publicly available literature in institutional repositories, in online publications, and even from published webliographies.[37] The result is a database that is large and broad but lacking the discriminating standards that Web of Science and Scopus maintain. Nonetheless, as a product of the ever-popular Google-verse, Google Scholar Citations has proven an invaluable resource for many researchers who are unable to find citation counts or journal rankings through other databases.

Google Scholar also offers author-level (Level 3) metrics through its Scholar Profiles. Using this tool, researchers can self-identify their own publications and then see their respective h-index and i10-index scores based on these publications. These profiles underwent a slight redesign in August 2014, but continue to be a good way for scholars to enhance their online presence.

Other Free Resources

In addition to the web-based resources now available to researchers at low or no cost, there are also a small number of bibliometrics resources available to users as free downloadable programs. Most of these programs are the pet projects of solo academics with coding skills who have sought to fill gaps in available metrics with freely available citation data. As most of these programs are fairly obscure, we will highlight the most well known of these resources here and leave some for readers to discover through the Further Reading section of this chapter.

Publish or Perish

Created by Anne-Wil Harzing, a former international management professor at the University of Melbourne, Australia, Publish or Perish (PoP) is a free software program that can be downloaded onto a computer. It is designed to help researchers manipulate Google Scholar citations to create their database of citations from which they can generate their own metrics, including times cited, h-index, and other author and journal-level metrics. As an impact measuring tool, Publish or Perish is appealing for a variety of reasons. For example, researchers whose citation counts suffer from inaccurate citation listings, such as problems associated with ambiguous names, misspellings, and duplicate entries, can correct such errors within the program. This same DIY approach can also be applied to the targeting of new author-level metrics as Publish or Perish allows users to move past h-index to more specific (and arguably more obscure) metrics such as g-index and hc-index.[38] For users with advanced questions or needs, the online manual serves as a helpful, concise guide to all the metrics available in the program.[39]

Figure 3.5. The Publish or Perish Interface

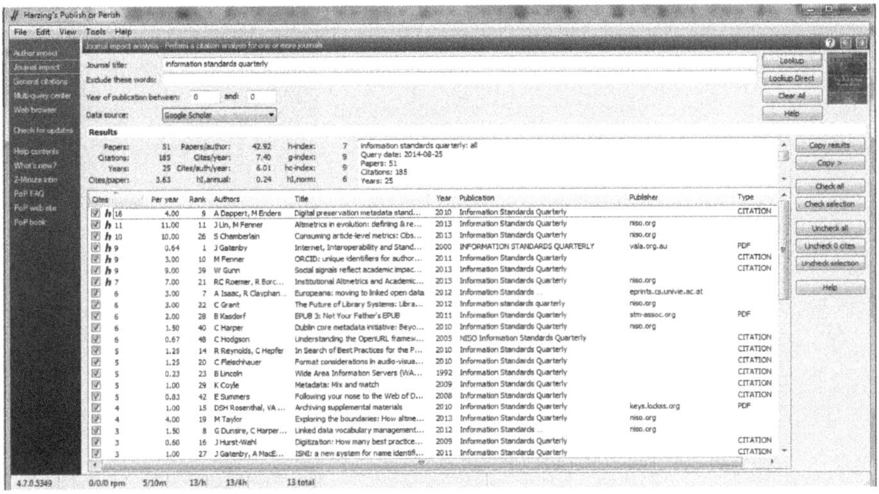

Other Proprietary Resources

As discussed at the beginning of this chapter, the early 21st century has seen a spike in demand for more diverse bibliometrics not only from users of journals and journal articles, but also from researchers whose fields value non-journal scholarly outputs like books, conference presentations, and data sets. Noting these trends, the big toolmakers in the bibliometrics market have strived to come up with new proprietary resources that stretch the citation-based model of measuring impact to cover these less well-documented contribution categories. In this section, we look at two of the latest offerings to fit this trend.

Book Citation Index

The Book Citation Index is one of the more recent Thomson Reuters offerings, though it is now included in the Web of Science core collection with other citation resources. Unlike journal citations, for which Thomson Reuters was the first to offer database coverage, Book Citation Index was created largely as an alternative to Google Scholar's book coverage (including Google Books), which was the first product to include citations contained within books. For disciplines that rely heavily on book publications to advance research in their fields, this ability to discover citations within books and see who has cited these scholarly books is paramount in moving these disciplines toward quantitative metrics.

The Book Citation Index indexes more than 60,000 books in the sciences and social sciences dating back as far as 2008, resulting in more than 15 million new citations within Web of Science.[40] Like other Thomson Reuters products, books are selected for the index through a selective process, which considers factors like publisher, date of publication, and evidence of "relatively high citation impact."[41] In our experience, this index still has a ways to go before it can reliably provide citation counts for book-writing scholars as it is only indexing a small fraction of scholarly books due to these criteria.

Data Citation Index

The Data Citation Index is another product offered by Thomson Reuters, but unlike the Book Citation Index, it is not currently included in the Core Collection (though we suspect that that may change with greater adoption of this resource). Unlike its other offerings, the Data Citation Index pulls together dataset citations from multiple sources, mainly online repositories like Figshare and government agency websites (see the Thomson Reuters' website to find out how data sources are selected for inclusion).[42]

One of the more intriguing aspects of this index is that one of its closest competitors is an altmetrics tool, Impactstory, which collects and unifies metrics related to datasets. However, in this case, the two resources serve complementary roles, with Data Citation Index displaying citations, including when a journal article cites a data set, while Impactstory focuses on other metrics such as views and downloads. With the increased demand for data curation services in libraries, this resource is one that many libraries may wish to investigate further.[43]

InCites Analytics

As mentioned earlier, InCites is Thomson Reuters' redesigned suite of metrics tools. With InCites Analytics, Thomson Reuters adds the ability to rank Level 3 and 4 metrics by offering a platform where users can self-select criteria, such as times cited or average citations per document, to make their own rankable list of authors or institutions. InCites Analytics does not, however, create new metrics, though the "Rank" column may be misleading. The list of authors or institutions are automatically ranked according to the chosen criteria, such as the number of documents attributed to that author or institution; however, it does not take any other criteria into account. It's important to understand these kinds of limitations so that the product's usefulness can be properly understood and contextualized prior to use.

Figure 3.6. InCites Essential Science Indicators

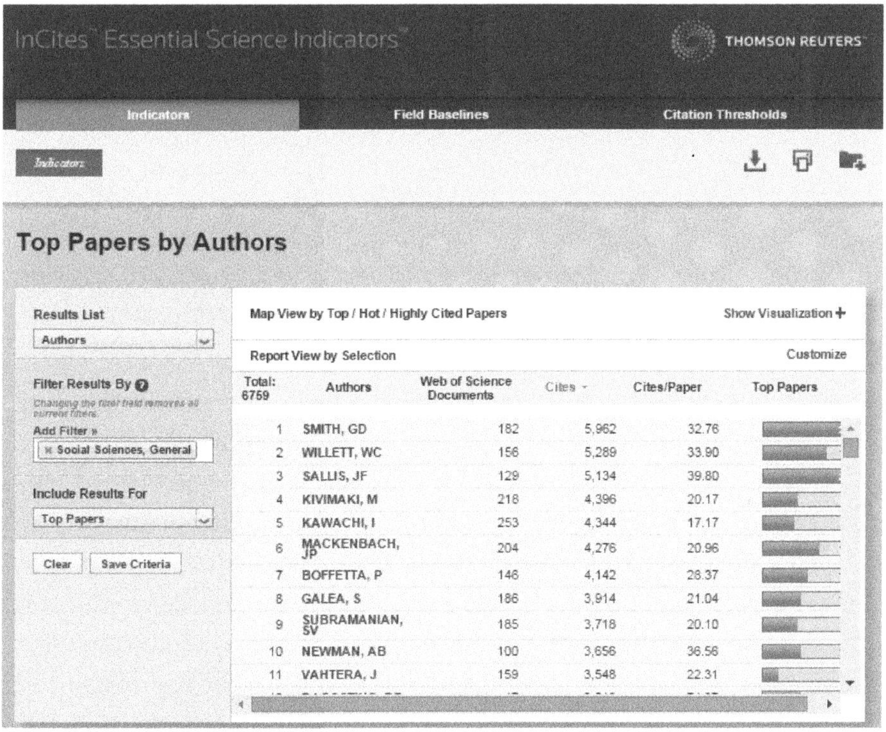

> "The journal impact factor, as calculated by Thomson Reuters, was originally created as a tool to help librarians identify journals to purchase, not as a measure of the scientific quality of research in an article. With that in mind, it is critical to understand that the journal impact factor has a number of well-documented deficiencies as a tool for research assessment."[44]
>
> —"The San Francisco Declaration on Research Assessment"

> "While there are illegitimate ways to achieve a higher impact factor—self-citation, citation rings, and denominator manipulations—most impact factors increase thanks to the hard work and careful choices of editors, reviewers, and publishers."[45]
>
> —Kent Anderson, "Exhibition Prohibition— Why Shouldn't Publishers Celebrate an Improved Impact Factor?"

Current Topics and Conversations about Bibliometrics

Now that we have reached the end of our long list of metrics and the major tools where one can find them, the question arises regarding each metrics' reputation, especially as deployed by researchers in the context of their actual evaluations and applications. For the most part, we can say that bibliometrics are viewed very positively by evaluating bodies, for capturing some measure (pun not intended!) of objectivity in the face of what can otherwise be a highly subjective presentation of quality is no small feat. However, as we have also hinted, there has been dissent within the academic ranks over the accuracy of some bibliometrics relative to certain fields, if not simply in general. Of these, the metric most often maligned is the golden stalwart, the journal impact factor, which paradoxically remains one of the oldest and most entrenched bibliometrics in higher education.

To some extent, we have already mentioned the controversy over impact factor as it exists across the disciplines in the sense that disciplines that are less focused on journals and journal articles are naturally disadvantaged in a comparative calculation of average citations per article. The arts and humanities are especially underserved by impact factor for this reason; to date, JCR doesn't even have an "arts and humanities" option, although theoretically one could calculate impact factor for journals within those fields, using Web of Science's Arts & Humanities Index. Yet there is more to the criticism of impact factor than its limited coverage of the academic research spectrum. For example, one of the biggest practical criticisms of impact factor's dominance is the ambiguity of what does and doesn't count as "citable material," and thus worthy of contributing to a journals' overall impact factor. On paper, citable materials should be scholarly works, such as original articles and reviews. But, as many commentators have pointed out, sometimes works published by journals like essays and extensive opinion pieces do have scholarly value and are arguably worthy of inclusion when assessing the reputation of a journal to the field as a whole. Another definitional criticism of impact factor is its insistence on using the printed date of publication as the basis for inclusion in the underlying journal data—not the date of online publication, which can precede the "official" publication date by months at a time. Both of these aspects gives impact factor the power to inflate or deflate a journal's relative impact significantly—a huge problem, given the importance that evaluators assign to the metric when trying to understand journal impact.

A third common criticism of impact factor goes to the monopoly that Thomson Reuters has on it—and what it means to calculate a journal's collective "times cited" in a sphere of knowledge that does not include scholarly portions of the Internet (e.g., Google Scholar) nor the ability to quickly fix errors in citations (e.g., Publish or Perish) nor the means to give input on journal impact as it changes between annual reports. For researchers in fields that have already branched out into venues not indexed by Web of Science or researchers who specialize in fields that are not well represented by JCR's title list, the lack of information and slow rate of change can be incredibly frustrating and cut directly into the usefulness of adopting impact factor as a standard. There is also a fourth line of criticism, represented in the literature of bibliometrics, about the possibility of "gaming" impact factor or of general impact factor inflation that can result from the less than genuine need to cite articles within a given paper.[46] Certainly both these practices exist, although measures are in place within JCR to combat the most blatant incidents of the former, such as rampant journal self-citation.

Overall, the decision to use impact factor—and *how* to use it—is up to the researcher, and in most cases, where available, it's likely the researcher will choose to use it, particularly if it helps fill out the picture of their impact in a way that reflects positively on their record. Still, as librarians, it is worthwhile for us to keep an eye on these issues and remind faculty, and connected administrators, that no single metric is sufficient for telling the story of their role and influence within the field. We can also help by reminding researchers that impact factor can and does change from year to year—and that the impact they see today may not be the one they see tomorrow as new journals enter the field and as the trends within disciplines wax and wane. We can also encourage users to update themselves on the latest pros and cons in the widespread discussion of impact factor, which vary across the disciplines.

> "So now, at least for some types of [web-based citation] data, gathering the data is the easy part.... With large data sets, you can also detect small effects and interactions that you wouldn't be able to detect in a sample. But honestly, the more that I work with statistics...the more deeply I've come to think of what the data can tell us, can't tell us about our world. Beneath the details and the techniques of the statistics themselves are some really profound ideas."[47]
>
> —Phil Davis, "Bibliometrics in an Age of Abundance"

The Future Outlook of Bibliometrics

In this chapter, we looked at the diversity of bibliometrics, from how it has developed over the last 50 years as a field of research to the many ways that scholars have used it, particularly in the sciences. We examined the patterns that exist in the types of bibliometrics that toolmakers have adopted and the relatively small number of companies that are actually behind the tools that scholars use most. Finally, we saw that bibliometrics is, in almost all cases, a school of impact dependent on journal citations—and therefore firmly grounded in a very traditional form of scholarly communication, often to the exclusion, for better and for worse, of other, more experimental formats and modes that are not so easily tracked and measured. Bibliometrics thus presents for us something of an artificially clean perspective on the identification and calculation of impact, useful for creating rankings (which require clean calculations) and powerful for tenure file evaluations (which value objective data as a shorthand for intradisciplinary values).

Yet all is not safe, stable, or static when it comes to the future of bibliometrics as companies and institutions alike are recognizing the potential of combining established bibliometrics with less easily tracked formats and indicators that go beyond exchanges that happen via citation. As we see in the creation of new indices for books and data sets and of portals that combine various research activities into one space, we will see a messier and arguably more compelling version of bibliometrics coming to the fore. That we will continue to have metrics like impact factor and times cited is virtually guaranteed. But it will be a far different place for researchers when they have richer tools that allow them to glimpse a more accurate picture of impact as it happens in their fields as well as in the context of their own work. In the meantime, as librarians, it is up to us to counsel researchers, faculty, and graduate students to continue to look for impact widely, seeking it in both tidy rankings and untidy bundles alike. As we learned in the last chapter, true impact is essentially impossible to measure, and to shy away from this fact is to do great disservice to the countless ways that scholars are making a difference in the eyes of their peers, and possibly in even greater circles as well.

Additional Resources
BOOKS AND JOURNALS
Blaise Cronin and Cassidy R. Sugimoto, eds., *Beyond Bibliometrics: Harnessing Multidimensional Indicators of Scholarly Impact* (Cambridge, MA: MIT Press, 2014).
> Despite the title, this newly published collection edited by Cronin and Sugimoto is focused on the past, present, and future of bibliometrics within the context of higher education. With chapters written by recognizable names such as Paul Wouters (The Citation Culture), Jevin West (Eigenfactor.org), and Jason Priem (Impactstory.org), this book is a great source of information on the latest research on impact as written for other scholars.

Nicola De Bellis, *Bibliometrics and Citation Analysis: From the Science Citation Index to Cybermetrics* (Lanham, MD: Scarecrow Press, 2009).
> By all accounts a solid introduction to bibliometrics, suitable to researchers as well as graduate students interested in the empirical, mathematical, and philosophical foundations of the field. The timing of the book's publication, just prior to the altmetrics movement, also means that it captures a unique moment in the development of "cybermetrics."

Ann-Wil Harzing, *The Publish or Perish Book: Your Guide to Effective and Responsible Citation Analysis* (Melbourne, Australia: Tarma Software Research, 2011).
> Written by the creator of the Publish or Perish software program, this companion book, an extension of the online guide, helps readers understand the in-depth ins and outs of the tool, from how it retrieves and analyzes academic citations to its various recommended uses.

Scientometrics
> The premiere journal for impact research across the sciences since 1978, *Scientometrics* is an excellent resource to read or browse when looking for articles on the quantitative features and scholarly communication. Based in Hungary but published in English, *Scientometrics* is copublished by Akadémiai Kiadó and Springer; it releases four volumes of 12 issues annually.

ORGANIZATIONS AND PROJECTS

Association for Information Science and Technology (ASIS&T) Special Interest Group on Metrics

An ASIS&T listserv dedicated to metrics papers, discussion, and announcements. Highlights include regular e-mails from Eugene Garfield featuring recent "publications of interest" and fierce debates on controversial metrics issues. SIGMETRICS@LISTSERV.UTK.EDU

Leiden Institute Center for Science and Technology Studies (CWTS)

CWTS is the independent organization in Leiden University (in the Netherlands) responsible for SNIP and one of the main driving organizations behind bibliometrics research. Its website features training and events, news, products, and services. *http://www.cwts.nl/Home*

International Society for Scientometrics and Informetrics (ISSI)

ISSI is a major society dedicated to the study of bibliometrics, particularly in the sciences. Highlighted features include a biannual conference, abstracts of bibliometric journals, and an electronic e-mail list. *http://www.issi-society.info*

BLOGS

The Citation Culture

The Citation Culture blog is the creation of Paul Wouters, director of the Centre for Science and Technology Studies at Leiden University (LU), and it is dedicated to discussion of academic impact from citation analysis to the broader evaluation of research across universities. While posts can be infrequent, they are notable for their depth and the wide range of topics they touch. *http://citationculture.wordpress.com/*

The Scholarly Kitchen

The Scholarly Kitchen is an independent, moderated blog that presents ideas on current topics of scholarly publishing and communication. Established by the Society for Scholarly Publishing, the blog features posts by "chefs" who boast expertise in the intersection between impact and publishing. Common topics include open access, impact factor, and policies related to journal publication in general. *http://scholarlykitchen.sspnet.org/*

Additional Tools

While we have tried to highlight the major tools associated with bibliometrics in this chapter, there remain even more citation-based tools that scholars have occasionally found useful in calculating their impact. The following is a list of some of those tools, which readers may choose to pursue at their own discretion and interest.

▼ **BibExcel.** A data generating tool designed to assist a user in analyzing bibliographic data. *https://bibliometrie.univie.ac.at/bibexcel/*

▼ **CiteSpace.** A network analysis and visualization tool that allows users to answer questions about the "structure and dynamics of a knowledge domain." *http://cluster.cis.drexel.edu/~cchen/citespace/*

▼ **Leiden Institute's list of institutional rankings.** An online ranking resource that covers 750 universities worldwide based on factors and uses a sophisticated set of bibliometric indicators. *http://www.leidenranking.com/*

▼ **Pajek.** A Windows program that allows for the visualization and analysis of large networks and can be freely downloaded for non-commercial use. *http://pajek.imfm.si/doku.php?id=pajek*

▼ **Science of Science (Sci2) Tool.** A modular toolset for scientists that supports the temporal, geospatial, topical, and network analysis and visualization of scholarly datasets. *https://sci2.cns.iu.edu/user/index.php*

▼ **SITKIS.** A free bibliometric tool that works on both Java and Microsoft Access. *https://sites.google.com/site/sitkisbibliometricanalysis/*

▼ **Scholarometer.** Formerly Tenurometer, this browser extension that provides a smart interface for Google Scholar and allows for additional features like user filtering and social tagging. *http://scholarometer.indiana.edu/*

Notes

1. Eugene Garfield, "Journal Impact Factor: A Brief Review," *Canadian Medical Association Journal* 161, no. 8 (1999): 979–80, *http://www.cmaj.ca/content/161/8/979.full*.

2. Alan Prichard, "Statistical Bibliography or Bibliometrics?," *Journal of Documentation* 25, no. 4 (1969): 349.
3. Mike Thewall, "Bibliometrics to Webometrics," *Journal of Information Science* 34, no. 4 (2008): 605.
4. Eugene Garfield, "Citation Indexes to Science: A New Dimension in Documentation through Association of Ideas," *Science* 122 (1955): 108–11, *http://garfield.library.upenn.edu/papers/science1955.pdf*.
5. "The SCI's use as a tool in measuring scientific productivity has often overshadowed its primary function as a search engine. Many people think bibliometrics is its main reason for existing"—Eugene Garfield, "The Evolution of the Science Citation Index Search Engine to the Web of Science, Scientometric Evaluation and Historiography," presentation, University of Barcelona, Barcelona, Spain, January 24, 2007, *http://garfield.library.upenn.edu/papers/barcelona2007.pdf*.
6. Eugene Garfield, "The Evolution of the Science Citation Index," *International Microbiology* 10 (2007): 65, *http://garfield.library. upenn.edu/papers/barcelona2007a.pdf*.
7. According to Garfield, the potential of citation searching for researchers was clear to him and ISI from the beginning, "but it took 40 years for the technology to advance to the point that allowed his vision to be fully realized"—Paula J. Hane, "Interview with Eugene Garfield: Eugene Garfield Turns 80," *InformationToday,* October 2005, 24, *http://garfield.library.upenn.edu/papers/infotoday102005.pdf*.
8. Lynn C. Hattendorf Westney, "Historical Rankings of Science and Technology: A Citationist Perspective," *The Journal of the Association of History and Computing* 1, no. 1 (1998): *http://quod.lib.umich.edu/cgi/p/pod/dod-idx/historical-rankings-of-science-and-technology-a-citationist. pdf?c=jahc;idno=3310410.0001.105*.
9. "The Complete Citation Connection," Web of Science, accessed January 6, 2015, *http://wokinfo.com/citationconnection/*.
10. Leslie S. Adriaanse and Chris Rensleigh, "Web of Science, Scopus and Google Scholar: A Content Comprehensiveness Comparison," *The Electronic Library* 31, no. 6 (2013): 727–44.
11. Henk F. Moed et al., "Citation-Based Metrics Are Appropriate Tools in Journal Assessment Provided That They Are Accurate and Used in an Informed Way," *Scientometrics* 92, no. 2 (2012): 376, doi:10.1007/s11192-012-0679-8.

12. "The Thomson Reuters Impact Factor," Web of Science, accessed January 6, 2014, *http://wokinfo.com/essays/impact-factor/*.
13. "Cited Half-Life," Journal Citation Reports, last modified May 22, 2012, accessed January 6, 2015, *http://admin-apps.webofknowledge.com/JCR/help/h_ctdhl.htm#jrnlctdhl*.
14. "A Model of Research," Eigenfactor.org, accessed January 6, 2015, *http://www.eigenfactor.org/methods.php*.
15. Just as Article Influence Score helps contextualize Eigenfactor at the article level, it's worth mentioning that the researchers behind Eigenfactor.org have also shown that the score can be adapted to help rank the outputs of scholars, scholarly institutions, and countries, in this case using data from the Social Science Research Network (SSRN, see ch. 5). However, because this use of Eigenfactor is hardly common, we have chosen not to detail it here. More information can be found in Jevin D. West et al., "Author-Level Eigenfactor Metrics: Evaluating the Influence of Authors, Institutions, and Countries within the SSRN Community," *Journal of the American Society for Information Science and Technology* 64, no. 4 (2012): 787–801, doi: 10.1002/asi.22790.
16. "About Us," SCImago Journal & Country Rank, accessed January 6, 2015, *http://www.scimagojr.com/aboutus.php*.
17. Ibid.
18. Borja González-Pereiraa, Vicente P. Guerrero-Boteb, and Félix Moya-Anegón, "The SJR Indicator: A New Indicator of Journals' Scientific Prestige," arXiv.org, Cornell University Library, December 21, 2009, *http://arxiv.org/ftp/arxiv/papers/0912/0912.4141.pdf*.
19. "SNIP Indicator," CWTS Journal Indicators, accessed January 6, 2015, *http://www.journalindicators.com*.
20. For anyone who needs a memory jog, median is the middle number in a series of numbers that has been ordered from lowest to highest. The median helps avoid outliers—in this case, an article with an unusually high citation count compared to other articles.
21. For a list of Cabell's Directories available for online subscription, see *http://cabells.com/directories.aspx*.
22. Many libraries subscribe to WorldCat, but a free version is also available at *http://www.worldcat.org/*.

23. Jorge E. Hirsch, "An Index to Quantify an Individual's Scientific Research Output," *Proceedings of the National Academy of Sciences of the United States of America* 102, no. 46 (2005): 16569, doi:10.1073/pnas.0507655102.
24. Garfield, "Journal Impact Factor."
25. For a good list of variations on h-index, see SCI²S Thematic Public Websites' "H-Index and Variants" website at ***http://sci2s.ugr.es/hindex/***.
26. Henk F. Moed et al., "Is Concentration of University Research Associated with Better Research Performance?," *Journal of Informetrics* 5, no. 4 (2011): 650, doi:10.1016/j.joi.2011.06.003
27. "SIR Methodology," SCImago Institutions Rankings, accessed January 6, 2014, ***http://www.scimagoir.com/methodology.php***.
28. "Overview of Institutions," Essential Science Indicators, last modified October 31, 2007, accessed January 6, 2015, ***http://esi.webofknowledge.com/help/h_datins.htm***.
29. "SIR Methodology," ScImago Institutions Rankings'.
30. "Home," Snowball Metrics, accessed January 17, 2015, ***http://www.snowballmetrics.com/***.
31. Robin Kear and Danielle Colbert-Lewis, "Citation Searching and Bibliometric Measures: Resources for Ranking and Tracking," *College & Research Libraries News* 72, no. 8 (2011): 470, ***http://crln.acrl.org/content/72/8/470.full***.
32. "Web of Science Core Collection," Web of Science, accessed January 6, 2015, ***http://wokinfo.com/products_tools/multidisciplinary/webofscience/***.
33. "ResearcherID," ResearcherID, accessed January 6, 2015, ***http://www.researcherid.com/***.
34. This redesign also introduces a new product, Essential Science Indicators, which also has some article-level metrics such as "Highly Cited" and "Hot" papers within large disciplines.
35. One notable example of Elsevier's outside partnerships is the Metrics Development Program, where researchers can apply to gain access to Scopus data for use in their metrics research. More information is available through its website: ***http://emdp.elsevier.com/***.
36. Lokman I. Meho and Kiduk Yang, "Impact of Data Sources on Citation Counts and Rankings of LIS Faculty: Web of Science versus

Scopus and Google Scholar," *Journal of the American Society for Information Science and Technology* 58, no. 13 (2007): 2105, doi: 10.1002/asi.20677.

37. More information on Google Scholar's inclusion criteria is available here: *http://scholar.google.com/intl/en-US/scholar/help.html#coverage*.
38. Introduced in a 2006 paper, g-index gives you *g*, which is the number of publications that have been cited g^2 times—Leo Egghe, "Theory and Practise of the G-Index," *Scientometrics* 69, no. 1 (2006): 131–52; the "contemporary h-index" more heavily weights recent citations—see Antonis Sidiropoulos, Dimitrios Katsaros, and Yannis Manolopoulos, "Generalized Hirsch H-Index for Disclosing Latent Facts in Citation Networks," *Scientometrics* 72, no. 2 (2007): 253–80, *http://link.springer.com/article/10.1007%2Fs11192-007-1722-z#page-1*.
39. "Publish or Perish 4 User's Manual," accessed January 5, 2015, *http://www.harzing.com/pophelp/metrics.htm*.
40. "The Book Citation Index," Web of Science, accessed January 6, 2015, *http://wokinfo.com/products_tools/multidisciplinary/bookcitationindex/*.
41. James Testa, *The Book Selection Process for the Book Citation Index in Web of Science*, accessed January 6, 2015, *http://wokinfo.com/media/pdf/BKCI-SelectionEssay_web.pdf*.
42. Figshare is a free online repository where works, particularly datasets, can be uploaded, assigned DOIs, shared, and cited: *http://figshare.com/about*; "The Data Citation Index," Web of Science, accessed January 6, 2015, *http://wokinfo.com//products_tools/multidisciplinary/dci/selection_essay/*.
43. That said, the future of tracking usage and citation of data goes far beyond Thomson Reuters, Impactstory, and libraries. DataCite is an organization that exists for the purposes of examining and standardizing this very issue: *https://www.datacite.org/*.
44. "San Francisco Declaration on Research Assessment," American Society for Cell Biology, accessed January 5, 2015, *http://am.ascb.org/dora/*.
45. Kent Anderson, "Exhibition Prohibition—Why Shouldn't Publishers Celebrate an Improved Impact Factor?" *The Scholarly*

Kitchen (blog), September 11, 2014, *http://scholarlykitchen.sspnet.org/2014/09/11/exhibition-prohibition-why-shouldnt-publishers-celebrate-an-improved-impact-factor/*.

46. Benjamin Althouse et al., "Differences in Impact Factor across Fields and Over Time," *Journal of the American Society for Information Science and Technology* 60, no. 1 (2009): 27–34, doi:10.1002/asi.20936.
47. Phil Davis, interview by Stewart Wills, "Bibliometrics in an Age of Abundance," *The Scholarly Kitchen* (blog), podcast audio, July 10, 2013, *http://scholarlykitchen.sspnet.org/2013/07/10/scholarly-kitchen-podcast-bibliometrics-in-an-age-of-abundance/*

Chapter Four

Bibliometrics in Practice

Now that you've been introduced to the major metrics and tools used in bibliometrics, it's time to take a more applied, hands-on approach. Think of these In Practice chapters as the workshop portions of the book—a chance to put your new knowledge to use as well as to survey how libraries and librarians are tackling research metrics today. That said, we fully understand that many of the specific details in this chapter are quite likely to change over time, so some of the details of our walk-throughs may or may not remain accurate. Nevertheless, the concepts and ideas behind the walk-throughs should remain valid, important, and useful.

We start our practical tour with a hands-on look at the three major tools currently available—Web of Science, Scopus, and Google Scholar—to find relevant metrics using a real-world example.

Walk-Through #1: Citations and Times Cited

One of the best ways of testing out new bibliometrics tools is to choose an actual person, either of sufficient reputation or appropriate acquaintance, and use him or her as a sample subject across a variety of resources. In this first walk-through, we've chosen to use Eugene Garfield, the father of scientometrics and one of the driving forces behind the 20th-century adoption of bibliometrics like impact factor. (If his name doesn't sound familiar, we suggest taking a quick look back at Chapter 3.) Garfield has a long publication history related to the topic of bibliometrics and, more generally, to library and information science. Additionally, his body of scholarship provides us with an entertaining opportunity to meta-analyze the very concepts that Garfield helped establish—an approach we like to think Garfield would only approve of.

We begin our walk-through by examining the process of gathering citations and times cited data for Garfield using one of the most popular tools available to scholars: Web of Science.

Web of Science

As discussed in Chapter 3, Web of Science is the best-known proprietary bibliometrics tool for scholars in search of citation data and the most commonly available (at least in terms of priority subscriptions managed by academic libraries with sufficient populations of science researchers). The first step in our walk-through is to perform a search on Garfield's name in the Web of Science database. Using the resource's Author Index, we find that we can identify and compare citations affiliated with all the scholars listed under the abbreviated name "Garfield E"—a nod to the prevalence of APA style, which truncates authors' first names to only display their initials. Eventually, we decide to select the index options of "Garfield E" and "Garfield Eugene" for a total of 1210 articles.

At this point in our search, however, we run into our first limitation: Garfield has been publishing since the 1950s, but the basic online subscription to Web of Science only includes citation coverage back to 1983. Due to this incomplete subscription coverage, we soon discover that only 605 of the citations affiliated with Eugene Garfield can be displayed, not the full set of 1200+ articles. This experience teaches us an important lesson: If seeking citations for an older author, it may be necessary to seek out print indices for more complete coverage or gain access to more complete online coverage at another institution. In the meantime, we must make do by working with our 600+ results in the hopes that we can still identify some of the most impactful articles authored by Garfield that have been cited since 1983. To do this, we sort the list of results by times cited. This reveals that of the 605 articles that we have access to via Garfield's

Figure 4.1. Author Index Results in Web of Science

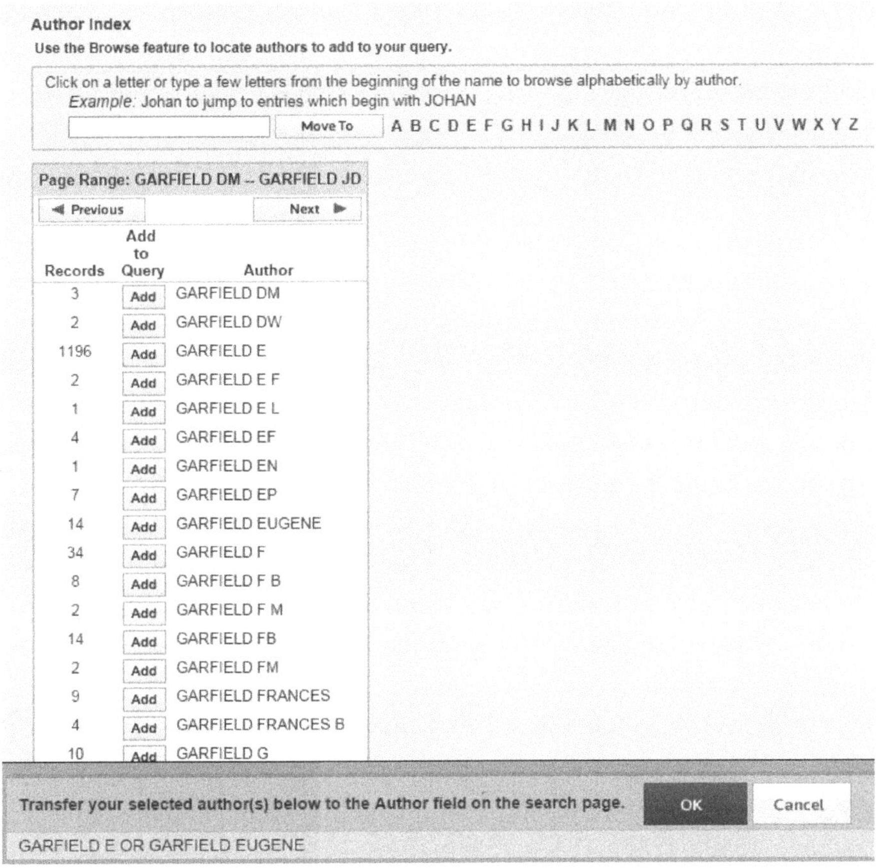

post-1983 citation record, the most frequently cited is a *Science* article published in 1972; it has been cited 1091 times.

Now, if our goal were to come up with a comprehensive list of Garfield's publications and times cited, we might choose to download all the available citations from Web of Science into a program like Excel or EndNote for later comparison with results derived from tools like Scopus and Google Scholar. Additionally, we might internally compare these citations collected via Web of Science to identify and eliminate any overlapping citations that may exist within that data set. Unfortunately, in the case of a scholar as prolific as Garfield, these steps could take many hours, much more time than most of us are willing to spend on a theoretical example. At the same time, both of these options are available to researchers who place a strong priority on a thorough examination of their respective scholarly records. Certainly this type of exhaustive searching and editing can help yield the most accurate author-level metrics later on, such as the calculation of Garfield's h-index.

Scopus

Now that we have completed a basic examination of Garfield's citations and times cited data in Web of Science, we repeat the process with Scopus, the second most popular proprietary bibliometrics tool. Not surprisingly, Scopus operates very similarly to Web of Science; it also offers convenient features like an Author Search tool. Using this tool now, we once again try searching both "Garfield, E" and "Garfield, Eugene" in order to identify all results relevant to Garfield's publication record. However, as with Web of Science, we quickly discover that Scopus's limited coverage of historic citation data significantly hampers the accuracy of our results. Even when searching on both the author profiles "Garfield, E" and "Garfield, Eugene," we only find 213 publications affiliated with Garfield here—a fraction of what we saw in Web of Science. Nevertheless, because Scopus may cover citation data derived from publications not indexed by Web of Science, it's important for us to proceed and learn more about these 200+ citations. To do this, we select both of these relevant author profiles and click Scopus's option to view their Citation Overview. This step gets us a display of the publications along with their citations counts and a few options to refine or change the display. Again, if we were interested at this point in performing a comprehensive analysis, we might download these results and check them for duplication, both as they currently stand and when combined with the results from resources like Web of Science.

Google Scholar

Having completed a tour of both of the major proprietary sources of citations and times cited bibliometrics, we head to Google Scholar, the "wild card" in our times cited equation due to its relationship with the Internet at large. Google Scholar offers a distinctly different interface from Web of Science and Scopus: a single stark search field, almost identical to the general Google Search tool, along with tiny icons that denote advanced search features. Using this basic search option, we perform an initial keyword search for "Eugene Garfield" to see what happens. This search returns "about 21,600 results," a number so bloated we know that it cannot be correct for our purposes. To increase our accuracy, we take advantage of Google Scholar's advanced search page, which includes a "Return Articles Authored by" search field that better mirrors our searches in Web of Science and Scopus. Repeating our search in this advanced author field, we discover 927 results for "Eugene Garfield," a number that clearly stands between the numbers offered by the other two bibliometrics tools. The gap between this number and Web of Science's count is not unexpected as it's reasonable to assume that many of the older publications that cite Garfield's research (prior to the 1990s) may not have found their way to the digital realm. However, we must once again consider the fact that as a tool based in the online realm, we may also be seeing citation results in Google Scholar that point to objects that are simply not indexed in either Web of Science or Scopus. For instance, because Google Scholar includes citations for an extremely wide variety of scholarly outputs, it's possible that our 900+ results include citations to Garfield's work derived from items such as books, reports, patents, conference proceedings, and online journals that Web of Science or Scopus may have missed. To discover whether this is the case, of course, we would need to perform a thorough analysis of the data, which would mean (as before) downloading the Google Scholar citations and carefully checking their times cited numbers. At this point, we'd also need to make a decision about what sort of citations we consider to be impactful. For example, do we include Google Scholar citations of Garfield's work that come from sources other than scholarly publications? Should citations from presentations be included in our times cited calculation? All these nuances would need to be decided and, ideally, put in writing as we continue to create a detailed statement of Garfield's citation-based impact.

> **Activity #1: Comparing Times Cited in Web of Science, Scopus, and Google Scholar**
>
> Regardless of the databases that you have access to, the process of searching, downloading, and reviewing publications' information and times cited data is a good technique for familiarizing yourself with the intricacies of any bibliometrics resource. To continue this exercise on your own, pick a researcher at your institution—or perhaps a well-known researcher in your field—and use him or her as your test case when exploring Web of Science, Scopus, or Google Scholar. See how the person's citation results change depending on search options available in the tool. Is a middle initial needed to identify his or her citations accurately? How does restricting the search to the tool's author field change your results? What options are you given to help discern which publications belong to your researcher and which ones do not? Investigating these questions for yourself will help you feel more prepared when similar questions inevitably arise as you help others in your library.

Discussion: Journal Rankings

In this section, we look at the application of Level 2 metrics, the real-world use of journal-level bibliometrics resources. As discussed in previous chapters, metrics, like times cited, often suffer from a lack of context: information that explains how "good" a metric is or how a given journal compares to other journals (if it can be compared). To create meaningful comparisons, discipline-specific journal rankings are often invoked to provide the necessary context to what can otherwise be disembodied numbers swimming in a page of numbers.

Before we jump to our next walk-through, let's take a moment to review what we know about journal rankings and the tools that offer users access to journal rankings.

What Are Journal Rankings?

Journal rankings are list-like resources that take journals with calculated metrics (impact factor, SJR, and h5-index) and divide them into subjects or disciplines as defined by each publisher (Thomson Reuters, SCImago, and Google Scholar, respectively). The reasons for these divisions are multiple, and they include the opportunity to provide specific user audiences with context for each metric and reveal the relative coverage strengths of each rankings resource (see the "Comparison of Subject Categories" sidebar). Consequently, studying these divisions and categories may help a researcher decide which resource best fits his or her research focus. It can also help librarians make meaningful comparisons between different rankings resources—a useful skill for working with a community or researchers.

What Are the Tools Most Commonly Used to Find Journal Rankings?

The tools researchers use for discovering journal rankings are intimately tied to the journal-level metrics themselves since all that the publishers are adding is a meaningful grouping of metrics based on a subject classification for each journal. As such, the most common providers of rankings are the same companies that provide major bibliometrics data: Journal Citation Reports (JCR) for rankings based on Thomson Reuters metrics like impact factor and other Web of Science-based times cited data; the ScImago website for rankings based on ScImago's internal journal rankings metric (SJR), Source Normalized Impact per Paper (SNIP), and other Scopus-based times cited data; and Google Scholar Metrics for rankings based on their h5-index, h5-median rankings, and other Google-based times cited data.

Journal Citation Reports Journal Rankings: Times Cited and Impact Factor

As discussed in the previous chapter, JCR can be used for finding journal-level metrics, most notably Web of Science-based times cited. These same metrics can also be grouped into discipline or subject-specific rankings based on Web of Science's Science Citation Index and Social Science Citation Index. Given Web of Science's strong focus on the science discipline, these subjects tend also to include much more specific categories for STEM disciplines than for the social sciences, though they do exist. Additionally, JCR includes both broader and narrower subject categories, which can often confuse scholars looking for information within and across a discipline. For example, environmental

Comparison of Subject Categories: Journal Citation Reports, SCImago Journal Rankings, and Google Scholar

Just as a database's subject headings give users clues about the subject coverage and specificity of the database, a citation database's subject categories for journals can provide librarians with clues as to the relative subject strengths and weaknesses of the database. However, differences in the way that categories are structured in each bibliometric tool can make direct comparisons difficult in practice. For instance, Thomson Reuter's rankings tool, Journal Citation Reports (JCR), starts with only two main academic categories: Science and Social Science. Within each of these root categories, the JCR tool lists academic subjects alphabetically—a design decision that makes additional research groupings inconvenient. By contrast, SCImago's rankings tool, SCImago Journal Rankings (SJR), starts with 27 root categories, which are each then broken down into five to ten specific subject categories. This decision to broaden the tool's root groupings is also reflected in the design of Google Scholar Metrics' rankings, which starts with eight main academic categories but narrows down to anywhere from 10–70+ subject categories each. What a mess!

Below, we give a comparison of similar subjects (and their structure) in JCR, SJR, and Google Scholar metrics. Use this table to get a basic sense of how three sample subjects are broken down by subdiscipline by each tool.

Table 4.1. Subject Category Comparison between Journal Citation Reports (JCR), SCImago and Google Scholar (GS)

CHEMISTRY

JCR	SCImago	GS
Category: Science	Category: Chemistry	Category: Chemical & Material Sciences
Chemistry, Analytical	Analytical Chemistry	Analytical Chemistry
Chemistry, Inorganic & Nuclear	Chemistry (miscellaneous)	Biochemistry
Chemistry, Medicinal	Electrochemistry	Chemical & Material Sciences (general)
Chemistry, Multidisciplinary	Inorganic Chemistry	Chemical Kinetics & Catalysis
Chemistry, Organic	Organic Chemistry	Crystallography & Structural Chemistry

Chemistry, Physical	Physical and Theoretical Chemistry	Dispersion Chemistry
	Spectroscopy	Electrochemistry
		Inorganic Chemistry
		Medicinal Chemistry
		Organic Chemistry

PSYCHOLOGY (EXCLUDING PSYCHIATRY)

JCR	SCImago	GS
Category: Social Science	Category: Psychology	Category: Health and Medical Sciences
Psychology, Applied	Applied Psychology	Child & Adolescent Psychology
Psychology, Biological	Clinical Psychology	Psychology
Psychology, Clinical	Developmental and Educational Psychology	Social Psychology
Psychology, Developmental	Experimental and Cognitive Psychology	
Psychology, Educational	Neuropsychology and Physiological Psychology	Category: Social Sciences
Psychology, Mathematical	Psychology (miscellaneous)	Academic & Psychological Testing
Psychology, Multidisciplinary	Social Psychology	Cognitive Science
Psychology, Psychoanalysis		Educational Psychology & Counseling
Psychology, Social		

HISTORY

JCR	SCImago	GS
Category: Social Science	Category: Arts and Humanities	Category: Humanities, Literature & Arts
History	History	African Studies & History
History & Philosophy of Science	History and Philosophy of Science	Asian Studies & History
History of Social Sciences		Canadian Studies & History
		Chinese Studies & History
		Epistemology & Scientific History
		History

scholars may initially browse JCR's "Environmental Sciences" category to discover top journals in their field, but then may wonder, "What about broader high impact publications like *Nature* and *Science*?" (Yes, we have been asked this exact question!) While *Nature* and *Science* are indeed journals that contain environmental science articles, they are classified by JCR under the easily overlooked category of "Multidisciplinary Science." Indeed, many science disciplines have an "interdisciplinary" category in addition to subcategories like "Interdisciplinary Chemistry", "Biochemistry," and "Organic Chemistry." As seen in the figure below, the number of journals listed within different JCR subject categories can be easily compared and displayed via JCR. This tool can give clues as to the breadth of a selected subject category, while the table below the visual display shows metrics for those categories, such as aggregate and median times cited. Users can also access information about subject categories by looking at a specific journal listed in JCR; it will display all the subject categories the journal is listed under. Any of these categories can be clicked on for easy viewing. As many readers will find, it's not unusual for a journal in JCR to appear in two more or categories.

When viewing an individual journal, JCR will also display the journal's rank within all subject categories for the past five years as well as its quartile (Q1, Q2, etc.), which is 25% (a quarter) of all the journals in the category that this journal falls into. Q1 places the journal within the top 25%, while Q4 places it in the bottom 25%. As seen in Figure 4.2, *Journal of Psychology* falls into Q2, ranking 65th out of 129 journals in the "Psychology, Multidisciplinary" category in 2013.

Figure 4.2. Journal of Psychology Category Ranking

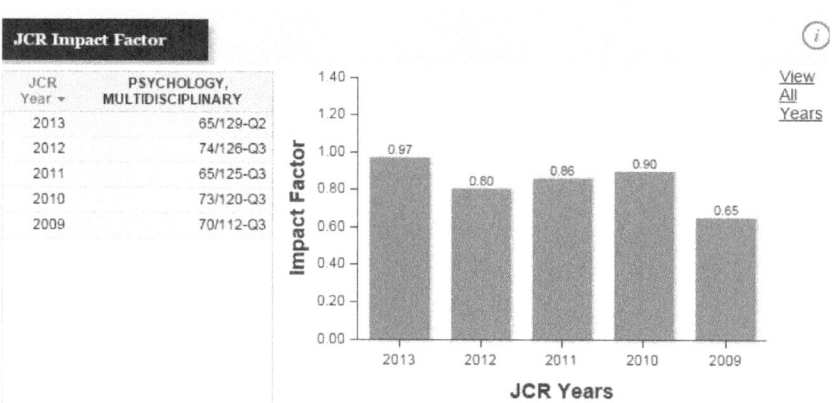

Chapter Four 81

Scopus Journal Rankings: SJR and SNIP
In the Compare Journals section of Scopus, SJR and SNIP are listed on an individual journal's page along with its assigned categories. From this page, journals can be compared using the Journal Analyzer. The Journal Analyzer allows for the direct comparison of two or more journals based on their SJR or SNIP values over several years (and creates a nice-looking graph of the comparison). However, at the time of writing this book, the full rankings of different journals by subject and SJR value could only be accessed through the SCImago Journal Rankings website (freely available at *www.scimagojr.com*) and not the Scopus analyzer itself. That said, once on the main ScImago Journal Rankings home page, we can easily view the comprehensive SJR rankings, delving into entire subject areas and subcategories via a simple search interface. Journals can also be ranked according to their adapted h-index (similar to Google Scholar's h5-metric) or their average citations per item. Unfortunately, there is no way as of yet to create journal rankings using SNIP, although technically you can directly compare a handful of journals' SNIP values using Scopus's Journal Analyzer as discussed.

Google Scholar Metrics Journal Rankings: H5-Index and H5-Median
In Chapter 3, we surveyed the tools and metrics that are provided through Google Scholar, including its two journal-level metrics: h5-index and h5-median. While these metrics are slightly simpler in their design than impact factor, SJR, or SNIP, these rankings can provide us with additional information about journals, particularly journals not included in Web of Science or Scopus, and thus lacking impact factor, SJR, or SNIP metrics. When searching Google Scholar Metrics, we find that we can search for individual journal titles to retrieve their h5-index and h5-median metrics on the Google Scholar Metrics home page. We can also click on their h5-index number to get more details about a journal, including any categories where the journal ranks in a discipline's top 20. Alternately, on the Google Scholar Metrics home page, one can also browse by broad discipline or click on a discipline to select a subdiscipline. Finally, journals indexed by Google Scholar can also be searched by keyword in Google Scholar Metrics to bring up a more specific comparison (e.g., searching for

all journals with "intercultural" in the title), but like the journal analyzer in Scopus, it may require some explanation for the venture away from the discipline and subdiscipline rankings. Keep in mind, Google Scholar Metrics comes with two major downsides:

1. While the metrics are frequently updated, historical metrics are not retained.

2. Though h5-index and h5-median are available for many journals, Google Scholar Metrics' categories only display the top 20 journals in each category, making journal rankings difficult for many journals.

Walk-Through #2: Journal Metrics and Rankings

In our first walk-through, we began creating a statement of impact by collecting citations and times cited. For our second walk-through, we continue our statement of impact by turning from article-level metrics to journal-level metrics and discipline rankings. For this walk-through, we turn to a different example: our friend and colleague, Matt Hartings. Dr. Hartings is a chemistry professor at American University, and he has published on interdisciplinary topics such as chemistry communication. Like the previous walk-through, we start by delving into the three major tools for retrieving citation-based metrics: Web of Science, Scopus, and Google Scholar. However, this time, instead of focusing on the number of times an author has been cited, we will focus on the impact of the publications that a specific scholar has been affiliated with. To make things easier, we'll start at the point where we have already used these sources to gather information about the journals that Hartings has published in, totaling 12 unique journal titles. What's more, because information about some of these journals is listed in multiple tools (e.g., both Web of Science and Scopus), we should be able to see some comparative journal metrics in action.

For those following along with this walk-through on their own, one excellent question to ponder before starting is whether to pull the most recent journal metrics for each publication or try to find metrics from the year of the scholar's specific interaction with the publication. In our case, we decided to pull the most recent metrics because this seems to be the most common practice among actual faculty. This decision also allowed us to include in this walk-through Google Scholar Metrics because it does not include historical metrics. Now it's time to start collecting some Level 2 metrics!

Journal Citation Reports

We start our search for journal-level metrics in Web of Science's JCR tool. Using JCR's Journal Profile search, we can search for individual journal titles indexed in Web of Science and retrieve their impact factor and discipline rankings. So, for example, searching the Journal Profile for "Journal of the American Chemical Society" (*JACS*) brings up the correct journal, which we then click on to get more details. At the top of this page, we get basic information about the journal, such as the ISSN and publisher information. Further down, we see the Key Indicators section, which includes metrics like journal impact factor—11.444 for this journal in 2013. Further down, we get the relevant categories and the ranking in each category. Note that if the journal belongs to multiple categories, the small display in the left side of the screen scrolls horizontally to show each ranking as shown in Figure 4.3. For *JACS*, there is only one category associated with the journal,

Figure 4.3. Scroll Bar for Multiple Category Rankings

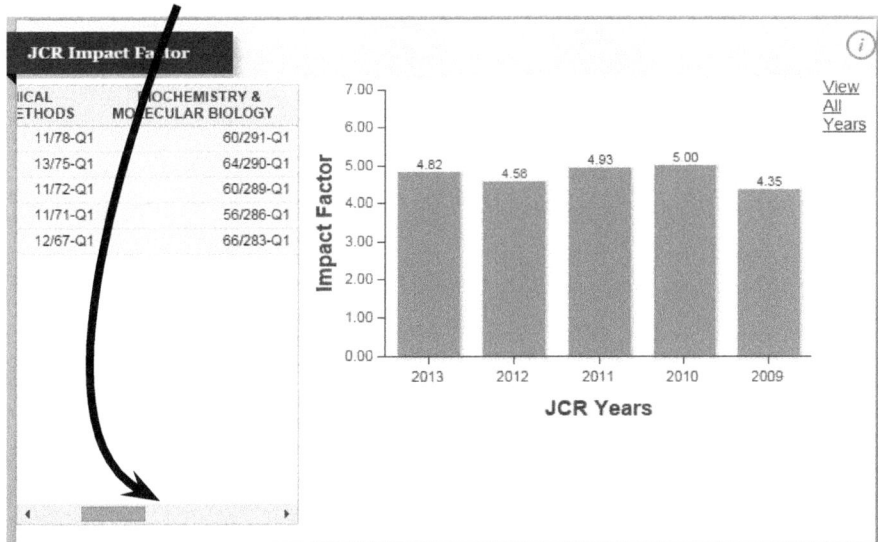

"Multidisciplinary Chemistry," and *JACS* is 10th out of 148 journals in this category. We add both the impact factor and discipline ranking to our spreadsheet and continue through all of the journals, adding metrics and rankings to the journals that are included in JCR.

SCImago

Next we turn to SCImago Journal Rankings (SJR), the rankings that drive the journal-focused data available in Scopus based on Scopus citations. To efficiently collect metrics for all 12 journals, we decided to use the free SCImago Journal and Country Rank website (scimagojr.com) to collect our data. On the website, there are options to look at Journal or Country Rankings, perform a Journal Search or Country Search, compare two or more journals or countries, and generate a map of co-citations for a particular country. Selecting the Journal Search directs us to a basic keyword search for journals, which then pulls up relevant metrics for the selected journal. By searching for and then selecting, "Journal of the American Chemical Society," we can view the detailed information for *JACS*. Near the top, subject areas and categories are displayed along with the quartile information for each subject category. For journals with many categories, like the one in the image, we like the idea of including this chart in a statement of impact as a quick demonstration of quartile impact as the list of rankings gets a bit cumbersome! To see exactly where a journal falls in its assigned subject areas, each subject area must be clicked on and browsed to find the journal. *JACS* has four assigned subject categories, appearing in the top quartile (Q1) in each of them. By clicking on each category individually and looking for *JACS*, we can add the rankings for each category to our statement of impact, such as the 7/417 ranking of *JACS* in "Chemistry (miscellaneous)."

Slightly further down below the subject categories, there are two tabbed options in the upper-right corner, Charts and Data, with Charts automatically displayed as the default. However, by clicking on the Data tab to switch from Charts to Data, we get a list of SJR and other data sorted by year (and remember that for SNIP values, we need to go to Scopus or journalmetrics.com).

Figure 4.4. Display of Multiple Journal Categories in SCImago

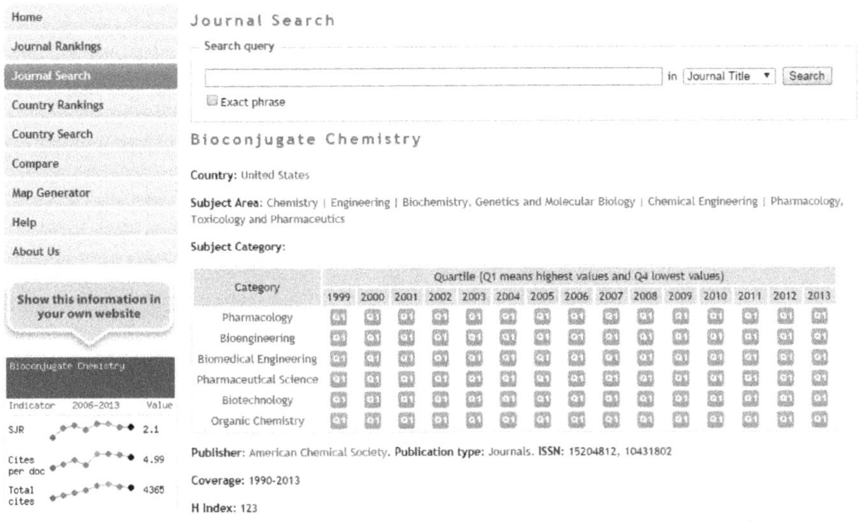

Google Scholar Metrics

Having successfully looked at the data available for Hartings' journals via the two most traditional providers of citation-based metrics, we proceed to round out our rankings with a look at Google Scholar's increasingly popular journal-focused metrics. As mentioned earlier, Google Scholar metrics are more limited than those in Web of Science or Scopus as they only include rankings information for journals that fall in the top 20 for a given subject category. We begin this last part of the compiled statement of impact by searching for "Journal for the American Chemistry Society" in the search box on the Google Scholar Metrics' home page. After finding the correct record for *JACS*, we can also see the h5-index and h5-median for *JACS*, 190 and 250, respectively. By clicking on the h5-index (190), we then view more specific information, including the most highly cited articles included in the rankings along with any top 20 category rankings. For *JACS*, we learn that it's ranked second in "Chemical & Material Sciences" and "Chemical & Material Sciences (general)" categories.[1] Due to the top 20 limitation for discipline rankings, these metrics don't shine much additional light to our existing information, but it could certainly be an option, particularly when a specific subject category (like "Asian Studies &

History," for example) matches up well with the researcher's publications and research interests.

All of this information was compiled into Microsoft Excel, as shown in Table 4.2, with the understanding that this raw chart may need further refining, explanations, or revisions before Dr. Hartings would choose to use this information for something like an application for tenure. Also note that this spreadsheet provides another real-world example of how widely categories can vary, even for a STEM field.

> **Activity #2: Compiling Journal Metrics and Rankings from Journal Citation Reports, SCImago Journal and Country Rank, and Google Scholar Metrics**
>
> Building on the information gathered in Activity #1, we can continue our hands-on training, moving from Level 1 metrics to Level 2. As you do this, there are decisions to be made: Are you aiming for comprehensive metrics, or do you want to only include what seems the most relevant (or flattering)? Do you want to include publications without any metrics (such as the published proceedings in our example) in your list?

Walk-Through #3: Self-Calculating Metrics

As evidenced in this chapter's first walk-through, one of the most common problems that scholars face when investigating their bibliometrics online is that of misinformation—duplicate entries, small typos that incorrectly generate multiple records, and issues of correct author name or affiliation. While Excel can be a useful solution to these issues when they occur across different bibliometrics providers, another solution is the use of a provider-specific data manipulator like the free downloadable program Publish or Perish. Discussed in detail in Chapter 3, Publish or Perish (PoP) is a great option for creating DIY metrics—so long as the DIYer accepts that all metrics generated will be derived from Google Scholar information.

With this limitation in mind, let's walk through two scenarios where the use of PoP could be an appropriate solution: first, for calculating

Chapter Four 87

Table 4.2. Chart of Dr. Harting's Journal Impact Metrics

Journal	Impact Factor	JCR journal Ranking	SJR	SJR journal Ranking	H-5 index	Google Scholar Ranking
Abstracts of Papers of the American Chemical Society	N/A		N/A		N/A	
Journal of the American Chemical Society	11.444	10/148 in Multidisciplinary Chemistry	6,317	1/47 in Catalysis, 1/19 in Colloid and Surface Chemistry, 6/390 in Biochemistry, 7/417 in Chemistry (miscellaneous)	190	#2 in Chemical and Material Sciences, #2 in Chemical and Material Sciences (general)
Nature Chemistry	23.297	4/148 in Multidisciplinary Chemistry	9,137	6/417 in Chemistry (miscellaneous, 1/333 in Chemical Engineering (miscellaneous)	99	#6 in Chemical and Materials Sciences (general)
Chemical Engineering News	N/A		N/A		14	
Science and Technology of Advanced Materials	2.613	51/251 in Multidisciplinary Materials Science	0,729	123/529 in Materials Science (miscellaneous)	29	
Proceedings of the National Academy of Sciences of the United States of America	9.809	4/55 in Multidisciplinary Sciences	7,048	3/112, Multidisciplinary	217	#3 in Life Sciences and Earth Sciences (general), #3 in Health and Medical Sciences (general), #4 in Life Sciences and Earth Sciences, #4 in Health and Medical Sciences

Table 4.2. Chart of Dr. Harting's Journal Impact Metrics

Journal	Impact Factor	JCR journal Ranking	SJR	SJR journal Ranking	H-5 index	Google Scholar Ranking
Journal of Physical Chemistry B	3.377	39/136 in Physical Chemistry	1,575	16/263 in Materials Chemistry, 6/123 in Surfaces, Coatings and Films, 170/1827 in Medicine (miscellaneous), 22/147 in Physical and Theoretical Chemistry	74	#9 in Chemical and Material Sciences (general)
Journal of Biological Inorganic Chemistry	3.164	121/291 in Biochemistry and Molecular Biology, 9/44 in Inorganic and Nuclear Chemistry	1,116	132/390 in Biochemistry, 8/64 in Inorganic Chemistry	32	
Coordination Chemistry Reviews	12.098	1/44 in Inorganic and Nuclear Chemistry	4,624	11/417 in Chemistry (miscellaneous)	78	#1 in Inorganic Chemistry
Bioconjugate Chemistry	4.821	11/78 in Biochemical Research Methods, 60/291 in Biochemistry and Molecular Biology, 24/148 in Multidisciplinary Chemistry, 7/58 in Organic Chemistry	2,105	26/346 in Pharmacology, 15/159 in Bioengineering, 11/325 in Biomedical Engineering, 5/211 in Pharmaceutical Science, 19/260 in Biotechnology, 12/172 in Organic Chemistry	57	
Applied Optics	1.649	29/82 in Optics	1,142	29/212 in Atomic and Molecular Physics, and Optics	45	#12 in Optics and Photonics
Science and Technology of Advanced Materials	2.613	52/251 in Multidisciplinary Materials Science	0,729	123/529 in Materials Science (miscellaneous)	29	

author-level metrics, and second, for calculating journal-level metrics. Following our earlier walk-through order, we'll start with the calculation of author-level metrics, using as our example one of the authors of this book—Robin Chin Roemer! PoP is ideal for researchers publishing in fields that aren't well covered by Web of Science or Scopus, so Robin, a librarian who has published in professional venues, is an excellent candidate.

Calculating Level 3: Author-Level Metrics

The first step, of course, is to download the PoP software for Windows, Mac, or Linux from its website (*http://www.harzing.com/pop.htm*), a relatively painless process. Once launched, the main area of the program is blank (but will contain results after a search is performed) with tabs along the left side that include Author Impact, Journal Impact, General Citations, and Multi-Query Center. If we click on the Author Impact tab, we find a search display that looks quite similar to Google Scholar's advanced search options (with good reason since we're searching Google Scholar!). By searching for "Robin Chin Roemer" in the Author's Name field, we pull up 18 results, including journal articles, published reviews, and library subject guides. Since reviews and subject guides are rarely cited, we remove these citations by unchecking the appropriate boxes. After "cleaning" our data, we are left with six articles we can gather metrics from. As shown in Figure 4.5, PoP automatically calculates several metrics, including cites

Figure 4.5. Calculating Author-level Metrics in Publish or Perish

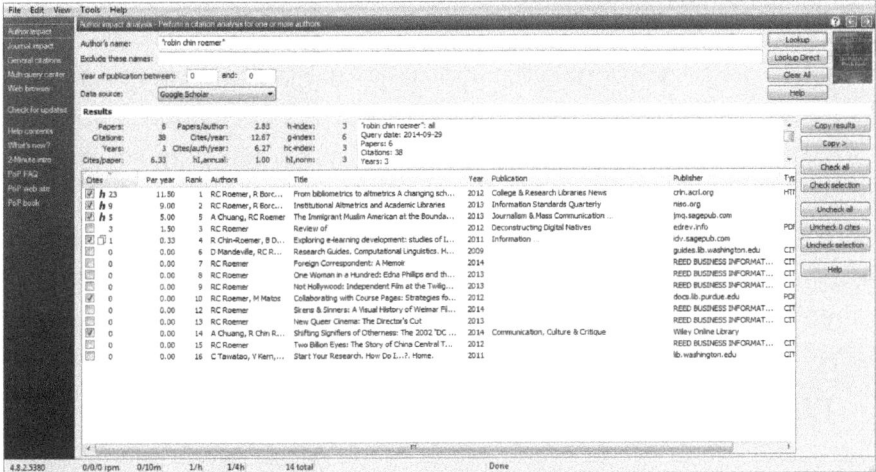

per year and several h-index variations. In Robin's case, the g-index may be a good Level 2 metric to use in the future since it gives more weight to highly cited papers. In this case, Robin's most highly cited paper has significantly more citations than any other paper with 23 citations compared to the next-highest cited paper with only nine citations.[2]

Calculating Level 2: Journal-Level Metrics

Taking Robin's example one step further, we will next focus on one of her more recent articles, "Institutional Altmetrics and Academic Libraries," published in the open access journal *Information Standards Quarterly* (*ISQ*). Although well known within LIS as a scholarly publication of National Information Standards Organization (NISO), *ISQ* isn't listed in JCR, SCImago/Scopus, or Google Scholar Metrics. How, then, can we retrieve any contextual metrics for this journal? Publish or Perish features the Journal Impact tab that allows users to calculate journal-level metrics based on Google Scholar information. In this case, Publish or Perish can find citations to *ISQ* articles in Google Scholar, and based on these entries, can calculate things like average times cited per article, times cited per year, h-index, and more; these can then be directly compared to peer journals or to Google Scholar's h5-index. While calculating metrics this way doesn't carry the same level of recognition or rigor as pointing to a journal's JCR-based impact factor or SCImago-based SJR, for authors like Robin publishing in journals with little to no alternative metrics, it can at least provide some useful and objective information beyond a simple citation count. Since Robin has no other metrics to support the impact of *ISQ*, she could manually calculate the h5-index for *ISQ* by searching for "Information Standards Quarterly" between the years of 2009 and 2014. By doing so, Publish or Perish gives us the h-index of eight (effectively, the h5-index, since we're already limited to the last five years of publication), which we can then directly compare to similar journals like *College & Research Libraries News*'s h5-index of 14, where another of Robin's articles was published.

Library Practices for Supporting Bibliometrics

Finally, to conclude this In Practice chapter, we take one more look at what other libraries and librarians are doing to incorporate concepts related to bibliometrics into their professional practice. Anecdotally, we know that librarians are already supporting bibliometrics through a variety of techniques such as the creation of research guides, the offering of consultations, and the purchasing of related databases. However, at the time of this book's publications, no recent studies could be found that detailed how common each of these practices were among interested librarians. Accordingly, in Fall 2013, we decided to conduct an online survey of individuals with online research guides related to metrics support to get a better sense of what librarians were doing to support metrics needs on their campus. We will refer to this survey several times since it informs many of our In Practice chapters.[3]

Thirty of 33 responders (91%) reported that they had worked to support bibliometrics—the highest number of any of the areas, indicating that the area of bibliometrics is one that the most libraries support overall, possibly because it has a longer history in academia than other types of metrics. By contrast, only 9/34 (27%) reported supporting "book metrics," making it the area of research metrics with the lowest percentage of support.

We also asked what types of activities these librarians were engaged in. The two most popular activities were the creation of subject guides and one-on-one appointments. We think that these two activities are the most frequent for two reasons. One, we surveyed people with guides, so we were not surprised to hear that they reported creating a guide! Two, as librarians, we are often asked for individual assistance from our users with many library-related subjects, including metrics. It is not surprising, then, that many of these librarians have worked with users, but it is unknown how these individuals came to seek individual assistance or why they turned to the library. Nonetheless, for libraries and librarians looking for places to begin, an online research guide is a natural place to start, and it is also a natural place to offer contact information for one-on-one assistance.[4]

So what does a good research guide look like? We turn to a guide that is often used as a model for other libraries, the University of Pittsburgh's "Citation Searching and Bibliometric Measures" guide by Robin Kear.[5] Kear, along with Danielle Colbert-Lewis, wrote a *College & Research Libraries News* (*C&RL News*) article in 2011 outlining bibliometric tools, so it's no wonder that Kear's guide is a frequently used template.[6] The guide contains basic information and introductions to many of the same key metrics and tools we discuss in Chapter 3, but it also includes discussion of relevant issues, related concepts, and plenty of links to other sources with additional information. We particularly like the printable handout version, which can easily transition to a handout given to individual faculty members or attendees of a workshop or instruction session.

Speaking of handouts, Curtin University's metrics research guide, "Measure Research Impact and Quality," links to a double-sided handout with a succinct listing of available services, which includes some specific services related to publication that libraries may not always associate with metrics, such as assistance with creating or modifying an EndNote style for publication in a specific journal.[7] Such a handout introduces services from a faculty member's perspective and is designed to entice the researcher into seeking more information and/or assistance.

While we're looking at the ways that libraries support metrics, it is also important to remember that libraries are also consumers of metrics. Use of Level 4 metrics can tell libraries which researchers, departments, or schools are frequent (or infrequent) publishers, which can help inform outreach services and determine where they may need additional assistance. Level 2 metrics can also still adequately perform their original function—that is, to assist librarians in making collection development decisions. Many librarians often use impact factor in conjunction with other data, such as usage statistics and faculty input, to make strategic decisions regarding their journal and database offerings and to ensure that if a collection needs to be trimmed that the library continues to retain high impact journals (by whatever definition of "high impact" they have chosen). And, as we'll discuss more in Chapter 8, librarians can also use metrics to measure the impact of their own research.

Moving Forward

Moving forward with bibliometrics on a practical level takes time and dedication from librarians who may not have much experience with them. As such, we end this chapter with a quick list of tips to help you move forward, based on our exercises and discussions above.

- ▼ **Practice creating a bibliometric "statement of impact."** By choosing a researcher of interest and piecing together the walk-throughs in this chapter, you can create an impact statement that includes citation counts, Level 2 and Level 3 metrics, and journal rankings for the researcher's publication.

- ▼ **Explore non-journal metrics.** While many bibliometrics are based on journal articles, there are other metrics for non-journal items, particularly books and datasets. This includes book metrics in Book Citation Index and Google Scholar, book reviews, publishers' acceptance rates, library holdings in WorldCat, and data metrics in Data Citation Index.[8] Familiarity with these metrics will help assist faculty in disciplines less reliant on journal publications (or anyone looking for book or data metrics).

- ▼ **Talk to researchers about their needs and concerns regarding bibliometrics.** Assessing researchers' level of comfort and familiarity with bibliometrics will allow you to successfully find metrics that work for them and their departments while also educating them to possibilities they may not have considered.

- ▼ **Explore discipline-specific metrics.** Many disciplines have plenty to say about the application of bibliometrics to their particular fields. While we will discuss discipline considerations in greater detail in Chapter 7, now is the time to start looking for these discussions in journal articles, blogs, or peer network communities. This will allow you to package your information for presentation to audiences within varying disciplines.

- ▼ **Plan a presentation.** Consider setting up a meeting with faculty and/or administrators and develop key messages to match the audience.

This could include new faculty, graduate students, grant holders, or administrators who evaluate files and/or grants. For example, Robin and Rachel used to co-teach a metrics workshop as seen in Figure 4.6.

Figure 4.6. Librarian-hosted Workshop Description

> 1004: Bibliometrics and Impact Factor (Anderson B-14)
>
> *Rachel Borchardt (Library) & Robin Chin Roemer (Library)*
>
> Want to learn how to find, measure and track your own research output? This workshop will introduce the topic of bibliometrics, or the analysis of scholarly literature and impact. An overview of major bibliometric research tools will be provided (e.g. Web of Science, Scopus, and Google Scholar), along with a demonstration of some alternative tools for use by individuals. Time will be given for a hands-on exploration of these tools.

Additional Resources

My Research Impact

A product of four Irish academic institutions, this "train the trainer" website is full of videos, handouts, and more educational resources to help librarians and other practitioners instruct others on bibliometrics. The materials are governed by a Creative Commons license, which encourages users to adapt the materials for their own needs. *http://www.ndlr.ie/myri/*

Chris Belter's Institutional-Level Work at National Oceanic and Atmospheric Administration (NOAA)

While Chris Belter is one of two recently hired bibliometrics specialists at NIH, the body of his work currently focuses on institutional-level analyses of NOAA publications.[9] One of his publications, "A Bibliometric Analysis of Articles Sponsored by NOAA's Office of Ocean Exploration and Research," shows how you can use bibliometrics to showcase your institution's publications. *http://www.lib.noaa.gov/bibliometrics/pdfs/jul2013_OER_citationreport.pdf*

SlideShare
    Searching SlideShare for terms like *bibliometrics*, *research impact*, or *impact factor* can give you ideas on how others have presented on similar topics (including Rachel's recent presentations to faculty and other audiences).[10] ***http://www.slideshare.net***

ALA's Librarian and Researcher Knowledge Space (LARKS): Research Methods
    Along with other research methods and methodologies, this ALA site links to several useful pages related to bibliometrics, including our 2012 *C&RL News* article, "From Bibliometrics to Altmetrics: A Changing Scholarly Landscape." ***http://www.ala.org/research/larks/researchmethods***

ACRL EBSS Presentation: "Measuring Impact Across the Disciplines: Tools and Strategies for Supporting Faculty"
    This recorded webinar, originally offered by in December 2012 by the authors of this book and University of South Florida-Tampa education librarian Susan Ariew, provides a brief introduction to the application of metrics within the context of education and the behavioral social sciences. ***http://connect.ala.org/node/194943***

Notes

1. No, we don't know the difference between these two categories! The collective mind of Google Scholar is, at times, rather incomprehensible.
2. For more information about the g-index according to Publish or Perish, check out their metrics guide: ***http://www.harzing.com/pop help/metrics.htm#gindex.***
3. All of the graphs and full data from the survey are covered in Chapter 8—check there to learn more.
4. But beware! Inclusion of contact information can sometimes lead to unsolicited e-mails with invitations to contribute to a survey.
5. Robin Kear, "Citation Searching and Bibliometric Measures," University [of Pittsburgh] Library System Course & Subject Guides, last modified January 1, 2015, ***http://pitt.libguides.com/bibliometrics.***

6. Robin Kear and Danielle Colbert-Lewis, "Citation Searching and Bibliometric Measures: Resources for Ranking and Tracking," *College & Research Libraries News* 72, no. 8 (2011): 470, **http://crln.acrl.org/content/72/8/470.full**.
7. "Measure Research Impact and Quality," Curtin University Library, last modified October 10, 2014, **http://libguides.library.curtin.edu.au/content.php?pid=333035&sid=2794979**; Curtin University Library, *Research Quality and Impact Service at Curtin*, **http://lgdata.s3-website-us-east-1.amazonaws.com/docs/1470/1208397/Research-impact-2014.pdf**.
8. More resources for data metrics are covered in Chapter 5.
9. A complete list of Chris Belter's works is available here: **http://nihlibrary.campusguides.com/chrisbelter**. We expect to see more bibliometrics support materials coming from Chris and his NIH colleagues in the future—keep an eye out!
10. Rachel Borchardt, "AU Library Support for Sponsored Research: Increasing Research Impact" (presentation slides, American University, Washington, DC, Fall 2014), **http://www.slideshare.net/Plethora121/**.

Section 3
ALTMETRICS

Chapter Five

Understanding Altmetrics

> "No one can read everything. We rely on filters to make sense of the scholarly literature, but the narrow, traditional filters are being swamped. However, the growth of new, online scholarly tools allows us to make new filters; these altmetrics reflect the broad, rapid impact of scholarship in this burgeoning ecosystem. We call for more tools and research based on altmetrics."[1]
>
> —Jason Priem, Dario Taraborelli, Paul Groth, and Cameron Neylon, "Altmetrics: A Manifesto"

The first thing one discovers when looking closely at the field of altmetrics is that it is, and has always been, about so much more than the pursuit of any single method of measuring impact. As evidenced by the opening lines of "Altmetrics: A Manifesto," first published online in October 2010, the coining of *altmetrics* was part of a larger call for new and improved tools for filtering scholarly information—a context that connects it to the coining of impact factor by Eugene Garfield more than 55 years earlier. However, like impact factor, the reputation of altmetrics has come to be shaped more for how such metrics have been used than how they *can* be used. For this reason, they have been frequently placed in a position at odds with other measures of impact and targeted by critics for attempting to upset the "natural" order of citation-based rankings, which have been the basis of so much of the academy's judgments about individual scholar productivity.

In this chapter, we take a closer at the school of impact measurement known as altmetrics, including its history, diversity, and development as a 21st-century academic movement.

The Definition of Altmetrics

The term *altmetrics* is the brainchild of Jason Priem, a graduate student at University of North Carolina at Chapel Hill who has since become one of its best-known public advocates. It first gained widespread attention within the impact community through the publication of the "Altmetrics: A Manifesto" on the website Altmetrics.org, which Priem registered in September 2010. As a term, altmetrics is a portmanteau, formed from the combination of "alternative" and "metrics" (originally hyphenated as "alt-metrics"). On Altmetric.org, the definition of altmetrics is given as "the creation and study of new metrics based on the social web for analyzing and informing scholarship."[2] This definition reflects three distinctive characteristics for all metrics within this school of impact. First, altmetrics is inseparable from the Internet, and more specifically, from the social aspects and areas of the Internet known as the *social web*. Second, altmetrics is driven by the new, both in the sense of the necessary creation of new metrics and the availability of new data related to the social web. And third, altmetrics is always tied back in some way to scholarship. While the first two of these characteristics have gained most of the attention for the territory they stake out jointly beyond the world of print, the third is equally essential for reminding us of how much altmetrics still shares in common with its predecessor movements in impact measurement, including bibliometrics. In this way, altmetrics is less "alternative" than it is an extension of the same impulse to measure, track, and analyze scholarly activity as befits the practices and tools of the current age.

For purposes of this book, we will use a slightly modified version of Altmetrics.org's definition of altmetrics: a set of methods based in the social web used to measure, track, and analyze scholarly output.

"The web has given rise to new forms of scientific discourse. Web 2.0 tools provide scientists with faster, less formal ways for conversation inside and outside the scientific community."[3]

—Hadas Shema, Judit Bar-Ilan, and Mike Thelwall, "Research Blogs and the Discussion of Scholarly Information"

The Practical History of Altmetrics
From World Wide Web to Social Web

Much as in the case of bibliometrics, the story of altmetrics begins not so much with the coining of a term but rather with the invention of a whole new set of tools and scholarly practices.

Following the birth of the World Wide Web in the early 1990s, journal publishers moved slowly but inevitably to embrace the online environment—a shift that led researchers from across the disciplines to reassess the Internet's value as a place for conducting research, not merely a place to chat with friends or discover funny pictures of cats. Libraries, too, played their part in this first-round transformation, both by making "big deals" with journal publishers to provide online access to large bundles of scholarly titles and, with the advent of search engines like Google, by acknowledging and investigating the scholarly potential of websites, blogs, and "born digital" information in general. It was, in many ways, the beginning of a total reinvention of the way people looked at and expected to find information—yet beyond the quiet coining of the *webometrics* subgenre in 1997, bibliometric experts were not unduly ruffled at first. Indeed, from their perspective, the rise of electronic journals was just further verification of the legitimacy of existing journal-based systems of impact calculation. After all, the landscape of use still looked familiar, even if the format had shifted away from print.

In the mid-2000s, another key round of transformation took place in the online sphere, this time in the form of the social media and networking revolution. Drawing in part from the Web 2.0 movement—an almost embarrassingly popular topic with librarians for much of the early

'00s—social media acknowledged online users' shared desire for communication and connection, yet refined its format by creating distinct hubs around which users could gather, share information, and interact. From Delicious and MySpace to Facebook and Twitter, general purpose social media and networking tools quickly broke into mainstream consciousness, drawing the attention of academics and librarians, many of whom were looking for more robust personal and professional networking spaces online. From this more specialized interest was born a secondary set of networking sites, aimed explicitly at the needs of researchers and scholars to find and communicate information via the web. In 2008, just four years after the launch of Facebook, at least three academic networks made their appearances online: Academia.edu, Mendeley, and ResearchGate. And while the idea of an online network of researchers was not in itself revolutionary—tools such as the Social Science Research Network had been around in some capacity since the early stages of the web in 1994—the practice of building such networks on top of unique researcher identities was as of yet very new. The birth of the social web thus changed not only the shape of the Internet, but also the shape of scholarly practice, bringing in new ideas of how researchers could find, filter, read, and share information in reference to their personal and professional lives.

Alternatives to Bibliometrics

Following this mid-2000s change in the use and popularity of online networks came waves of new discussion within the field of bibliometrics. As impact scholars began to look more closely at the flow of information on the Internet at large, they began to recognize innovative practices and tools for scholarly communication—practices such as the saving or bookmarking of online works for later reading and the availability of article-level metrics (ALMs) from prestigious online journals, such as *PLOS ONE* in 2009.[4] The growing reputation of online publications and institutional repositories as viable methods of distributing scholarly information both quickly and while "in progress" also caught the attention of researchers who had long complained about the inefficiency of formal models of peer review favored by print-based venues of production.[5] By the late 2000s, these myriad realizations had combined with other maturing complaints about the limits of existing citation-based metrics to become an identifiable call for action: the development of a set of impact metrics beyond the existing field of bibliometrics—a set of metrics better suited for tackling the web. This alternative set of metrics was discussed under many different names, including *web-based bibliometrics*, *Scientometrics 2.0*, and the aforementioned *webometrics* term.[6] That *altmetrics* eventually prevailed as the name most favored by members of the impact community is more likely a reflection of the content and timing of the altmetrics manifesto than an endorsement of the term itself. In any case, the result was the sudden recognition of the field of altmetrics in 2010.[7]

Thus, while altmetrics is still undoubtedly a young field, it is also a field with incredible force and momentum, fueled by dozens of tools and metrics that have been churning and developing, in some cases, for over a decade. As we will see, it is this energy and entrepreneurial spirit that makes the current state of altmetrics so compelling, and yet—from some researchers' perspective—so hard to follow and predict.

The Categories of Altmetrics

In the second chapter of this book, "Impact in Practice," we discussed the strategy of organizing impact metrics into four different levels of focus, which we have already used to organize the metrics most frequently associated with bibliometrics (see Chapter 3). These levels of focus are as follows:

▼ **Level 1:** Metrics focused on individual scholarly contribution.
▼ **Level 2:** Metrics focused on the venues that produce individual scholarly contributions.
▼ **Level 3:** Metrics focused on author output over time.
▼ **Level 4:** Metrics focused on group and institutional output over time.

In this section, we will once again attempt to break down the larger concept of altmetrics into these four categories, in part so that the metrics within the two chapters can be easily compared. However, before we dive into the levels, it is worth taking a moment to remind readers that this four-part division is only one way to organize metrics, particularly when it comes to altmetrics. Most altmetrics, for instance, represent an attempt to trace the impact of a single identifiable scholarly entity across an online

Altmetrics Milestones by Year
▼ 1990: Tim Berners-Lee writes the first web browser as part of the World Wide Web.
▼ 1994: Social Science Research Network (SSRN) launches.
▼ 1997: Tomas C. Almind and Peter Ingwersen coin the term *webometrics* in a published paper.
▼ 1998: International DOI Foundation (IDF) is created to develop the digital object identifier (DOI) system.
▼ 2003: Social bookmarking service Del.icio.us (now known simply as Delicious) is founded.
▼ 2004: Online social networking service Facebook launches at Harvard University.
▼ 2004: Richard Cameron begins developing academic social bookmarking site CiteULike.
▼ 2006: The first full version of Twitter becomes available to the public.
▼ 2006: Open access peer-reviewed journal *PLOS ONE* is established.
▼ 2008: Academic networks Academia.edu, Mendeley, and ResearchGate launch online.
▼ 2008: The ResearcherID author identification system is introduced by Thomson Reuters.
▼ 2010: The Open Researcher and Contributor ID (ORCID) nonprofit is founded.
▼ 2010: Dario Taraborelli launches ReaderMeter.
▼ 2010: Jason Priem coins the term *altmetrics* via Twitter.
▼ 2010: Jason Priem, Dario Taraborelli, Paul Groth, and Cameron Neylon publish "Alt-Metrics: A Manifesto."
▼ 2011: Mark Hahnel launches the online digital repository Figshare.
▼ 2011: Andrea Michalek and Mike Buschman start altmetrics-focused Plum Analytics.
▼ 2011: Euan Adie founds Altmetric, an altmetrics aggregator site.
▼ 2012: Jason Priem and Heather Piwowar launch Total-Impact (later renamed Impactstory).
▼ 2012: Elsevier partners with Altmetric to add altmetrics data to Scopus.
▼ 2013: Elsevier acquires Mendeley.
▼ 2014: EBSCO Information Services acquires Plum Analytics.
▼ 2014: Wiley officially partners with Altmetric to add altmetric data to its journals.
▼ 2014: Impactstory announces a new individual subscription model.

network due mostly to the opportunities for public data collection afforded by such networks. However, from here there arise many complexities that frustrate the idea of simple levels of focus. To begin with, there is an inherent flexibility in terms of what a "scholarly entity" can be within the online environment that goes far beyond the world of bibliometrics and formal citations. Some entities may appear to be traditional scholarly materials, like journal articles and books, while others may be online slide decks, conference posters, recorded lectures, blog posts, podcast episodes, video links, infographics, datasets, and so forth. Furthermore, while many online entities qualify as individual scholarly contributions, others are in fact closer to venues, authors, groups of authors, or even whole institutions. In light of these variations, many altmetrics developers have built their tools around the online activity generated by a scholarly entity, not the specific characteristics of that entity—an approach that cuts against the idea of a focus-based organization of impact. At the same time, activity-centered metrics clearly do not apply equally across all types of scholarly entities. Rather, they have emerged from the "tools up"—as new types of activities become possible in different tools, they are then customized for different entities. Therefore, while we continue to use our four original levels in this book to organize altmetrics for consistency's sake, we will also incorporate a secondary set of groupings—based on online activity—that gives a slightly different picture of how such metrics can be organized within each level of focus. We encourage each of you as readers to consider the use of either (or both) of these grouping strategies when explaining altmetrics to researchers, as best fits your users' familiarity with impact, metrics, and online tools.

> "Today we have more ways to capture engagement with research outputs and more providers operating in this space than ever before."[8]
>
> —Jennifer Lin and Martin Fenner, "Altmetrics in Evolution: Defining and Redefining the Ontology of Article-Level Metrics"

Level 1: Individual Contribution Level Metrics

Despite the seemingly infinite variety of individual scholarly contributions that exist on the web, this first level of altmetrics activity is in certain ways the easiest for new users to access. This is because Level 1 reflects an approach to metrics that is familiar from the world of bibliometrics and highly visible within the dashboards of most online social spaces. To help further organize each of the metrics within this class, we have borrowed some of the categories used by Plum Analytics in the design of its PlumX tool (see the Categories of Altmetrics Tools section later in this chapter), which in our minds does the best job of identifying the types of altmetrics best suited to individual contributions. Even so, there will still be some overlap between our subcategories of metrics as many similar-seeming altmetrics sources actually provide different kinds of unique data about impact on the social web. (Head spinning yet? Don't worry, it's harder to explain than it is to recognize in practice.)

Finally, as scholarly communication continues to evolve and altmetrics continues to gain in popularity, we fully expect that the number of contribution- level metrics available to researchers will continue to grow and shift. For this reason, we recommend that readers consult with the resources listed at the end of this chapter for more information about new metrics aimed at individual contributions that may have emerged since the publication of this book. That said, the groupings below represent some of the most popular, stable, and foundational altmetrics of the present day. As such, they will almost certainly continue to bear on the works and activities of researchers in the future.

Usage Metrics

This altmetric grouping is the most straightforward, and the one that seems to tie into discussions of citation-based metrics the most seamlessly. Usage metrics reflect the options users have within online tools to interact directly with individual scholarly contributions, whether that contribution is a journal article or a recorded conference presentation. These action-oriented metrics include the following:

▼ **Clicks/Views.** Today, many scholarly websites and online publications take advantage of analytical tools like Google Analytics to provide information about how many unique users have visited a URL or clicked on a particular link within a site. Information about clicks and views can also be gathered for informal research contributions, such as personal blogs, video channels, and podcasts. In the case of time-dependent contributions, the view count can be accompanied by metrics for "average length of time viewed," information that can provide a useful double-check on the level of user interest in a work. Some online tools even allow the harvesters of text-focused altmetrics to distinguish between an item's "abstract views," "full-text views," "figure views," "HTML views," "PDF views," and so forth.

▼ **Downloads.** Similar to views, many websites with downloadable scholarly content will tell users how many times people have downloaded an item from the site. This metric provides a level of impact measurement that lies somewhere between citation count (definite evidence

Figure 5.1. PLOS Article Level Metrics

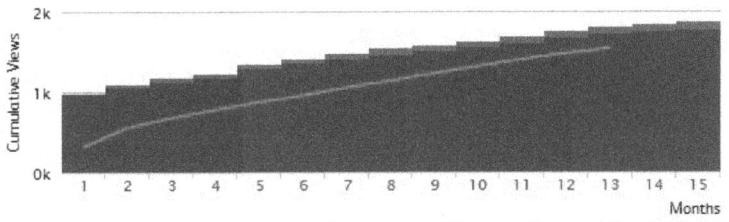

of impact) and times viewed (early potential evidence of impact). As with views, downloads of scholarly material are not typically restricted to just other scholars, so a high download count may be a reflection of a scholarly item's interest to a diverse online audience, including not only scholars but students, professionals, and the general public.

▼ **Sales/Holdings.** Originally discussed in Chapter 3 as a "fuzzy" metric, sales (or holdings in the case of libraries) is an example of an "alternative" measure of impact that has already found acceptance within some bibliometrics circles due to its value for tracking individual contributions like monographs. While monographic impact can be partially tracked via citations in journal articles, such as Thomson Reuters' Book Citation Index, monographs are still much less likely to generate citations than journal articles—so a count of how many people or institutions have purchased a work can provide a more comfortable quantitative measure of vetted quality. Indeed, the success of an item's distribution via Amazon sales and WorldCat library holdings can be seen as both a measure of community endorsement and a test of how widely an item's reputation has spread. As we like to tell our book-writing faculty and patrons, sometimes these metrics provide an important backdrop for discovering qualitative measures, such as *which* libraries own your publication. To show that libraries with prominent research populations have bought your book can be a powerful story in itself, even if it's a relatively small number of libraries.

Capture Metrics

Capture metrics is a subcategory that represents a more subtle interaction with an individual scholarly contribution than usage metrics, one that sees us take our first major step away from the certainty of use so valued by bibliometric indicators. With capture metrics, we see how online spaces have given users new options for planning their longer term interactions with individual scholarly contributions, "capturing" them for future use or reuse as the case may be. In a print-based view of impact, this sort of interaction—the printing of an article to read later or the physical collecting of articles deemed most relevant to one's interests—would be impossible to track quantitatively. For online toolmakers, however, this information is essential to understanding the sort of works that 21st-century users want and value, either in addition or in contrast to what they eventually "use." In this sense, capture metrics provide a fascinating complement to usage metrics and can help identify everything from hot topics within a field of research to the range of disciplines that may be interested in a specific scholarly work. The following are popular capture metrics currently available across the social web:

▼ **Bookmarks.** Social bookmarking sites, such as Delicious and CiteULike, function by allowing users to save and organize the URLs of sites to a single, personalized online location. As such, bookmark counts is a metric similar to downloads as it shows a level of interaction somewhere between the early stage indicator of views and the late-stage indicator of citations. At the same time, it's important to keep in mind that social bookmarking is not a universally standard practice for scholars, so any bookmarking numbers generated around a certain work by a tool are likely to have relatively little meaning unless they're compared to bookmark counts for other works. It is also our observation that since the rise of citation management tools like Mendeley, which combine academic communities with more powerful tools for saving and organizing academic works, the use of social bookmarking by academics has dwindled. This suggests that numbers of bookmarks around a work should also be balanced with capture metrics, such as Saves/Readers (see below).

▼ **Forks.** Forks are a unique capture metric and refer to the impact of a work in inspiring new "branches" or similar work projects. Forks are most common in the world of software development, where programmers may use the source code of one project to create new standalone programs. Some online code repositories, such as the wildly popular GitHub, help users track the number of forks that each of their projects generates as well as the popularity of those subsequent forks (see Favorites below). Note that while fork metrics can apply to other parts of the social web, most altmetrics aggregators focus exclusively on this software context when providing that information, and even then typically from just GitHub.

▼ **Favorites.** As the name suggests, favorites refers to the number of times that users within an online tool or community score, rank, or otherwise tag a work as being one of their favorites within the limits of the site. Often there is no limit to the number of works that users can mark as favorite, meaning there is no way to translate the number of times a work has been favorited to a specific ranking within a site unless one has access to comparable data or additional levels of detail. Still, one of the advantages of the favorites feature is the opportunity it occasionally offers researchers to identify *who* has favorited their work within a community. This can in turn lead to greater awareness of the people impacted by or interested in their work. Favorites also helps translate into quantitative terms a sense of a work's qualitative value to users, making it similar to scores/rankings (see its section later in this chapter), albeit more focused on the positive end of the implied comparison spectrum.

▼ **Saves/Readers.** Reader metrics—also sometimes indicated as number of saves by readers—are usually gathered from academic peer networks that support communities around readership, such as Mendeley, ResearchGate, or the Social Science Research Network (SSRN). While similar to other interest metrics like views, the saves/readers metric is somewhat unique in that it only counts interactions within a tool's closed network of users. By contrast, both views and downloads can often be generated by anyone with access to a contribution's online page or space. Thus, the saves/readers metric can be reasonably assumed to be a measure of interest from within a given community, albeit a community that may have different demographics and interests than the whole of academia. Other closely related metrics include "watchers" (i.e., the number of community members who want to track changes or developments in the work) and "subscribers."

Mentions

Arguably the most qualitatively connected of the metrics grouped under Level 1, mentions are altmetrics that point to the discussion of a scholarly work within and across the social web. As mentioned earlier, with the advent of the Internet, references to scholarly works can appear in a variety of settings that are generally not included in citation analysis, including books, presentations, websites, course syllabi, in Facebook or Twitter, or on *Wikipedia*. These mentions can be counted or detailed in a researcher's statement of impact as further evidence of a contribution's use. The following represent the most common types of mentions currently tracked by altmetrics tools:

▼ **Blog Posts.** Blogs have become one of the most popular ways to share information on the web—information based in research or information targeted at an audience of researchers. With the blog posts metric, we see the tracking of this form of sharing via links in posts that refer back to an original scholarly contribution. Because there are so many blogs, this metric is often limited to posts on specific blogs or blog networks, such as well-reputed research blogs, blogs associated with scholarly journals, and so forth.

▼ **Comments.** Comments, in some ways, provide a deeper level of insight than many other metrics, in that they speak directly to how users are interpreting, reacting, and incorporating a work into a larger understanding or narrative. While qualitative in nature, a comments altmetric can supplement the qualitative content of comments by helping track the number of comments generated by particular contributions. This can then be compared to comments generated by other works within a network. Keep in mind though that comments collected from different places are likely to be making different statements about impact (e.g., a YouTube comment may speak to a more general appeal than a scholarly comment on Faculty of 1000).

▼ **Reviews.** The word *reviews* has many meanings in academia, from the reviews scholars write for journals about new books and items in the field to the reviews scholars receive in private from peer evaluators after submitting works for publication. In the case of altmetrics, however, reviews is a term that encompasses something much less formal and more quantitative: the number of reviews an individual contribution receives with a specific site, tool, or online social space. Within the context of PlumX, for example, review metrics are harvested from two tools: online goods retailer Amazon and the Amazon-owned social cataloging book site Goodreads. While neither of these sites is scholarly in nature, their review counts are also exponentially higher than those currently available on any academic network. What's more, for researchers in certain fields, these review sites can provide important, otherwise hidden information about the impact of a work on the wider public consciousness.

▼ **Attributions.** The attribution metric applies mostly to attributions arising from non-journal works, but it could include things like the use of part of a written work in a presentation, on a blog, or in a guide. Attribution is related to but distinct from other mentions in that an attribution requires a more substantial use of an original work, not just a reference to it. Visual images are probably the most common form of attribution, but datasets, original music, quotes, or any other type of information could also be given attribution. Attribution can be very difficult to capture through metrics as many times the attribution must be discovered before it can be added to a portfolio of metrics. Still, in a world of quickly changing altmetrics possibilities and the growth in standardized practices of object and author identification, attribution is worth—dare we say it?—a mention here.

> "Typically, different data sources are required to measure different types of impact. For example, to measure impact on policy, you may need to look at government documents. Or to look at how work has influenced practitioners, you may need to monitor the online communities in which they congregate. To see how successful public outreach has been, you may want to look at Twitter and Facebook."[9]
>
> —Jean Liu and Euan Adie, "Five Challenges in Altmetrics: A Toolmaker's Perspective"

Social Media Metrics

Social media metrics are one of the most divisive inclusions for researchers considering the relevance and use of altmetrics. Proponents of their inclusion point to the power of social media to both capture and spread information to a larger public, creating non-frivolous movements targeted at reflection, action, and social change. Detractors, on the other hand, argue that social media interactions are most often used for personal purposes and are fraught with issues of inaccuracy, insincerity, and "gaming" (i.e., artificial strategies for self-promotion and popularity). Both of these perspectives have their merits, and we will discuss them in more detail later in this chapter. For the moment, however, we will point out that, like it or not, the academic world has overwhelmingly begun using social media to discover, promote, and discuss information, including individual scholars, students, administrators, journal publishers, research centers, and universities. To ignore the metrics associated with this investment does not change the level of participation in the slightest, and thus, for us, these metrics are worth examining for all the caveats one must insert. We now proceed to look at a few of the altmetrics most commonly associated with social media.

▼ **Likes.** Another largely self-explanatory metric, likes refer to the number of times that someone has indicated they enjoyed a work or (presumably) found it valuable within a specific online social network. Similar in this way to favorites, likes are found on many social media sites in some form or another, including Facebook, SlideShare, YouTube, and many peer networks like Faculty of 1000 or ResearchGate. Particularly for digital-born, self-published content, this metric can be one of the only indicators of audience reaction to a work, especially when combined with baseline usage metrics like page views or downloads. However, it stands to reason that to some degree, these kinds of metrics are also influenced by the activity of the person posting the work within that social network (e.g., a very active Twitter user with many followers may be more likely to receive more retweets and favorites from a post than a less active Twitter user). Thus, when issues of "gaming" come up as they relate to altmetrics, critics often point to mentions and social media as prime examples of how scholars could artificially inflate their metrics or where natural variations may occur independently of the relative quality of the content.

▼ **Shares and Tweets.** Shares and tweets are metrics largely born out of the dominance of Facebook and Twitter as social networks for sharing links and other short snippets of information. Indeed, as of 2014, Facebook has over 1.23 billion active users and Twitter approximately 284 million active users.[10] One of the consequences of this market dominance was the development of a free Facebook "Share" button, which developers can add to a website to encourage readers with Facebook accounts to automatically create a post about the website content. Twitter offers code for a similar button, which encourages readers with Twitter accounts to "Tweet" about website content with a single click. Many content sites, including online journals, now display the stats for the number of times an item has been shared or tweeted. In light of the popularity of these networks and practices, altmetrics toolmakers created the shares and tweets metrics to track the number of times a link to a work has appeared on Facebook or Twitter, respectively. Over time, these metrics have expanded to encompass sharing on other social media networks as well, including LinkedIn and Google+.

Scores and Rankings

This final grouping under the individual scholarly contribution level is a sort of catchall, meant to showcase the unique analysis provided by some altmetrics tools that allows for the comparison of similar items' impacts within that tool. Each of these tools has its own formula for assigning "weight" to a scholarly item, which depends on the metrics collected by the tool, as well as the toolmaker's perspective on which metrics are most indicative of influence and importance. Here, we highlight two of the most popular altmetrics tools that provide these rankings, which we will return to later in this chapter's Categories of Altmetrics Tools section.

▼ **Altmetric's Altmetric Score.** Altmetric is a fast-growing company that sells access to multiple article-focused altmetrics products, each of which features the assignment of an Altmetric Score, a metric that equates quantitatively to the "attention that a scholarly article has received."[11] According to the website, this score is based on the balance of three factors: (1) volume—the overall extent to which people are mentioning an article; (2) sources—types of places where the article is mentioned, some of which are valued more highly due to audience or prestige; and (3) authors—who is mentioning the article and to what extent these authors may be biased or engaged with scholarship. Users may test the calculation of this score by downloading the free Altmetric bookmarklet and testing it on select article URLs. However, as Altmetric makes clear, many perfectly legitimate articles will score 0 on its scale, both because many articles are not mentioned on the social web and because sometimes Altmetric doesn't have access to data that accurately portrays an article's online presence. For example, "if the article was published before July 2011 …its score won't be accurate [due to transient activity not captured by Altmetric] and will represent a lower bound of the attention received."

Figure 5.2. Altmetric Score Displayed for an Article in PubMed

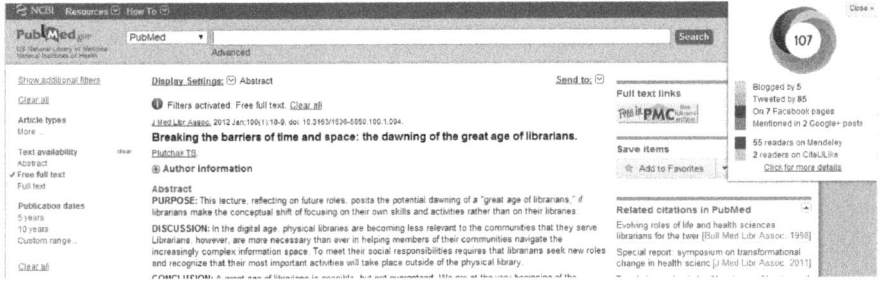

▼ **Impactstory's Altmetrics Percentiles.** Impactstory is an open source web-based tool that provides another toolmaker's perspective on what it means to compare scholarly output on the basis of altmetrics. Rather than assign a comprehensive impact score to a given scholarly contribution (identified by authors who create "collections" of items to be measured by the tool), Impactstory assigns percentiles to each contribution within the frame of a single altmetric. For instance, when Impactstory retrieves the number of readers that a scholarly item has on Mendeley, Impactstory will also calculate how this number ranks in comparison with the number of readers retrieved for other items being tracked by Impactstory. An article with 73 readers on Mendeley might include an alert that, within Impactstory, it is in the 91st percentile for number of Mendeley readers.[12] Percentiles are provided across a wide range of Impactstory sub-metrics, and are highlighted with a series of shorthand badges such as "Cited" and "Highly Cited" (based on Scopus data); "Saved" and "Highly Saved" (based on Mendeley and Delicious data); "Discussed" and "Highly Discussed" (based on Twitter data); and "Viewed" and "Highly Viewed" (based on Figshare and internal Impactstory data). We will look at Impactstory and its percentiles again in this chapter's Categories of Altmetrics Tools section.

> "Journal editors can immediately see which articles are gaining traction online, which they may use to inform future editorial decisions."[13]
>
> —Graham Woodward, "Altmetric Is Now on Board for All Wiley Journals"

Level 2: Venue-Level Metrics

As noted elsewhere, altmetrics as a field caters primarily to individual scholarly contributions (Level 1) with metrics concentrating on evidence of the discussion and use of specific scholarly works. This concentration is captured quite nicely in the altmetrics manifesto, which argues explicitly for the value of concentrating filters on ferreting out "the impact of the article itself, not the venue." We won't go into the pros and cons of ignoring venue-level altmetrics in favor of contribution-level ones right here, but suffice it to say, thus far, no altmetrics have seriously challenged the almighty impact factor to describe the relative impact of individual journals. That said, as article views and downloads become more common, we predict that journal-level metrics based on aggregated article-level data will begin to serve as a useful alternate way to look at the frequency with which users are interacting with journal content. Already, a few notable venues such as the Public Library of Science (PLOS) and journals published by John Wiley & Sons have taken the major step of adding some altmetrics to all its online content. Additionally, in late 2013, Elsevier announced a pilot program with Altmetric to display altmetrics for the top three rated articles in 33 of its journals.[14] Such aggregated metrics, should they gain traction, would naturally be a reflection of all user interactions with a journal, regardless of whether the person accessing the content was scholarly or not. As such, a theoretical criticism of venue-level altmetrics is that journals with a more "popular" appeal would likely benefit disproportionately to their journal peers. Still, as savvy readers of this book will have already discovered, all metrics come with their own benefits and limitations, and knowing how to identify those limits is part of telling the story of impact.

For purposes of example, we will now take a brief look at the two aforementioned venues that have begun to incorporate altmetrics across the board.

Public Library of Science

The Public Library of Science, more commonly known as PLOS, is a scholarly nonprofit aimed at "transformation in research communication" through the collection and publication of open access content, particularly as relates to the science and medical fields.[15] Active since 2000, PLOS is especially well known as the publisher of the seven PLOS-branded journals, including *PLOS ONE*—a unique peer-reviewed journal that emphasizes post-publication discussion and ratings over prepublication content restrictions. As a well-respected online scholarly publisher, PLOS has helped draw attention to altmetrics via its pioneering use of ALMs, which have helped authors and readers track online usage for individual articles within PLOS journals since 2009. These metrics include "Viewed," "Cited," "Saved," "Discussed," and "Recommended," and they are updated for each article over time. Because of its across-the-board use of these metrics, PLOS also offers access to venue-level "journal summary usage data," which users can view or download (as an Excel file) to get a better sense of benchmarks within each journal as well as for different topics tagged within a single PLOS journal.[16]

Wiley Journals

Wiley Journals is the periodical publishing wing of John Wiley & Sons, a centuries-old company that specializes in global publishing solutions for academics as well as professionals. With over 1500 journals in its online library service, Wiley is recognized by librarians as one of the largest and most important publishers of scholarly content, particularly in the areas of science, technology, and medicine. In May 2013, Wiley announced a six-month trial partnership with Altmetric, during which altmetrics were added to articles in six journals published by the company.[17] By the trial's end in November 2013, nearly 2200 articles received an Altmetric score with 40% of these achieving a score of 10 or higher, "indicating that a high proportion of articles were receiving attention and making an immediate impact."[18] Wiley also announced that a poll of website visitors during the 2013 trial indicated that 88% of users felt that altmetrics were useful or somewhat useful and that 77% of readers agreed that altmetrics enhanced the value of the articles in Wiley's journals. On the strength of these results, Wiley announced the permanent addition of Altmetric metrics to its open access journals in March 2014, followed by the addition of such metrics all Wiley journals in July 2014.[19] This pattern of altmetrics adoption—from a trial of six journals to a feature in 1500 journals in a single 14-month period—is yet another sign of the speed with which publishers and other scholarly venues are beginning to recognize the potential of altmetrics as an across-the-board tool for complementing their practices of impact measurement. As other key publishing groups continue to adopt altmetrics, such as Nature Publishing Group and Stanford's Highwire Press, we will likely see more aggregated data and statistics on the relative impact of scholarly venues and the responses of venue users to the inclusion of such metrics, similar to Wiley's poll.

> "The greatest opportunity for applying these new metrics is when we move beyond just tracking article-level metrics for a particular artifact and on to associating all research outputs with the person that created them."[20]
>
> —Mike Buschman and Andrea Michalek, "Are Alternative Metrics Still Alternative?"

Level 3: Author-Level Metrics

Not surprisingly, due to the incredibly wide range of individual contribution metrics available via the social web (Level 1), the world of altmetrics has yet to come up with a meaningful way to summarize altmetrics for researchers interested in author-level values. Still, unlike the dismissiveness shown to the idea of venue-level metrics within the altmetrics community, several prominent toolmakers are catering to researchers by giving them access to author-level altmetric portfolios, which serve at least as a personal dashboard for altmetrics and encourage researchers to monitor their changing altmetrics values over time. For example, both Impactstory and PlumX have begun providing authors with unique URLs that bring together altmetrics information for them on an individual basis. Nevertheless, as of yet, both of these products stop short of contextualizing their values and scores, such that authors' altmetrics-based impacts could be directly compared.

Peer networks, by contrast, have indeed begun to produce author-level metrics within their own systems. Most notable of these networks is ResearchGate, an academic peer network designed primarily to connect authors in the sciences. Each scholar within ResearchGate is given an RG Score based on metrics related to interactions with an author's contributions within ResearchGate.[21] We anticipate that as the demand for higher-level metrics continues, more products will develop their own "brand" of author-level metrics to try and make comparisons and benchmarking easier for administrators and other decision makers. But for now, the h-index is still the primary metric for describing a scholar's academic publishing career quantitatively.

We will now summarize briefly three of the major altmetrics features most closely associated with author-level metrics.

Impactstory Profiles

At the core of Impactstory's popularity is its ability to create "profiles," collections of links and altmetrics-generating identifiers ostensibly related to a single researcher's output (although this is by no means an enforced method of forming collections). Profiles begin with users identifying themselves—filling out their basic information—and then are created through a combination of linked accounts (e.g., GitHub, ORCID, SlideShare) and user-submitted product IDs (e.g., DOIs, URLs, PMIDs). The resulting profile page organizes the author's work into different groupings according to his or her respective contribution types, with visible buttons next to individual contributions to indicate their relative level of altmetric impact within the tool (see Impactstory's Altmetric Percentiles under the Scores and Rankings section earlier in this chapter). Each profile has its own unique and stable URL, which makes sharing profiles particularly easy and appealing. Users can set up their Impactstory profiles to send them e-mail alerts as soon as their altmetric values change or simply at regular intervals.

PlumX Sunbursts

In addition to providing author-level profiles similar to those provided by Impactstory, PlumX's provides its users with a unique author-level feature called "sunbursts." Sunbursts are circular graphics that are designed to

Figure 5.3. PlumX Sunburst

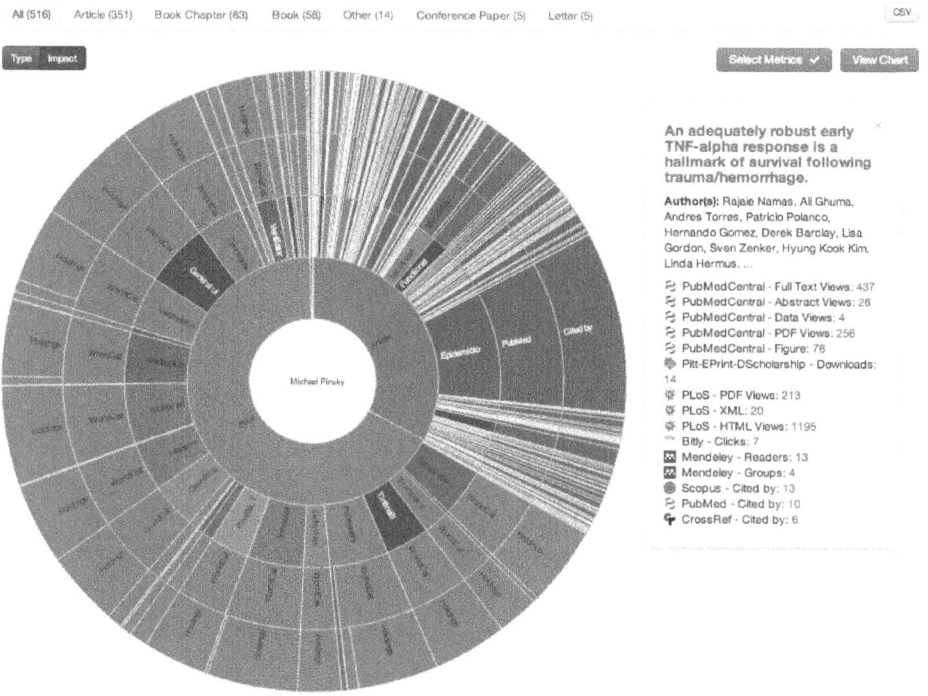

function as visual summaries of the relative impact of a researcher's output. Similar to a four-tiered pie chart (think smaller pies, embedded and centered in bigger pies), sunbursts come with two basic views (or settings): types or impact. Within the impact setting, there are tiers for (1) types of researcher output, (2) specific researcher outputs, (3) data sources related to each output, and (4) altmetric interactions gathered by the data sources about each output. By visualizing these levels of information, users can get a sense of the internal proportions of researchers' activities and impacts. This can then be compared to the proportions of other researchers within the tool. Practically speaking, of course, this is a lot of information to take in at once; the fourth tier of the sunburst is close to unreadable unless filtered, and it gets even worse when set to "type" mode. Nevertheless, we find that sunbursts can be a quick and easy means of seeing the balance of outputs and impacts achieved by actual, practicing researchers and understand the way in which certain types of outputs produce impact in different ways.

ResearchGate RG Scores
RG Score is a metric unique to the academic social networking site ResearchGate, and it purports to measure "scientific reputation based on how all of your research is received by your peers."[22] RG Score is calculated based on an internal algorithm that combines the number of contributions authored by a researcher; who is interacting with each contribution on ResearchGate (i.e., the reputations of those interacting with contributions); and how these researchers are receiving and evaluating these contributions. For this reasons, if users with high RG scores are interacting with your research, your RG score will see an increase. This also means that users with high RG scores know that they can leverage this reputation to increase the reputations of fellow ResearchGate users—an interesting take on channels of impact that may more accurately reflect certain academic dynamics and yet may also less accurately capture influence for fields with less ResearchGate penetration.

Unique Author Identifiers

Author disambiguation can be a major issue when calculating any author-level metrics. In some cases, the researcher's name is unique, so searching by name will only bring up relevant articles. More frequently, however, there are multiple researchers with similar (or identical) names. Searching by institution often alleviates this issue; however, it fails to properly track researchers should they ever move from one institution to another, and it doesn't eliminate the possibility of two identically named researchers publishing from the same institution.

One of the first companies to create a solution was, not surprisingly, Thomson Reuters. They created ResearcherID, a service to help give authors unique identifiers, which makes author searches more effective in Web of Science.[23] Since then, other databases including Scopus and arXiv have created their own author identifiers.[24] However, as more information moves to the Internet, it's obvious that one single identifier is needed. In 2012 ORCID (Open Researcher and Contributor ID) was created to address this need. It creates a single author identifier that researchers can use to identify their research publications across platforms.[25]

While many researchers remain unaware of author identifiers, ultimately such identifiers work best when a researcher takes control of his or her own author profile. As we will see in Chapter 8, the issue of author identifiers can be added by librarians to workshops or presentations that teach researchers how to use metrics to ensure that researchers are getting the most accurate metrics possible in the long run.

"The first and most obvious challenge that must be addressed for altmetrics to penetrate the broader realm of higher education is the development of more sophisticated tools for aggregate-level altmetrics and comparative institutional analysis."[26]

—Robin Chin Roemer and Rachel Borchardt, "Institutional Altmetrics and Academic Libraries"

Level 4: Institution-Level Metrics

As mentioned back in Chapter 3, institution-level impact metrics pose serious challenges for toolmakers of all kinds, from the lack of an ability to meaningfully compare metrics across the disciplines to the potentially different research cultures of different institutions or internal departments. With altmetrics, these challenges continue, bolstered by the array of available altmetric indicators mentioned earlier in the level introductions. (For a more detailed analysis at the present difficulties and future benefits of developing institutional altmetrics, we recommend that readers take a look at our jointly authored article on the subject, "Institutional Altmetrics and Academic Libraries," published in *Information Standards Quarterly's* 2013 special altmetrics-themed issue.[27]) In the meantime, we urge institutions to use strong caution when using aggregated impact metrics to directly compare one department or discipline to another, altmetric or otherwise, though they can be very useful as part of larger, more holistic benchmarking efforts. Indeed, in the long run, we see the development of institutional altmetrics as an area where librarians can make a difference by educating administrators about what altmetrics can and can't do at the institutional level. This sort of outreach by librarians can prevent the misuse or even abuse of these aggregated metrics.

The following three sections describe current features or initiatives focused on the use of altmetrics at the institutional level.

PlumX Group Metrics

Just as PlumX provides author-level profiles that collect and summarize altmetrics gathered from a researcher's individual scholarly works, it also offers pages dedicated to large groups of affiliated researchers, such as publishing employees of universities and museums. By aggregating the works and metrics of a group in the same way one would treat the work of a prolific individual researcher, PlumX provides a window into the type of outputs and impacts that an institution produces without forcing the assignment of a higher-level metric. Users can switch easily between institution-level views of impact by usage, captures, mentions, citations, etc., and toggle between sunburst charts and traditional tables of impact metrics. Because the calculation of institution-level profiles requires the same data necessary to complete author-level profiles, PlumX also displays icons to represent affiliated researchers on the institutional page, which users can click to jump to a specific author's metrics.

Altmetric for Institutions
Altmetric for Institutions, one of the five web-based products currently offered by Altmetric, offers researchers and administrators the ability to search, monitor, and measure "conversations about publications by people affiliated with your institution" with the goal of capturing what amounts to an institution's early stage impact.[28] This article-focused data is collected from a variety of sites to represent these conversations, including blogs, message boards (e.g., Reddit), communities (e.g., F1000), popular news sources, and social media sites (e.g., Twitter, Facebook, Google+, Pinterest, Sina Weibo). After processing, the data is displayed with breakdowns by metric source, distribution over time, and (where available) geographic distribution of the conversations in a "Summary Report" on the institution's dashboard. Users can also filter the data displayed in the report by unique categories like "Mentioned in the Past," "Funded by," "In these Journals," and "With Keyword." Filters thus become one of the biggest benefits of Altmetric for Institutions over competing institutional altmetrics products, although time will tell whether this or any other subscription-based institutional altmetrics product will take hold, or if altmetrics will continue to thrive mostly through integration into certain venues, databases, and academic online communities.

Snowball Metrics
While we originally detailed the UK-based initiative known as Snowball Metrics in the Level 4 metrics breakdown in Chapter 3, it also falls into the fourth level of this section for its endorsement of altmetrics in the second edition (2014) of its "recipe book" for institutional benchmarking. This latest version of the book includes 24 metrics that are organized into three categories: (1) input metrics, (2) process metrics, and (3) output and outcome metrics. Altmetrics are grouped under this third category and are called out for capturing impact in the form of online engagement not

only between scholars but also between scholarship and the general public. The recipe book mentions several primary data sources for engagement metrics, including Scopus, Web of Science, Google Scholar, Altmetric, PLOS, Impactstory, and Plum Analytics. However, the book leaves room for other sources of altmetrics data in future recipe book editions to be decided based on the will of project partners. For more information about Snowball Metrics, see its section in Chapter 3 or visit its website (*http://www.snowballmetrics.com*).

Accessing Altmetrics

When it comes to locating personal altmetrics, most researchers will find themselves turning to convenient, highly accessible sources of information, such as Twitter, for a record of related public tweets, or contribution URLs, for the number of shares or likes. However, as librarians, it's always good to remember that many useful altmetrics are only available to individuals through personal logins to certain sites, administrator dashboards, and personal requests for information. Examples of this include many peer network metrics, website analytics (like, say, page views for a blog or podcast), or obtaining evaluations following a conference presentation, workshop, or webinar. Accessing altmetrics is all about recognizing the various ways that impact can be captured and following up on them accordingly.

The Categories of Altmetrics Tools

Now that we've made it through our extensive and occasionally layered levels of altmetrics indicators, we can start to take a look at how these different metrics play out in the major products and tools that are available to researchers online. As we proceed, you will note that some of these tools cater to individual scholars, while others are designed with the needs of administrators and other academic representatives in mind. It's also important to note that despite the deep connection between altmetrics and ideals like openness and community, not all of these products are free. On the contrary, as altmetrics-focused start-ups have been acquired by larger companies or come to the end of their grant funding, we have seen an increasing trend toward for-cost tools, albeit nowhere near the high cost of their bibliometric equivalents. Still, this is likely an issue that will continue to evolve as altmetrics finds its footing and audience within academia.

For the benefit of readers new to altmetrics, we've divided the major tools into two types: (1) those that generate metrics based on information within their network, which we call "peer networks" and (2) those that largely gather information from external sources and then provide their own comparative analysis and/or metrics, which we call "harvesters."

> **Disclaimer**
> Please note that, as mentioned in many sections of this book, altmetrics development is a rapidly changing field. In a mere two year stretch between 2012 and 2014, users saw the rebranding of Total-Impact as Impactstory, the purchase of Mendeley by Elsevier and Plum Analytics by EBSCO, the disappearance of the early altmetric tool ReaderMeter, the integration of Altmetric into journals by Wiley and other publishers, and the announcement that Impactstory would be switching from a free tool to an individual subscription model. It is therefore almost guaranteed that some aspects of the tools below will have changed between the time this book is published and the time you start reading it. For this reason, we strongly suggest you view this chapter as a snapshot of the altmetrics landscape and use it to identify patterns in the latest direction of altmetrics tool development. The facts may change, but the story goes on!

"Article-level metrics data comes from somewhere—tweets from Twitter, citations from Web of Science or Scopus, bookmarks from CiteULike, etc. Provenance is concerned with the origin of an object, the ability to trace where an object comes from in case there is any need to check or validate data."[29]

—Scott Chamberlin, "Consuming Article-Level Metrics: Observations and Lessons"

Peer Networks

Peer networks represent one of the fastest growing trends for researchers as well as one of the most popular tool categories for producing altmetrics specifically for scholars. As the name suggests, peer networks are online spaces that allow users with similar interests, credentials, or skills to share information and interact with one another. Outside of academia, these networks include familiar online sites like Facebook, Flickr, Twitter, and Google+, most of which came into existence following the spike in growth of the social web in the early to mid-2000s. Since the late 2000s, however, a number of networks specific to the needs of researchers and academics have developed. In this section, we will review some of the most successful of these networks, and how they relate to impact and the spread of altmetrics.

Social Science Research Network
Social Science Research Network (SSRN, **http://ssrn.com**) is arguably the oldest free academic peer network currently available, founded in 1994 following the rise of the World Wide Web. Primarily an online article repository, SSRN is comprised of three parts: a database of more than 563,000 abstracts; a large electronic paper collection; and about 25 specialized subject networks that registered users can use to promote their work and connect to free abstracts and articles. Users can jump directly to any one of these networks from SSRN's home page or look for papers across the SSRN eLibrary using a centralized "Search" feature.

In terms of impact, SSRN offers a number of key altmetrics that are filtered at four levels: article, author, network, and whole site. For instance, for each article, SSRN offers users metrics for abstract views, downloads, and download rank as well as information about what other papers people who downloaded the paper have also downloaded, which could be used for more focused article benchmarking. Authors in SSRN are tracked according to aggregated downloads and citations, although these are broken up into the metrics for each individual contribution to allow for easy parsing of an author's statistics. Networks, by contrast, are at first only resolved according to total number of papers uploaded—a statistic that appears at first to have little meaning from an impact perspective, other than to show evidence of user activity. However, by delving into the scholarly subnetwork (e.g., the "Subject Matter eJournals" sections of each network), one discovers the metric for "Total Downloads," which can be compared to the number of papers within the subnetwork for additional usage context. Finally, at the whole site level, users can view an array of activity statistics, such as total number of abstracts, full-text papers, authors, and "Papers Received in Last 12 Months." Downloads information is also given at the site level and is broken up into totals for the last 30 days, 12 months, and all time—a helpful division for users curious about the continued relevance and currency of SSRN as an academic tool. Another key feature of SSRN is its monthly updated listing of "Top Authors," "Top Papers," and "Top Organizations," with the latter two partially broken up according to different networks.

Though praised for its ability to facilitate discovery of scholarship, SSRN has also been criticized for the strictness of its policies, which some see as stifling in comparison to emerging scholarly networks. However, in recent years, SSRN has helped addressed this criticism by adding a number of new networks and subnetworks, each of which help add new coverage or depth to areas of growing interest. Thus, SSRN's site-specific metrics remain key indicators of online interaction and impact to social science faculty, especially those in stronghold areas such as law, business, accounting, and economics.

ResearchGate

ResearchGate (***http://www.researchgate.net***) is a more recent example of a free and popular academic peer network, this time aimed toward the science disciplines. Founded in 2008 by two physicians and a computer scientist, ResearchGate is designed, like SSRN, to help researchers "connect, collaborate, and discover scientific publications, jobs and conferences."[30]

To use the site, researchers sign up for a free account that allows them to identify publications they have the authored, institutions they are affiliated with, disciplines and subdisciplines they work in, and areas of skill and expertise. Using this data, ResearchGate generates a researcher profile similar to Google Scholar Citations, in that users can get a quick sense not only of a researcher's background but also his or her contributions to the field and an array in-network use statistics. For example, each profile includes a Stats tab, which tracks and visualizes such output usage metrics as total publication views, total full-text downloads, total dataset downloads, and total full-text requests. Researchers also are informed via this tab how many publication views they have received recently and which of their publications have been viewed the most (based on daily, weekly, and total view counts). Profile views and question views (i.e., posts that the researcher has submitted to the site's internal discussion forums) are also tracked on the profile according to a similar schedule. Consequently, unlike SSRN, ResearchGate offer users the clear and focused opportunity to see subtle changes in their in-network influence and impact over time. Further, by adapting features from nonacademic networks such as an internal inbox and a "Requests" alert system, ResearchGate can help academics start private, semiprivate, or public conversations with peers about their research interests and projects. These conversations can themselves become valuable qualitative pieces within a researcher's portfolio and can lead to the discovery of audiences in unexpected subject areas. However, like many social networks, ResearchGate suffers from the problem of limited data in that it cannot track information about the identities of non-ResearchGate users who stumble across user profiles (something that naturally occurs via Google searching). Also, researchers outside the sciences may find their fields less than accurately populated with research due to inevitable imbalances in the adoption of ResearchGate across the disciplines.

Mendeley

Mendeley (*http://mendeley.com*) is a free peer network that combines the discoverability of peer networks with the organizational content of a citation management software program. Mendeley launched in 2008, initially funded by investors until its acquisition by Elsevier in early 2013.[31] By registering for Mendeley, users can search for articles, upload articles, create article citations, browse articles by discipline, or follow group topics of interest and other researchers' updates in Mendeley.

Once logged in, a Mendeley user's home page is similar to that of a Facebook feed with individual items comprised of recent updates from groups and researchers that the individual follows. By downloading

Mendeley's desktop program, users can take advantage of the citation aspect of the network, which allows users to store, organize, and cite articles of interest within a personally created citation library.[32] Still, from the perspective of altmetrics, the greatest value of using Mendeley is data that the tool produces and collects—namely, information about Mendeley's readership, which is freely available and can be harvested by various altmetrics tools. According to the Mendeley website, readership is defined as "the total number of Mendeley users who have [a specific] reference in their Mendeley personal library."[33] Readership as a metric is further categorized based on basic reader demographic information: readers' disciplines, academic statuses, and countries of affiliation. Despite the fact that readership data is only technically available for individual articles through the Mendeley platform, many altmetrics tools rework and aggregate this metric independently to provide readership metrics at the author, departmental or lab, and institutional levels.

One question that often comes up for new users of Mendeley is that of which disciplines use Mendeley most frequently, with the idea that the network's readership metrics will be more accurate if researchers in similar fields are already using it actively. Unfortunately, as of the time of this writing, a discipline breakdown of Mendeley users is not available. However, according to a 2014 study that compared coverage of a set of social science and humanities articles between Web of Science and Mendeley, only 44% of social science articles covered by Web of Science were also included in Mendeley and only 13% of the humanities papers from Web of Science.[34] These percentages suggest that Mendeley readership may not be entirely accurate for many research fields outside the sciences, particularly the arts and humanities. With this information in mind, we conclude that Mendeley readership metrics are best represented when compared to readership counts for similar articles.

Academia.edu

Academia.edu (***http://www.academia.edu***) was established in 2008 (a magical year for peer networks) with a stated mission to "accelerate the world's research" by creating a network of researchers and uploaded articles, and it has developed a strong and broad base of users, with over 11 million profiles created and nearly 3.5 million articles contained in its database.[35] Researchers can sign up for a free account on its website (which is not affiliated with a higher education institute—the domain name was registered several years before the .edu domain was regulated) and can then upload and tag citations and full-text articles to their personal profile as well as to the database of searchable research. Users can also follow other researchers as well as tagged keywords of interest. Searching for a topic will suggest tagged keywords, some of which have a great deal of overlap (for example, topics exist for both "Academic Libraries" and "Academic Librarians").

On the metrics front, Academia.edu provides researchers "analytics" based on all activity generated relative to their profiles and/or documents within the last 30 or 60 days. Users can choose to make these analytics publicly available, but users must manually select this option. Analytics include categories like "Profile Views," "Document Views," and "Downloads," each of which includes details like country of user origin or keywords users searched for to find the researcher's work. One of the features we particularly like is the ability to view institution-specific URLs, which lists the number of researchers that self-identify with a department or unit within the institution along with the number of documents associated with that department or unit. This makes it relatively easy for librarians to identify "core user" groups and gauge overall adoption of Academia.edu at their institution.

CiteULike

CiteULike (*http://www.citeulike.org*) is designed to be a social bookmarking site for researchers to save and organize citations of interest. CiteULike, first conceived in 2004 by researcher Richard Cameron, who was reportedly frustrated with the availability of similar tools, continues to be independently owned and operated. As a network, CiteULike relies on browser bookmarklets to allow registered users to save references from a wide range of recognized sites and to add custom keywords to create a personal database of citations—a "library."[36] These citation libraries can be set to display publicly or privately, which gives CiteULike users the ability to share their libraries with other colleagues. Users can also search CiteULike for individual articles and publicly displayed libraries of citations. Indeed, CiteULike can even generate a metric for how many publicly displayed libraries have a particular citation—a metric that several altmetrics harvesters include in their collections. However, issues with version control and low user counts have gradually limited the usefulness of data generated from CiteULike, making the tool's future uncertain from an altmetrics point of view.

Faculty of 1000
Faculty of 1000 (***http://f1000.com***), otherwise shorthanded as F1000, is a post-publication peer review service that highlights articles in the fields of biology and medicine based on recommendations made by a community of experts. Articles are nominated for inclusion by existing F1000 users (who must first create a paid account) and then rated by the site's larger community of approximately 6,000 faculty members, who can also provide commentary and feedback. Publications with the highest overall ratings are displayed in a regularly updated "Top 10" list (both "Current" and "All Time"). Users can browse these lists or search the article directory by keyword and interest topic. Some articles may be viewed for free, but the vast majority requires users to login with a valid subscription. In addition to F1000's "Prime" recommendation service, designed for use by individual subscribers, it also produces F1000 Research, an open publishing platform for science, and F1000 Posters, an open access repository of conference posters and presentations.

> "The fundamental question we try and answer with all of our metrics is 'What has happened?,' 'What is the impact of the research that's occurred in the last 18 months?' If you look at traditional metrics like all the citation-based metrics... they lag, and they cannot alone give insight into that question."[37]
>
> —Andrea Michalek, "Altmetrics in the Last Year and What's Next"

Harvesters

Impactstory

Impactstory, formerly known as Total-Impact, is a relatively high profile altmetrics tool created by Jason Priem and Heather Piwowar during a hackathon challenge in 2011 and later developed based on grants from the Alfred P. Sloan Foundation and the National Science Foundation. Geared toward the needs of individual researchers, Impactstory harvests free and open data from both social networks and traditional scholarly sources and presents the resulting metrics to authors using a system of scholarly profiles. For this reason, it may be easiest for researchers to think of Impactstory as an online supplement to a traditional CV rather than a means of looking up altmetrics for external articles, authors, or venues on demand.

To get started, researchers must sign up for an Impactstory account, at which point they must submit the basic information (e.g., full name, e-mail address) that becomes the basis for their online profile. Researchers can add a variety of scholarly outputs to their profile individually, manually, or by linking their profile to up to a supported scholarly venue, including Google Scholar, SlideShare, and ORCID—Impactstory will automatically allow new additions to be added to the profile from any of these venues. Once a researcher's scholarly outputs have been added to a profile, Impactstory will then look for any metrics associated with these outputs. Researchers receive badges that indicate the presence of certain types and levels of altmetrics; users can hover over these badges to learn more details. For instance, a researcher whose article has been saved two or three times via Mendeley may receive a "saved" badge next to his or her article, while an author whose work has been saved 100 times via Mendeley may receive a "highly cited" badge. These badges are an attempt to put altmetrics into context by comparing them statistically with similar outputs. In this way, Impactstory is attempting to answer the age-old question of "How good is that number?" without dwelling too much on the raw data behind each number. That said, because Impactstory has limited access to discipline-specific usage information (SlideShare views, for example, are compared to all SlideShare presentations uploaded that year), the badges are far from perfect indicators of impact.

One additional note on Impactstory—on July 31, 2014, the team behind the tool announced a change in its basic operational model: Impactstory users will be charged $5.00 per month for their profiles. Currently, users who cannot afford the fee can have it waived by filling out a form and adding to their e-mail signature a link to their Impactstory profile. Nevertheless, the fee highlights an open question regarding the sustainability of independent altmetrics tools in an era otherwise marked by acquisitions, mergers, and buyouts.

Voices from the Field
"Understand the strengths and shortcomings of various tools before you teach them or talk about them with users."

—Nazi Torabi, Health Sciences Librarian, McGill University

PlumX

PlumX is the name of a proprietary product created by Plum Analytics, which was recently acquired by EBSCO Industries. Because an institutional subscription is required for users to access PlumX, it can be called an institutional-level altmetric tool. However, the main function of PlumX is the creation of individual researchers profiles, which places it in practice closer to online data harvesting tools like Impactstory. For instance, in creating PlumX profiles, researchers can automatically retrieve "artifacts" (e.g., scholarly outputs) by connecting their profiles to external sources (e.g., ORCID) or by manually entering a specific DOI, PubMed ID, or direct URL. Users hoping to track journal articles can also import citation files downloaded from Web of Science or Scopus.

Once artifacts have been added to a profile, metrics for each artifact are displayed in a table with the option to sort the table by each metric category for quick comparisons. As previously mentioned, PlumX supports five categories of impact metrics: usage, captures, mentions, social media, and citations. As discussed earlier in this chapter, the resulting table can also be displayed as a "sunburst," which helps visualize which impact measures take up a larger proportion of an author's overall impact. However, as sunbursts have a tendency to compare wildly different impact measures (for example, PDF views vs. citations vs. tweets), this feature is best used for comparing authors with similar collections of artifacts, and thus similar arrays of harvested metrics. Tables and sunbursts are also available in PlumX at the group level, which PlumX creates by aggregating the outputs of researchers who share an affiliation across a department, labs, campus, or institution. Institutions that have become PlumX subscribers, like the University of Pittsburgh, are encouraging their researchers to add their own profile to PlumX and incorporate it into their habits of impact collection.

Altmetric
Altmetric (*http://altmetric.com*) is a London-based company founded in 2011 that has come to dominate the altmetrics product market due to its success in partnering with traditional publishing sources such as *Nature* and Wiley Journals. As a toolmaker, Altmetric offers a variety of products designed to account for both different metric levels and different academic audiences (and different audience price points). These products revolve its primary feature: the Altmetric "donut." This colorful circle shows users at a glance the altmetrics activity surrounding a particular article. The donut colors show the type of metric (tweets, blogs, Mendeley, CiteULike, etc.) and relative activity (the larger the color within the circle, the greater the activity), while the number inside the circle gives you the Altmetric score—a Level-1 metric to show the overall altmetrics activity level for that article. Two of its most popular products are as follows:

▼   **Altmetric Bookmarklet.** The Altmetric bookmarklet is technically a piece of code—a free resource that users can add to their bookmark toolbars in compatible browsers such as Firefox, Chrome, and Safari. Once installed in the toolbar from the Altmetric website, the bookmarklet can be used whenever users navigate to a URL that includes a findable DOI.[38] Once the URL has loaded, users can simply click the bookmarklet to run the code, which prompts a search for any altmetric indicators that Altmetric can discover for the findable DOI. However, it is important to explain to researchers that if a publication URL does not contain a DOI or if the DOI is not discoverable on the URL, then the program will return an error—regardless of the actual impact of the resource. For this reason, we recommend this tool mostly for the discovery of altmetrics for published journal articles with clearly marked DOIs.

▼ **Altmetric Explorer and Altmetric for Institutions.** Altmetric Explorer and Altmetric for Institutions gather and aggregate very similar data but package the data for different sets of users. Both gather freely available metrics about a set of journals defined by the user and display the donut for each journal. The altmetrics data can be filtered and compared by several fields and downloaded, or users can set up e-mail alerts with updates to the data. Altmetric Explorer is primarily designed for publishers wishing to sift through altmetrics data to learn more about attention and use of their journals, while a free version of Explorer is available to librarians wishing to gain similar insights for their library or institution. Altmetric for Institutions allows for additional functionality, such as the ability to group articles by author, department, or institution as well as the ability to save search filters and have updates periodically e-mailed. Altmetric for Institutions is not free, so interested librarians should contact Altmetric for trials and pricing.[39]

Harvesters vs. Peer Networks

While many altmetric sites can be categorized into harvesters or peer networks, a select few appear to cross the line between categories simply due to the openness of their approach to data. For example, the online citation manager Mendeley produces metrics that can be retrieved by users within the tool, which places it well within the category of an academic peer network. However, because Mendeley offers an open application programming interface (API) that allows toolmakers to retrieve those same metrics or create new impact metrics based on Mendeley data, many researchers are used to seeing Mendeley data primarily appear in the context of harvester tools and may decide to never sign up for a separate Mendeley account. Later, in Chapter 6, we will revisit the relationship between harvesters and peer networks and look closer at how issues of data accessibility are likely to play out in the future of academic altmetrics.

Figure 5.4. The Altmetric Explorer Interface

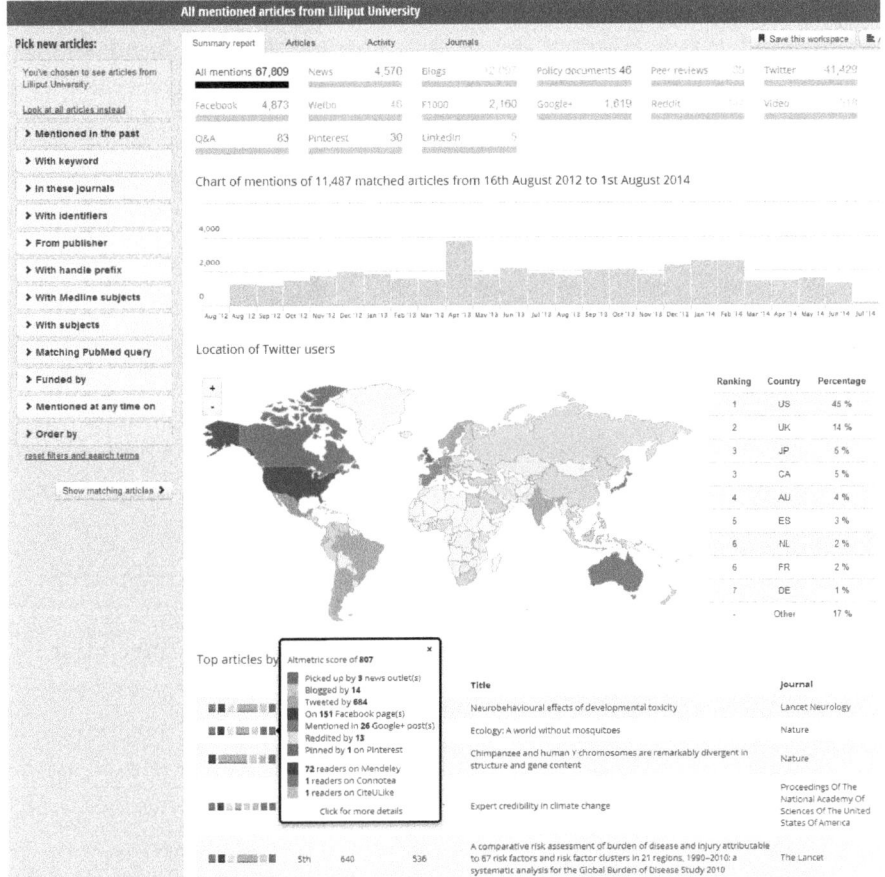

Current Topics and Conversations about Altmetrics

Since becoming a buzzword in higher education circles, altmetrics has generated a tremendous amount of discussion, especially regarding its value to researchers in addition to, or in lieu of, more traditional forms of scholarly impact measurement and information filtering. Just as bibliometrics generated its fair share of critics and proponents following the development of groundbreaking tools like journal impact factor, altmetrics has galvanized researchers into debating the use of online interactive spaces for purposes of intellectual discussion and development. Among detractors is a growing opinion that altmetrics poses too much of a risk when it comes to capturing in-depth scholarly engagement and that altmetric measures more likely to be "gamed" (i.e., increased through disingenuous interaction) than metrics based in patterns of citation. By contrast, those passionate about altmetrics have touted it as the approach that most accurately reflects the way the majority of researchers seek out and use information and the best collection of metrics for scholars seeking to promote and track engagement beyond the limits of formal citation—which can itself be "gamed" through unnecessary and largely reciprocal references.

We advise readers to be mindful of all of these conversations and look to reasoned arguments, objective information, and meta-research as a means of bridging philosophical divides that may exist within your library, institution, or larger professional community. For instance, on the topic of gaming (which doubtless exists in the context of pretty much any form of impact measurement), it may be helpful to look at how various metrics producers anticipate and address attempts at gaming their systems and evaluate whether these policies are sufficient to address most instances of gaming. Just as Altmetric must address the problem of Twitter bots by creating alerts when suspicious patterns of activity arise, Journal Citation Reports must address the problem of artificial citation and excessive self-citation by creating alerts when annual rates rise too far above a probable threshold. Curation and auditing are therefore inextricable parts of the field of impact measurement, even as actual incidents of academic gaming are relatively rare across both bibliometrics and altmetrics.

Let's now take a quick look at the some of the current conversations going on with regard to the future of altmetrics and where such topics are likely to head given recent developments in the field.

> "As article-level metrics become increasingly used by publishers, funders, universities, and researchers, one of the major challenges to overcome is ensuring that standards and best practices are widely adopted and understood."[40]
>
> —Martin Fenner, "What Can Article-Level Metrics Do for You?"

Duplication, Continuity, and Version Control

One major drawback of all altmetrics harvesters is their inability to address errors that may arise after a tool has finished automatically pulling together different types of altmetrics and integrating them into a single report. While playing around with our own profiles in the Impactstory harvester, for example, we had difficulty getting accurate metrics for items like our jointly authored 2012 *College & Research Libraries News* article, simply because in Mendeley the article appears at first to be two separate works due to associations with two separate (but equally valid) URLs. Altmetrics harvesters also have problems accurately representing items that are continuously updated, such as blogs, podcasts, and video series. Anyone wishing to measure the impact of one of these works must struggle to find a harvester that can accurately track both the indicators of impact for a general resource (e.g., the blog home page) and that resource's discoverable components (e.g., each blog post). Too often the only solution is to add each component URL to the harvester one by one—an inconvenience that one can only hope will be solved as harvesters update their methods of collection and integration. The same goes for situations in which a resource has been identified by a single URL or DOI and by a URL shortener such as bitly or tinyurl. Because so many harvesters rely on single identifiers to track online interactions—particularly social media interactions—the use of a shortener can divide the resulting metrics and make it difficult for users to discover the true extent of their web-based impact. For this reason, and from personal experience, we highly suggest that users perform manual searches for scholarly title mentions on social media sites, such as Twitter, as these will often surface additional tweets, retweets, and favorites that would otherwise be missed by altmetrics harvesters.

In the long run, it is almost certain that increasingly sophisticated altmetrics tool developers will come to address these bumps in the road surrounding duplication, continuously updated resources, and multiple resources versions—perhaps even in the short term, in light of increasing pressure to standardize the collection of altmetrics from organizations such as the National Information Standards Organization (NISO). However, for now, the takeaway message is similar to that of calculating an author's h-index or a work's number of times cited: Automatic harvesting of data is great, but for works that are in any way complex, a hands-on, manual approach to collecting metrics may also be necessary and is always recommended.

> ### What's the Deal with Twitter Citations?
> One category of altmetrics that has gotten a fair amount of attention is that of using Twitter posts as a way to measure a different type of impact, namely the "buzz" surrounding an article. But can Twitter posts predict later citation rates for an article? The article "Twitter Buzz about Papers Does Not Mean Citations Later," published in *Nature* in December 2013, suggests that little correlation between tweets and citations can yet be found.[41] In truth, researchers studying impact are still seeking to unpack what, if anything, Twitter and other altmetrics data can truly tell us about the academic world of citation-based impact. Another recent article, "Validity of Altmetrics Data for Measuring Societal Impact: A Study Using Data from Altmetric and F10000Prime," concludes that altmetrics may benefit from normalizing metrics based on topics that have more popular interest rather than normalizing based on subject (as metrics such as journal rankings are normalized).[42] While we believe all data is helpful to some degree, we agree with the articles: It's still difficult to tell what some data actually *means*, particularly when using metrics based on public social media, such as Twitter and Facebook.

> "Correlation and factor analysis suggest citation and altmetrics indicators track related but distinct impacts, with neither able to describe the complete picture of scholarly use alone."[43]
>
> —Jason Priem, Heather Piwowar, and Bradley H. Hemminger, "Altmetrics in the Wild: Using Social Media to Explore Scholarly Impact"

Relationships between Altmetrics and Bibliometrics

One of the more interesting questions recently to arise out of the popularity of altmetrics has been the exact relationship between altmetrics and bibliometrics—that is, "How well do altmetric values relate to bibliometric values over a specific period of time?" Because bibliometrics rely on citations that may take several years to populate sufficiently for purposes of comparison, while altmetrics can begin to be harvested within hours of a work's online availability, there is an understandable appeal to the idea of using altmetrics indicators to predict bibliometric success. However, the handful of studies have been conducted to date on possible correlations between a work's interactions in an online social space and the number of citations it eventually generates have been far from conclusive. For example, as discussed in the What's the Deal with Twitter Citations? sidebar, studies that have focused on social media altmetrics have shown no evidence of a strong correlation with citation metrics, which would seem to suggest that the number of tweets or likes a work generates has no real bearing on the number of citations that same article will receive in formal publication. However, a recent meta-analysis of studies investigating correlations between altmetrics and citations did find some correlation between articles' citation counts and their mentions on blog posts (r=.12) and peer networks, with Mendeley receiving the highest correlation (r=.51, which means that an article's Mendeley metrics and citation counts are roughly 51% similar).[44] A 2012 study by Jason Priem, Heather Piwowar, and Bradley H. Hemminger also found a nearly identical correlation of .5 between "social reference saves" and citation counts along with many other correlations.[45] Both articles are just two of many that have been done to try and correlate altmetrics with citations, but reading these two will provide an excellent foothold in the area (and of course, tracking who has cited these articles is likely to yield additional relevant articles in the future). Based on the current literature, it's accurate to say that research is still largely forthcoming on the full extent of the relation between altmetrics and bibliometrics. However, as librarians, it's also important to remind users that a strong correlation between all altmetrics and all bibliometrics is by no means a prerequisite for accepting the idea that both altmetrics and bibliometrics may contain valuable representations of impact for purposes of their work.

> "As tools improve, we can anticipate these early adopters [of altmetrics] will begin to incorporate a much wider range of altmetrics on a much wider range of products. However, if we expect these early adopters to be joined by their more cautious peers, scholars will need a clearly articulated case for use."[46]
>
> —Heather Piwowar and Jason Priem, "The Power of Altmetrics on a CV"

> "With any new concept or methodology there exist limitations and gaps that need to be addressed in order to facilitate its adoption."[47]
>
> —NISO, Altmetrics Initiative Phase 1 White Paper

Adoption and Use of Altmetrics

Another question that has not been fully answered is that of the extent to which altmetrics has been adopted, and by whom it has been adopted. As of late 2014, only a few surveys have been done to surface the number of researchers who are actively using altmetrics, and most of them only through the efforts of singular journal publishers. A poll conducted by Elsevier, for example, found that in October 2013, only 5% of responding researchers had heard of altmetrics, while 88% were familiar with impact factor. Those polled also indicated that overall they found more traditional bibliometrics to be more helpful.[48] By contrast, when Wiley Journals conducted its own poll of readers in late 2013 (for more details see Level 2: Venue-Level Metrics, Wiley Journals earlier in this chapter), it found 88% of responding users exposed to altmetrics data felt that altmetrics were useful or somewhat useful—a startling contrast that says as much about the uncertainty that surrounds the definition of altmetrics as it does the need for more information about the actual adoption and use of such metrics.[49] A more focused study asked bibliometricians at a 2012 conference to comment on the potential for specific altmetrics to evaluate articles or authors. Responses varied from a high of 72% responding favorably to "downloads or views of your article" down to a low of 18% responding favorably to "followers on Twitter or other networking sites," showing that even those that work most closely with altmetrics have varying views regarding altmetrics adoption.[50] Finding actual case uses of individuals who have successfully integrated altmetrics into an impact statement are relatively scarce. A 2013 *Nature* article, "Research Impact: Altmetrics Make Their Mark," by Roberta Kwok highlights one professor's use of altmetrics in his promotion file—a natural addition, considering that his PLOS article was "the most-accessed review ever to be published in any of the seven PLOS journals".[51] We think that more case uses and success stories will pop up soon, whether on blogs or curated by tools like Impactstory, to instill confidence and inspire creativity in altmetrics adoption and use.

In the meantime, there is an upside to the current uncertainty: the widespread recognition amongst altmetrics advocates that the time has come for more official consolidation and standardization around the terms that drive the altmetrics movement. In June 2013, NISO applied for and was awarded a multiyear grant from the Alfred P. Sloan Foundation to "explore, identify, and advance standards and/or best practices" around altmetrics.[52] The result is a two-phase initiative with the first phase already completed at the time of writing this book. During the first phase, NISO worked to "expose areas for potential standardization" and help members of the academic community prioritize standardization options.[53] In June 2014, NISO released a draft of its Phase One White Paper, in which it identified 25 potential action items for the second phase of the initiative, which is to develop appropriate standards and best practices to be approved and disseminated by key community members. Some of the highest priority actions include the following:

▼ develop specific definitions for alternative assessment metrics;
▼ identify research output types that are applicable to the use of metrics;
▼ define appropriate metrics and calculation methodologies for specific output types such as software, datasets, or performances;
▼ promote and facilitate use of persistent identifiers in scholarly communications; and
▼ agree on proper usage of the term *altmetrics* or on using a different term.[54]

Looking at even this short list of actions, it seems clear to us that the second phase of NISO's altmetrics initiative will go a long ways toward removing the barriers that exist for many users who are considering the adoption of altmetrics as well as strengthening the reputation of altmetrics in academic circles where it is already partially known. At the time of writing, work on the project's second phase has only just begun; it's due to be completed in late November 2015. Both in the meantime and afterwards, however, librarians can continue to play a role increasing research awareness about the existence of altmetrics and the opinions and attitudes surrounding its adoption and use, even as they change over time. We will talk more about the role of librarians in facilitating discussions about altmetrics when we get to Chapter 8.

> "Clearly, now is the time to capitalize on the interest and attention to finally bring assessment of research out of the systems belonging to the print era and into a more modern, multi-faceted system that takes advantage of the flexibility and scale of the web."[55]
>
> —William Gunn, "Social Signals Reflect Academic Impact"

The Future Outlook of Altmetrics

Over the course of this chapter, we've shown altmetrics to be both an exciting new area of data analysis for scholars and a category of practice that has yet to be tested or implemented to its full effect. On one hand, the overwhelming acceptance of web-based information in the world at large has opened up the door for 21st-century researchers to examine their own diverse practices regarding the filtering, gathering, and discussion of scholarly information online. On the other hand, a lack of understanding, information, and confidence in the place of altmetrics within established discussions about academic impact have left researchers uncertain about such metrics' strengths and weaknesses, even as they continue to desire and need their benefits. Now, however, with the recent spike in both the diversity and sophistication of altmetrics products, we believe that a turning point in this conversation is at hand. As altmetrics developers begin to market their products not just as "lone wolf" tools for use outside of mainstream campus resources but also as institutional assets for benchmarking and extending the quantitative picture of impact drawn by bibliometrics, we predict there will be a smoothing over of many concerns, particularly at the campus administration level.

While this is good news for altmetrics enthusiasts (and we'd like to think, researchers in general), this is not to say that significant shake-ups are not on its way for altmetrics as a field. On the contrary, in light of the NISO movement to further standardize the terms, methods, and practices surrounding altmetrics, it seems unlikely that all of today's web-based metrics will continue to be successfully packaged under the same umbrella designator of "altmetrics." Instead, in the near term, it is probable that the altmetrics that are more closely or directly tied to established impact metrics will be more rapidly defined and adopted than those that are more abstract or less clearly connected to academia. Specifically, we expect to see significantly more scholars and institutions start using page views, downloads, and metrics from respected peer networks to supplement bibliometrics such as citations counts and journal ranks. By the same logic, we see categories like social media metrics as more likely to achieve narrow adoption, specifically within fields that place a larger emphasis on the translation of research to a public audience (e.g., popular social sciences such as communication, journalism, social work, and political science). Whether these specific predictions turn out to be true or false, it remains clear that as the further scholarly communication moves away from peer-reviewed journal articles, the more prominent and necessary altmetrics will become—for researchers, administrators, students, and (lest we forget) academic librarians.

Further Reading

"Keeping Up With…Altmetrics," Association of College and Research Libraries (ACRL)
> Part of ACRL's "Keeping Up With" series, this brief online publication (authored by the same writers of this book) is a good quick

review of the general field of altmetrics, from major stakeholders to recent controversies. Useful as a communication tool with other librarians or faculty familiar with other impact measurement tools. *http://www.ala.org/acrl/publications/keeping_up_with/altmetrics*

"Altmetrics: A Manifesto"
The classic document of the altmetrics movement, the altmetrics manifesto is required reading for any researcher looking to become seriously involved in the field of altmetrics. In addition to the manifesto itself, the website is also useful for tracking recent publications and upcoming events and conferences related to altmetrics. However, be aware that the site is not updated regularly! *http://altmetrics.org/manifesto/*

"Article-Level Metrics: A SPARC Primer," Scholarly Publishing and Academic Resources Coalition (SPARC)
A resource of SPARC, this online PDF provides a thorough yet relatively brief introduction to the topic of article-level metrics (ALMs) and is a good starting point for librarians and researchers who are primarily interested in metrics targeted at individual scholarly articles in and across the sciences. ALM-friendly tools are discussed as is the relationship between ALMs, bibliometrics, and the tenure and promotion process. *http://www.sparc.arl.org/sites/default/files/sparc-alm-primer.pdf*

NISO Alternative Assessment Metrics (Altmetrics) Initiative
As mentioned earlier, the NISO Alternative Assessment Metrics (Altmetrics) Initiative is an Arthur P. Sloan Foundation funded project that seeks to tackle the standardization of key altmetrics components and the formation of community-approved best practices for further growth and development. Divided into two phases, the initiative began in June 2013 and is slated to be completed in November 2015. Information about the first phase of the project, including potential action items for the second phase, may be found on the initiative website. It's a great resource for librarians, faculty, and administrators looking to understand the reputation, value, and

interpretation of altmetrics across a wide spread of academia. *http://www.niso.org/topics/tl/altmetrics_initiative/*

PLOS ONE Altmetrics Collection
This curated collection consists of *PLOS ONE* articles specifically dealing with altmetrics issues. The collection was initially introduced via essay by many of the same individuals responsible for the "Altmetrics: A Manifesto" and contains an interesting mixture of articles researching metrics, including plenty of discipline-specific viewpoints. *http://www.ploscollections.org/altmetrics*

Additional Resources
BOOKS AND JOURNALS
Bulletin of the Association for Information Science and Technology (ASIS&T) Altmetrics Issue
The April/May 2013 issue of the ASIS&T *Bulletin* is a special issue dedicated to altmetrics. Its articles include many major names in the field, including articles from the founders of Impactstory, Altmetric, and PlumX along with several librarians. *https://www.asis.org/Bulletin/ Apr-13/AprMay13_Piwowar.html*

Information Standards Quarterly (ISQ) Altmetrics Issue
An open access NISO journal, *ISQ* devotes its Summer 2013 to altmetrics and features many of the same authors as in the *ASIS&T Bulletin* altmetrics special issue. However, since we were asked to contribute to this issue, we maintain some bias for this one! *http://www.niso.org/publications/isq/2013/v25no2*

ORGANIZATIONS AND GROUPS
Mendeley Altmetrics Group
This Mendeley group is one of the largest public groups devoted to sharing of altmetrics resources and discussion. Group members include both researchers and librarians interested in altmetrics. *http://www.mendeley. com/groups/586171/altmetrics/*

PLOS: Article-Level Metrics
PLOS's overview on the topic of article-level metrics includes plenty of good information and links to research articles, tools, videos, and more, all with a focus on metrics for journal articles. *http://article-level-metrics.plos.org/alt-metrics/*

WORKSHOPS AND CONFERENCES

Association for Computing Machinery (ACM) Web Science Altmetrics Workshop
This one-day workshop, delivered annually as part of the ACM Web Science conference, features a number of papers and presentations reflecting the latest in altmetrics developments (and uses Figshare to host and share the accepted papers). The conference can be easily followed with the #altmetrics14 (or #altmetrics15 and beyond) hashtag on Twitter. *http://altmetrics.org/altmetrics14/*

Altmetrics Conference
This conference, currently the only one specifically devoted to altmetrics issues and discussion, had its inaugural event in September 2014. The schedule of events featured many of the same discussion topics and questions central to this book and to altmetrics at large. The presentations are available for view on YouTube along with a conference blog featuring live posts from conference presentation sessions. *http://www.altmetricsconference.com/schedule/*

Additional Tools

While we have tried to highlight the major tools associated with altmetrics in this chapter, there is a near-constant stream of altmetrics tools that are emerging, gaining favor, merging with other tools, or being abandoned. The following is a short list of some altmetrics tools, both active and inactive. With time, we expect these and other tools to also change status, but it's worth keeping an eye on these for changes in the future.

- ▼ **CitedIn:** *http://www.programmableweb.com/api/citedin*
- ▼ **ReaderMeter** (currently inactive): *http://www.readermeter.org*

▼ **ScienceCard** (currently inactive—URL links to a blog post with more explanation): *http://blogs.plos.org/mfenner/2012/09/19/announcing-the-sciencecard-relaunch/*

Notes

1. Jason Priem et al., "Altmetrics: A Manifesto," version1.0, last modified October 26, 2010, accessed January 7, 2015, *http://altmetrics.org/manifesto*.
2. Jason Priem et al., "Altmetrics: About," accessed February 9, 2015, *http://altmetrics.org/about/*.
3. Hadas Shema, Judit Bar-Ilan, and Mike Thelwall, "Research Blogs and the Discussion of Scholarly Information," *PLOS ONE* 7, no. 5 (2012): e35869, doi:10.1371/journal.pone.0035869.
4. Cameron Neylon and Shirley Wu, "Article-Level Metrics and the Evolution of Scientific Impact," *PLOS: Biology* 7, no. 11 (2009): e1000242, doi:10.1371/journal.pbio.1000242.
5. Dario Taraborelli, "Soft Peer Review: Social Software and Distributed Scientific Evaluation," *Proceedings of the 8th International Conference on the Design of Cooperative Systems* (2008): 99–110, *http:// discovery.ucl.ac.uk/8279/1/8279.pdf*.
6. Jason Priem, "Scientometrics 2.0." *Jason Priem* (blog), July 10, 2010, *http://jasonpriem.org/2010/07/scientometrics-2-0/*.
7. The coining of the term *altmetrics* is generally attributed to a tweet by Jason Priem on September 28, 2010: *https://twitter.com/jasonpriem/status/25844968813*.
8. Jennifer Lin and Martin Fenner, "Altmetrics in Evolution: Defining and Redefining the Ontology of Article-Level Metrics," *Information Standards Quarterly* 25, no. 2 (2013): 20, *http://www.niso.org/apps/group_public/download.php/11273/IP_Lin_Fenner_PLOS_altmetrics_isqv25no2.pdf*.
9. Jean Liu and Euan Adie, "Five Challenges in Altmetrics: A Toolmaker's Perspective," *Bulletin of the Association for Information Science and Technology* 39, no. 4 (2013): 32, *https://www.asis.org/Bulletin/Apr-13/AprMay13_Liu_Adie.pdf*.
10. Active Facebook and Twitter users defined based on monthly use. "Investor Relations: Facebook Reports Fourth Quarter and Full Year 2014 Results," Facebook, January 29, 2014, *http://investor.fb.com/*

releasedetail.cfm?ReleaseID=821954; "About," Twitter, accessed January 7, 2015, *https://about.twitter.com/company*.
11. "What Does Altmetric Do?," Altmetric, accessed January 7, 2015, *http://www.altmetric.com/whatwedo.php#score*. This website also provides information about how the Altmetric score is derived.
12. This example is borrowed from a previous sample profile provided by Impactstory for Carl Boettiger: "Carl Boettiger," Impactstory, accessed January 7, 2015, *https://impactstory.org/CarlBoettiger/ product/yvvv1cjdnt7jydvhjtt54ncp*.
13. Graham Woodward, "Altmetric Is Now on Board for All Wiley Journals," *Exchanges* (blog), Wiley, July 8, 2014, *http://exchanges. wiley.com/blog/2014/07/08/ altmetric-is-now-on-board-for-all-wiley-journals/*.
14. Sarah Huggett and Mike Taylor, "Elsevier Expands Metrics Perspectives with Launch of New Altmetrics Pilots," Authors' Update, Elsevier, accessed January 7, 2015, *http://editorsupdate.elsevier.com/issue-42-march-2014/ elsevier-altmetric-pilots-offer-new-insights-article-impact/*.
15. "About," Public Library of Science, accessed January 7, 2015, *http:// www.plos.org/about/*.
16. "Journal Summary Usage Data," *PLOS ONE*, accessed January 7, 2015, *http://www.plosone.org/static/journalStatistics*.
17. "Wiley Trial Alternative Metrics on Subscription and Open Access Articles," Wiley, May 20, 2013, *http://www.wiley.com/WileyCDA/ PressRelease/pressReleaseId-108763.html*.
18. Verity Warne, "Wiley Introduces Altmetrics to Its Open Access Journals," *Exchanges* (blog), Wiley, March 19, 2014, *http://exchanges. wiley.com/blog/2014/03/19/ wiley-introduces-altmetrics-to-its-open-access-journals/*.
19. Woodward, "Altmetric Is Now on Board."
20. Mike Buschman and Andrea Michalek, "Are Alternative Metrics Still Alternative?," *Bulletin of the Association for Information Science and Technology* 39, no. 4 (2013): 38, *https://www.asis.org/Bulletin/ Apr-13/AprMay13_Buschman_Michalek.pdf*.
21. More information about the RG Score is available on their FAQ: *https://www.researchgate.net/publicprofile.RGScoreFAQ.html*.

22. "RG Score," ResearchGate, accessed January 7, 2015, *http://www.researchgate.net/publicprofile.RGScoreFAQ.html*.
23. "Researcher ID," Web of Science, accessed January 7, 2015, *http://wokinfo.com/researcherid/*.
24. "Scopus Author Identifier," Elsevier, accessed January 7, 2015, arXiv.org, Cornell University Library, accessed January 7, 2015, *http://arxiv.org/help/author_identifiers*.
25. "Home," ORCID, accessed January 7, 2015, *http://orcid.org/*.
26. It's our article! Robin Chin Roemer and Rachel Borchardt, "Institutional Altmetrics and Academic Libraries," *Information Standards Quarterly* 25, no. 2 (2013): 14–19, *http://www.niso.org/publications/isq/2013/v25no2/roemer/*.
27. Ibid.
28. "For Institutions," Altmetric, accessed January 5, 2015, *http://www.altmetric.com/institutions.php*.
29. Scott Chamberlin, "Consuming Article-Level Metrics: Observations and Lessons," *Information Standards Quarterly* 25, no. 2 (2013): 9.
30. "About Us," ResearchGate, accessed January 5, 2015, *http://www.researchgate.net/about*.
31. The acquisition prompted a large outcry from the Mendeley user base. A great summary of the response can be found here: Mathew Ingram, "The Empire Acquires the Rebel Alliance: Mendeley Users Revolt against Elsevier Takeover," Gigaom Research, April 9, 2013: *https://gigaom.com/2013/04/09/the-empire-acquires-the-rebel-alliance-mendeley-users-revolt-against-elsevier-takeover/*.
32. Citation management software is hardly the focus of this book, but we feel obliged to point out some of Mendeley's better software features, including users being able to "watch" folders on their computer; automatically add new downloaded PDFs to their Mendeley library; and rename and organize PDFs by author, journal title, year, and more. It's very handy for researchers with lots of PDFs!
33. "What Are Readership Statistics?," Mendeley Support, accessed January 5, 2015, *http://support.mendeley.com/customer/portal/articles/1626928-what-are-readership-statistics-*.

34. Ehsan Mohammadi and Mike Thelwall, "Mendeley Readership Altmetrics for the Social Sciences and Humanities: Research Evaluation and Knowledge Flows," *Journal of the Association for Information Science and Technology* 65, no. 8 (2014): 1627–38.
35. About Academia.edu," Academia.edu, accessed January 7, 2015, *https://www.academia.edu/about*.
36. A full list of recognized sources is available in CiteULike's FAQ: *http://www.citeulike.org/faq/faq.adp*.
37. "Altmetrics in the Last Year and What's Next," YouTube video 1:18:13, from Altmetrics Conference, London, September 25, 2014, *https://www.youtube.com/watch?v=_qcM6DkLDUU*.
38. "The Altmetric Bookmarklet," Altmetric, accessed January 7, 2015, *http://www.altmetric.com/bookmarklet.php*.
39. "Altmetric Explorer Plans & Pricing," Altmetric, accessed January 7, 2015, *http://www.altmetric.com/plansandpricing.php*.
40. Martin Fenner, "What Can Article-Level Metrics Do for You?," *PLOS Biology* 11, no. 10 (2013): e1001687, doi:10.1371/journal.pbio. 1001687.
41. Richard Van Noorden, "Twitter Buzz about Papers Does Not Mean Citations Later," *Nature*, December 12, 2013, *http://www.nature. com/news/twitter-buzz-about-papers-does-not-mean-citations-later-1.14354*.
42. Lutz Bornmann, "Validity of Altmetrics Data for Measuring Societal Impact: A Study Using Data from Altmetric and F10000Prime," arXiv.org, Cornell University Library, June 30, 2014, *http://arxiv.org/abs/1406.7611*.
43. Jason Priem, Heather A. Piwowar, and Bradley M. Hemminger, "Altmetrics in the Wild: Using Social Media to Explore Scholarly Impact," arXiv.org, Cornell University Library, March 20, 2012, *http://arxiv.org/html/1203.4745*.
44. Lutz Bornmann, "Alternative Metrics in Scientometrics: A Meta-Analysis of Research into Three Altmetrics," arXiv.org, Cornell University Library, last modified October 28, 2014, arXiv:1407.8010.
45. Priem, Piwowar, and Hemminger, "Altmetrics in the Wild."
46. Heather Piwowar and Jason Priem, "The Power of Altmetrics on a CV," *Bulletin of the Association for Information Science and Technology* 39, no. 4 (2013): 10, *https://www.asis.org/Bulletin/Apr-13/AprMay13_Piwowar_Priem.pdf*.

47. NISO, Alternative Metrics Initiative Phase 1 White Paper, June 6, 2014, accessed January 7, 2015, *http://www.niso.org/apps/group_ public/download.php/13809/Altmetrics_project_phase1_white_ paper.pdf*.
48. Michael Habib, "Research Awareness + Perception: A Year in Review" (presentation, NISO Altmetrics Project Meeting, Washington, DC, December 11, 2013), *http://www.niso.org/topics/ tl/altmetrics_ initiative/agenda_dc/Habib_NISOLightning_CNI. pdf*.
49. Warne, "Wiley Introduces Altmetrics."
50. Stefanie Haustein et al., "Coverage and Adoption of Altmetrics Sources in the Bibliometric Community," *Scientometrics* 101, no. 2 (2014): 1145–63, doi:10.1007/s11192-013-1221-3.
51. Roberta Kwok, "Research Impact: Altmetrics Make Their Mark," *Nature* 500, no. 7463 (2013): 491, *http://www.nature.com/nature-jobs/science/ articles/10.1038/nj7463-491a*.
52. "NISO Alternative Assessment Metrics (Altmetrics) Initiative," NISO, accessed January 7, 2015, *http://www.niso.org/topics/tl/alt-metrics_ initiative/*.
53. Ibid.
54. Based on the results of NISO's open community survey, "NISO Alternative Assessment Potential Action Items," which was available on SurveyMonkey August 11–29, 2014: *http://www.niso.org/apps/ group_public/download.php/13661/Altmetrics%20survey%20 input%20-%20selected.pdf*.
55. William Gunn, "Social Signals Reflect Academic Impact: What It Means When a Scholar Adds a Paper to Mendeley," *Information Standards Quarterly* 25, no. 2 (2013): 38, *http://www.niso.org/ apps/group_public/download.php/11275/IP_Gunn_Mendeley_ isqv25no2.pdf*.

Chapter Six

Altmetrics in Practice

In this In Practice chapter, we will focus on the practical application of the altmetrics principles, metrics, and tools we explored in Chapter 5. However, it bears repeating that due to the quickly shifting and ill- defined nature of altmetrics, setting up walk-throughs is far from a straightforward process. What constitutes as a tour of cutting-edge applications and tools today may not look as cutting edge tomorrow as the field of altmetrics continues to advance. With these restraints in mind, this chapter endeavors to take an in-depth look at the mechanics, uses, and real-life applications of some of the most popular altmetrics tools and measurements of the authors' present day. For readers more than a few years out from the this book's publication date, take a look at suggestions in Chapter 8 for staying up to date with altmetrics, which when combined with the practical knowledge gleaned from this chapter, should give a fuller picture of any subsequent best practices and uses within the scope of altmetrics.

Walk-Through #1: PlumX's Altmetrics Sources in Action

In Chapter 5, we discussed the lack of institutional-level altmetrics in today's impact landscape and how this gap represents a future area of development for the field. However, as we also made clear, a few toolmakers have begun gathering altmetrics generated from the outputs of individual researchers and grouping them together to make altmetrics summaries at the department, lab, and institutional levels. To gain a better understanding of what these grouped altmetrics look like and the information and level of detail these groups can provide, we turn now to one of the most successful of these early efforts, Plum Analytics' PlumX tool, to test the application of higher-level altmetrics summaries "in the wild."

We start at the PlumX website (***https://plu.mx***), which features links to institutions that are using PlumX applications, such as the Smithsonian. For those unaware of the Smithsonian, it's is a group of 19 museums and galleries (e.g., Library of Congress, National Museum of American History, National Museum of African American History and Culture); nine research facilities (e.g., Astrophysical Observatory); and the National Zoological Park—all based in Washington, DC. Due to its vast network of scholarly interests and research, the Smithsonian's scholarly contributions (or, as PlumX calls them, "artifacts") span across virtually every discipline. Additionally, because the Smithsonian's institutions are funded through taxpayer money, the public dissemination of its research is of particular interest. For these reasons, altmetrics tools like PlumX are a good choice for the Smithsonian because it allows Smithsonian-affiliated researchers to gain information and insight into the application and adoption of their scholarship.

From the PlumX website, we click on the Smithsonian example link (***https://plu.mx/smithsonian/g***) to see what PlumX looks like in practice—that is to say, how PlumX operates once an institution's affiliated author and publication information has been entered into the system. Now at the main dashboard, we see that PlumX has created sets of altmetrics across the entire Smithsonian Institution as well as links to individual researchers and separate groups that reflect the different Smithsonian sub-entities. The ability to combine and recombine altmetrics gives users easy ways to compare different groups of entities, authors, and publications within an institution. Additionally, the ability to create groupings may reveal trends within an institution, such as which entity or author is the most prolific, which individual is the most highly cited, and which articles or areas of research have received the most public attention, etc.

As we continue to browse PlumX's Smithsonian landing page, we find we can click on any of the five listed altmetrics categories—"Usage,"

"Captures," "Citations," "Social Media," or "Mentions"—to see how metrics from individual artifacts combine to form a broader altmetrics picture. Additionally, if we scroll a little further down on the page, we see that of the five altmetrics categories, "Usage" is by far the most common type of impact to result from works authored by Smithsonian researchers. By clicking on "Usage," we can start to unpack this institutional-level view, performing a more detailed analysis on the metrics that help shape the "Usage" category. (For those interested in seeing all the possible metrics that are combined into the five main categories, PlumX keeps a handy chart of its current metrics included on its website along with the category associated with each one: "Overview: Plum Metrics," ***http://www.plumanalytics.com/metrics.html***).

Figure 6.1. Sample PlumX Usage Chart

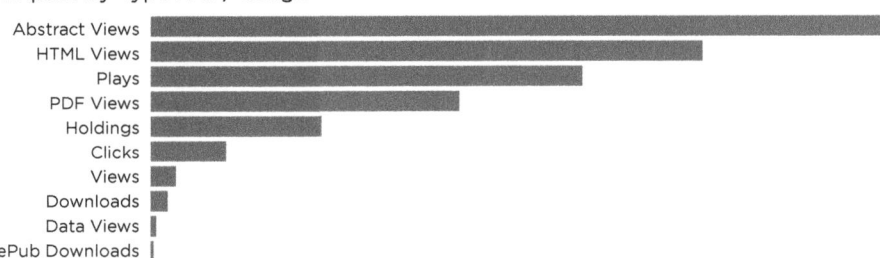

As we look closer at the Smithsonian's detailed usage information, we note that the largest individual metric within this grouping is "HTML Views" (about 1.7 million total), closely followed by the second largest usage metric, "Abstract Views" (about 1.6 million total). However, both of these views' values are much larger than the metric for the total number of citations generated from publications for the institution (about 106,000 total), which may point to a much broader general interest in the work of Smithsonian scholars than otherwise expected. Alternatively, this ratio may simply be proof that the spectrum of interaction with Smithsonian publications goes far beyond cited scholarship, something that is hardly surprising to anyone familiar with information-seeking behaviors in the digital age.

Having considered the metrics' basic breakdown within the "Usage" category, we can now try drilling down further to get even more detailed information about the contributing metrics. By clicking on the "Abstract Views" category, we discover the sources of the abstract views being generated: EBSCO and Smithsonian Digital Repository. (Remember, PlumX is an altmetrics harvester, not an original source of online metrics, so keep in mind that we are only seeing results based on information that other sites have made available to PlumX, either because they are already free to collect from or because of a special agreement between PlumX and that provider.) Because Plum Analytics is owned by EBSCO, PlumX features abstract views compiled directly from EBSCO databases. Still, like many usage metrics, EBSCO metrics only represent a portion of all abstract views, given that abstracts are widely available through many resources (Google Scholar, institutional repositories, publisher websites, other proprietary databases, etc.). PlumX's EBSCO-based abstract views serve well enough as a comparative metric for individuals and groups that stand within the Smithsonian research network. That said, when looking at sources of altmetrics data, it's important to consider not only the sources that are included but also the potential sources that are *not* included as this can potentially limit the ability to draw meaningful comparisons between institutions or arrive at definitive conclusions about the meaning of the metrics.

We insert here a quick note about the use of EBSCO data since this data represents an area where altmetrics has begun to overlap with the data that librarians collect for internal purposes, such as COUNTER (Counting Online Usage of Networked Electronic Resources) data. In sum, we find the idea of making COUNTER data available to researchers for impact purposes very interesting, and it's a potential area of collaboration between the altmetrics community, librarians, and publishers in the future. Of course, as many librarians are already aware, many large issues would need to be worked out before this could happen, including issues of proprietary access and standardization.

Discussion: When Should Altmetrics Be Used?

Because altmetrics tools are a novelty in the context of the impact market, many of the major altmetrics providers give basic online examples of how their tools work when put into action. For example, as we will see in our

> **Activity #1: Developing a PlumX Institutional Model**
>
> Surprisingly enough, one great way to develop a deeper understanding of an altmetrics tool's front end is to take some time to explore its back end.[1] PlumX, for example, is a powerful tool, but it requires significant input from users in order to run smoothly. When setting up a PlumX trial, you can create a hypothetical (or real life) PlumX model for your institution. To create such a model, start by choosing some researchers at your institution (or yourself!) and proceeding to walk through the steps of creating their PlumX profile, such as connecting their name with scholarly profiles (e.g., ORCID); uploading a citation file from Scopus or Web of Science; and adding individual artifacts by DOI, URL, or PubMed ID. What would the workflow of creating profiles look like if you implemented PlumX at your institution? Who would be responsible for creation and maintenance of these profiles? What steps could be streamlined or automated from existing sources? Once you've created some profiles, you may also want to examine what the aggregated altmetrics for your institution look like. What kind of information or trends can be gleaned from the collective data? How might this data be used by your institution? This kind of hands-on critical thinking can be useful when determining the relative "return on investment" for products like PlumX.

next walk-through, altmetrics leader Impactstory offers users access to a couple of sample profiles to give scholars some idea as to how the provider's metrics are synthesized and whether it would be worthwhile to include a link to an Impactstory profile in their evaluation or promotional file. Indeed, one of the main functions of altmetrics is to provide scholars with alternative ways to document and share their impact. Therefore, it follows that altmetrics could be considered useful in any situation that calls for some sort of impact statement, including the preparation of CVs, annual reports, merit reports, files for tenure or promotion, job applications, grant applications, and grant follow-up reports. However, the question remains of whether researchers *should* use altmetrics as part of specific evaluation scenarios—a question that is much more difficult and that can be answered with few, if any, certainties so long as altmetrics continues to be hotly debated across academia. For this reason, it may be helpful for librarians to walk through the following questions when considering the application of altmetrics on behalf of themselves or another researcher:

- What can altmetrics add to my submission?
- What is the culture or accepted standards regarding altmetrics in the discipline or institution that I am submitting to?
- Are there guidelines, templates, etc., that show best practices for my submission?
- How could my altmetrics be misinterpreted? Can I minimize or mitigate this risk?

In addition to these questions, a good general rule of thumb regarding the incorporation of altmetrics is to consider their inclusion when other metrics are unavailable or when they can supplement bibliometrics. Supplementing bibliometrics can include metrics for journals not included in major bibliometrics-providing tools like Web of Science or metrics for less traditional works, such as a presentation or blog. Scholars with recent publications may also be more inclined to include altmetrics as "emerging indicators of impact," even the hotly debated practice of using Twitter buzz as a loose, possible predictor of later citation counts. Finally, altmetrics may be appropriate to use when they give evaluators some sense of qualitative insight, such as specific comments or reviews made about an article, in addition to quantitative metrics.

Walk-Through #2: Impactstory's Author-Level Grouped Altmetrics

In our next walk-through, we step away from the institutional-level metrics we examined using PlumX and move to author-level metrics, demonstrated by the altmetrics tool Impactstory.

Groupings of altmetrics around authors generally predate the emergence of institution-focused groupings, but they are similarly built on the basis of aggregating altmetrics generated from a set of individual scholarly contributions. This order of emergence—individual contribution metrics, then author-level grouped metrics, then institutional-level grouped metrics—has helped reinforce the idea that altmetrics are most relevant to individual researchers who want to better discover and document their impact in new and interesting ways. Indeed, Impactstory was one of the first products to trumpet the connection between altmetrics and the needs and views of individual researchers. However, this is hardly a surprising perspective since the founders of Impactstory, Jason Priem and Heather Piwowar, have for years used the single-researcher narrative to lead conversations related to altmetrics, both in their published works and presentations.[2]

As an author-focused tool, Impactstory seeks to help individual scholars gather altmetrics related to their work in order to make visible their "spectrum of impact." Each scholar's spectrum of impact is inevitably different, depending on the nature of his or her scholarly contributions as well as on the fields of research involved. On a more practical level, the spectrum also depends on how well each scholar's scholarly contributions align with available altmetrics sources since an altmetrics tool is only as strong as the metrics it can provide for a researcher's scholarly works. To see a great example of an altmetrics profile that is well aligned with altmetrics sources, we need look no further than to an online profile recently featured on Impactstory's website: Carl Boettiger.[3] Boettiger is an excellent example for our walk-through because he has enjoyed success in both the scholarly and non-scholarly arenas, and he has also made some of his work publicly available through professionally recognized sites like GitHub. To top it all off, Boettiger maintains active accounts with several harvester-compatible altmetrics sources, including SlideShare, Twitter, and Figshare.

We begin the walk-through by opening a browser window and entering the URL for Boettiger's Impactstory profile: ***https://impactstory.org/CarlBoettiger***. (At one point, Boettiger's profile was linked off Impactstory's home page, but now it is only accessible by visiting the permalink.) Once on Boettiger's main profile page, we immediately see a box on the right-hand side of the page that says "Key Profile Metrics." These metrics provide a convenient summary of Boettiger's author-level metrics, sorted by type of work—articles, datasets, posters, slide decks, etc.; for Boettiger, his key profile metrics are 765 saves on 21 articles and 102 forks on 61 software products. By providing this basic information on each profile's home page, Impactstory allows viewers to quickly sum up the metrics affiliated with a given user. Meanwhile, on the left-hand side of Boettiger's page, we see types of individual research contributions that have been used in calculating his metrics, including the key profile metrics. In the main, central portion of the profile, we see a list of "Selected Works" that Impactstory has auto-generated based on Boettiger's key contributions (though authors can change the items that are displayed here to highlight works of their own choosing). Through these key metrics and selected works, we start to see the power that Impactstory brings to collecting *and* contextualizing altmetrics.

Using badges, Impactstory provides the highest level of contextualization by classifying each selected work with badges that include values such as "Cited" and "Highly Cited;" "Discussed" and "Highly Discussed;" and "Saved" and "Highly Saved." These badges serve to convey to viewers several important messages about each Impactstory author. First, the color of the badges indicates the type (or "flavor") of altmetrics being displayed for the author: scholarly or public, reflecting altmetrics' broader scope as discussed earlier in Chapter 4. Designated with a green badge, scholarly metrics includes activities such as page views, downloads, Mendeley readership, and GitHub views and forks. By contrast, public metrics, designated by blue badges, include Facebook mentions, Twitter tweets, Delicious bookmarks, and Impactstory views (which are counted when someone goes to an author's profile URL, as we are doing now, and subsequently clicks through to view a scholarly work).

The word *highly* in some of Impactstory's badges also has a special definition, which is where we start to see the contextualization potential of the tool really come in play. According to the toolmakers, any altmetric that falls in the 75th percentile or above as compared to the altmetric for similar works is considered "Highly—", such as "Highly Viewed" or "Highly Saved." Hovering over a given tag tells you the exact percentile a work has earned as well as what collection of items the work is being compared to. For instance, if we look again at Boettiger's profile, we see that his 2012 article "Is Your Phylogeny Informative? Measuring the Power of Comparative Methods" has four badges: "Highly Cited," "Highly Saved," "Highly Viewed," and "Discussed." By hovering over the "Highly Cited" badge, we learn that because this article has generated 34 Scopus citations to date, ranking higher than "98% of [articles published in 2012] on Impactstory." Do note, however, that these contextual comparisons can

Impactstory and Twitter Metrics

Impactstory takes a slightly different approach to measuring Twitter altmetrics that some users may find confusing at first glance. One of the main metrics they collect and share is "impressions," which doesn't match standard Twitter language: *tweets, retweets,* and *favorites*. What, then, does it mean for an Impactstory user to have Twitter impressions, and why are these numbers so high compared to other altmetrics in the tool?

The answer to this question lies in the unique connection that altmetrics recognizes between social media and the largely academic world of scholarship. As mentioned in Chapter 1, the definition of altmetrics is deeply entwined with the social web and the discussion and dissemination of scholarship—albeit not always in ways that are easy to articulate. Accordingly, Twitter impressions in Impactstory come from tweets that are generated in relation to an author's scholarly work. For example, if PLOS were to tweet about an article that Boettiger has written, the resulting impression metric is equal to the number of followers that PLOS has since, presumably, all of those followers have now been exposed to Boettiger's work through this one-time PLOS tweet. So, if PLOS has 50,000 followers, it follows that Boettiger's Twitter impression metric is now 50,000, even though this number comes from sending just one tweet. Impressions offer a way for users to measure how widely academic tweets are being sent and received rather than just the sheer number of tweets that have been generated in relation to a work. After all, a tweet from an account with 50,000 followers will presumably have a different impact than a tweet from an account with only 50 followers. All it takes is one tweet from a very popular account for a Twitter impression score to rise rapidly! Perhaps if adoption of Twitter impressions as a metric really takes hold in academia, we'll start to see scholars soliciting the likes of famous celebrities and other notable Twitter accounts in search of that one tweet that can really increase their impression metric.

differ depending on the information available from the original source. For example, in the metrics-provider tool Mendeley, articles are categorized by field and year, so Impactstory will only compare the readership metric to other articles in Mendeley in the same field and published in the same year. This two-pronged contextualization makes for a more accurate comparison of readership data in Impactstory than, say, data pulled from SlideShare, which does not have separate subject categories for its publicly available slide decks. SlideShare-generated views for a particular slide deck are, therefore, compared with all other slide decks uploaded to that site in that same year, regardless of their topics. Thus, while contextual comparisons can get us closer to the ideal of cross-discipline metric accuracy, there remains plenty of room for misinterpretation stemming from inaccurate comparisons.

Finally, certain Impactstory badges can also have numbers listed on them, such as "+10." While these numbers can easily be mistaken as indicators of activity on the social network Google Plus, which often uses the "+1" designation as an in-tool synonym for likes, here it indicates a change in the metric during the past week. Knowing more about changes to the metrics displayed on Impactstory's profiles can be helpful in discerning which of an author's scholarly products are currently receiving community attention and at what rate.

For viewers looking for more granular information about an item, any badge can be clicked on to display more details, including the source(s) the item's information was retrieved from. Interestingly, some Impactstory metrics are harvested from the Altmetric bookmarklet, but most are harvested directly from original sources, like peer networks.

Discussion: The Limitations of Harvesters

In Chapter 5, we discussed the difference between a tool that generates altmetrics, a peer network, and a tool that collects and summarizes altmetrics, a harvester. Let's now take a closer look at the features and limits of a harvester by tracing a scholarly source as it generates altmetrics through two well-known peer networks and into a prominent harvester.

In this case, we will imagine an article that has been published and uploaded to both ResearchGate, a closed peer network system (data only available to members), and Mendeley, an open peer network system (data available to the public). In ResearchGate, we can see the number of article views and bookmarks, two indicators of interaction within the ResearchGate network. In Mendeley, however, the view is different, with information about the article's number of readers broken down by

> **Activity #2: Developing an Impactstory Profile**
>
> As discussed in the last activity, hands-on development within an altmetrics product is one of the best ways of assessing its value, strengths, and weaknesses. In the case of Impactstory, an online tool marketed to individual researchers rather than institutions, we can easily apply this technique by setting up a profile and using it to explore the development of a profile for just one individual. However, because our choice of individual will have a tremendous impact on the complexity and richness of the resulting Impactstory profile—we can't all be Carl Boettiger, after all—you may want to start by choosing someone for whom you can input a variety of *types* of scholarly items: URLs as well as DOI-linked articles, online presentations, and one or more researcher IDs. You may even want to start by looking at yourself, assuming you have done some of this work, to ensure that the profile is as complete as possible. Alternately, you could choose a high profile researcher at your institution, or perhaps one early in his or her career, to get a sense of how a user's Impactstory profile might change over time. As before, pay attention to what information can be imported from other sources into Impactstory versus what needs to be entered manually. You will also note that you can e-mail publications directly to Impactstory to add them to a profile!
>
> Once you have added some items, we recommend you check to see what the tool automatically selects to be a "Featured Work," and then try clicking on individual categories of works on the left-hand side, which allows you to star or unstar the works that are featured. If you discover works with no altmetrics, consider whether there's a better way to import the record (e.g., by DOI instead of URL), whether you should delete the record, or whether it's best to wait in case altmetrics are generated in the future. When finished, survey the resulting record. How well does it serve as a complement to an existing CV? How accurately does it capture the total impact of the sample researcher? Using these questions, you can start to gain a better sense of the researchers for whom Impactstory may hold greater value and the situations that you might recommend its use.

discipline, academic status, and country of viewership. While both of these sets of metrics arguably demonstrate useful ways that each system's users are interacting with our article, only Mendeley allows altmetrics harvesters like Impactstory to collect and process its metrics. Meanwhile, the ResearchGate metrics remain out Impactstory's reach, so contextual comparisons for ResearchGate article metrics can't be listed alongside Mendeley metrics.

Combining Sources to Measure Nontraditional Publications

Between 2009 and 2012, one of this book's authors, Rachel Borchardt, was one of three cohosts of the *Adventures in Library Instruction* podcast, a work she considered an unconventional form of scholarship in the field of librarianship.[4] For Rachel, a science librarian, it was difficult to demonstrate the podcast's impact because readily accepted metrics, like citations or impact factor, aren't applicable to the podcast medium. Her solution to this problem was a collated "statement of impact," which she used in her library's reappointment and merit files for several years. The statement, as shown in the figure below, included information on subscriber statistics, descriptions and links showing the integration of the podcast into online book and course materials, and links to notable librarians' blog posts that featured the podcast.

Finding these sources was not simple—it required Rachel to monitor several online sources to collect sources from multiple sites. These sources included the following:

▼ FeedBurner for gathering subscriber statistics;
▼ the podcast blog's internal analytics and Google Analytics for referring websites;[5]
▼ Google for finding links, using "link:[website];" and
▼ Impactstory for monitoring social media.[6]

Figure 6.2. Feedburner Subscriber Statistics

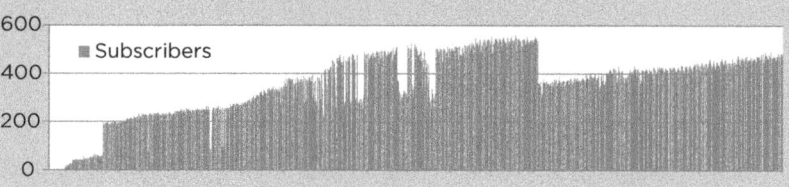

The accessibility of this generated data ultimately determines the limitations of altmetrics products like Impactstory since they are barred from accessing data generated by closed networks like ResearchGate. It remains to be seen how these limitations will play out in the future, but for now, there is no altmetrics product that can truly offer all available altmetrics so long as closed systems exist. Ultimately, peer networks will need to balance the value in keeping metrics within their systems (and thus forcing its users to register and log in to access their metrics) versus the potential for increased visibility that they would receive by partnering with harvesters like Impactstory.

Walk-Through #3: Altmetric and Scopus, Partners in Action

As discussed in Chapter 5, one of the more interesting developments in altmetrics over the last few years has been the integration of some altmetrics tools into existing websites and applications. One of the best examples of this is the integration of the Altmetric "donut" badge into individual article records within Scopus. Scopus also recently began integrating Mendeley readership statistics into its records, but that was expected since Elsevier now owns both Scopus and Mendeley. By contrast, Altmetric remains an independent company (interestingly, Mendeley and Altmetric were both founded out of an Elsevier-sponsored programming competition).[7] In this third walk-through, we take a look at how the Mendeley and Altmetric programs work together from the perspective of Scopus database users.

We start our walk-through by navigating to Scopus through a library website that provides access to it as part of its online subscriptions. While not all academic libraries provide access to Scopus, readers who wish to follow along may request a trial of the product to continue with this exercise. In any case, once reaching the Scopus home page we are prompted by default to begin a document search by article title, abstract keyword, first author, etc. As we play around with some searches, we find that Scopus's results look remarkably similar to other science-focused databases like Web of Science. This changes, however, once we click through to an individual record, at which point we may begin to see new options for impact alongside expected information related to article citations (though you may need to scroll down a bit to confirm the new options' presence or absence). For purposes of demonstration, let's use Impactstory cofounder Heather Piwowar's 2013 *Nature* article, "Altmetrics: Value All Research Products," which provides a good example of the donut in action. We recommend that readers search for this article by title to get to the record quickly.

Having located and clicked on the record for Piwowar's article, we scroll down toward the bottom of the page to reveal a kind of rainbow-colored Altmetric donut. Note that the donut itself is a quick visualization of impact: Each color in the circle represents a different source of altmetrics that has been tracked for this particular article. For this reason, some Altmetric donuts only have one or two colors, while others can have seven or more. As of the time of our writing, the Altmetric donut for Piwowar's article has four colors: dark blue, light blue, yellow, and magenta. The size of each color band in the circle is a rough approximation of the percentage of the data that comes from each individual source. Piwowar's circle, like many other circles, has a dominant light blue band, which indicates metrics data from Twitter. Not surprisingly given what we know about the relative size of social media metrics, the light blue band is often the largest one within the Altmetric donut for Scopus articles. In Piwowar's case, using the conveniently provided color legend, we see that her article's 270 affiliated tweeters (light blue) eclipses its nine mentions from Facebook users (dark blue), 12 affiliated science blogs (yellow), and 13 mentions from Google+ users (magenta).

Looking below at the "Altmetric for Scopus's Color Legend," we notice here a small "Saved to Reference Managers" section, which is kept separate from the colors in the donut visualization. For this record, we note that this section includes the article's number of CiteULike users (23) and Mendeley users (198)—essentially, instances where users have presumably saved Piwowar's article to read or perhaps cite in a future publication. Finally, at the bottom of the Altmetric box, we see links that read "See Details" or "Open Report in New Tab." Here's a professional tip for readers—both links take you to the same information! "See Details" opens a pop-up that displays more information from Altmetric about the article, while the other link opens the same information in a new browser tab. Either way, we can use these links to take a closer look at how Altmetric collates and contextualizes its altmetrics sources for Piwowar's article. Pick your preferred link, and click it to continue the walk-through.

Along the left-hand side of the newly revealed detailed display, we see essentially the same information available about Piwowar's article from the Altmetric donut in Scopus, including the color legend. Along the top of the pop-up (or page) are seven tabs, each of which, with the exception of Help, provides more granular detail about the source from the perspective of a specific metric. The Twitter tab, for example, shows the total number of tweets, tweeters, and combined followers (i.e., number of followers reached by all of the tweets sent about an article, comparable to Impactstory's impressions metric) along with the most recent tweets that were taken into the calculation. For Piwowar, we see that the large light blue band is made up of 305 tweets from 270 accounts with 1,301,023 combined followers. The Score tab is where we find the article-level metric calculated by Altmetric as discussed in Chapter 5: 243.36 for Piwowar's article. The Score tab also displays a complete list of contextualized percentiles for the article, some of which are displayed near the donut along the left side, but they're not nearly as comprehensive. As we learn from the descriptions provided within this tab, these percentiles take the article's Altmetric score and compare it to other articles published in the same journal other articles published during the same year or all articles from both the same journal and the same year.. For some articles, this can provide an interesting take on context, particularly with the comparison of other articles published in the same journal during the same year. However, for larger and more interdisciplinary journals, these comparisons may not be as appropriate as comparisons based on discipline (such as those provided by Impactstory), though they still may prove interesting as a way to show how an item relates to similar articles. We also notice that alongside each percentile, Altmetric also shows the article's raw ranking, which indicates the total number of articles that Piwowar's article is being compared to. Consequently, when we read that Piwowar's article places in the 99th percentile for "All Articles of a Similar Age," we can also understand this is another way of saying that the article ranks 401st out of 276,133 articles of a similar age (401/276,133 = the top 0.145%).

Figure 6.3. Altmetric Score Details

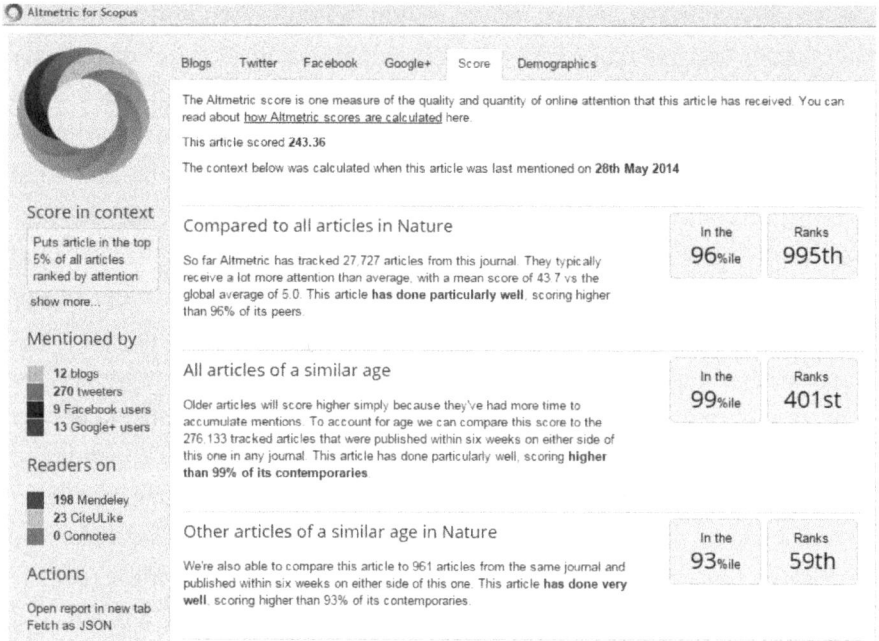

Before we leave this detailed view of the Piwowar article's altmetrics, we will look at one final bit of data hidden within the detailed Demographics tab. While many of the article's demographics are relatively expected, including Twitter's geographic location and Mendeley's demographics taken directly from the network's readership data, one additional demographic is added: Twitter's user demographics. In this demographic, Twitter users are broken up into categories. Clicking on the Demographics tab for Piwowar's article, we see that 56% of the tweets for the article were generated by "Members of the Public," 28% by "Scientists," 12% by "Science Communicators," and 2% by "Practitioners." In other words, the Altmetric for Scopus tool is taking Twitter data, a source that is often seen as purely an indicator of public impact, and breaking it down into finer categories of public and scholarly interest. That said, in looking at the actual tweets related to the 2013 article, we suspect that many of the so-called "Members of the Public" are actually academics, perhaps tweeting from their personal accounts. Doubts like these suggest that the demographic information provided by Altmetric could stand a bit of refinement if users want to pursue demographic data as a serious factor in academic impact.

In concluding this walk-through, it's useful to point out that not every article result in Scopus will be as successful as Piwowar's example when it comes to generating analyzable altmetrics data. As Scopus users soon discover, the colorful Altmetric donut only appears in the records of some articles, presumably those with significant altmetrics. Because Scopus displays results for articles that are still in press, your best bet when seeking a donut is to search for a fairly broad topic (like "altmetrics"), and then to choose an older article or, even better, click on the "Cited By" option under "Sort On" in the upper-right corner of the screen. This click will re-sort the citations listed on the page by times cited instead of by date. Sorting by times cited also allows for an excellent comparison of citations and altmetrics for individual articles. A motivated reader could even start his or her very own correlation study between times cited and altmetrics indicators such as page views, downloads, and Twitter buzz, similar to studies examining these correlations discussed in Chapter 5.[8]

Library Practices for Supporting Altmetrics

Just as librarians have proven themselves to be ardent supporters of researchers in the search for indicators of bibliometric impact, some librarians have already recognized in altmetrics an opportunity to further extend the reach of their support or rethink their approach to discussing impact with stakeholders. According to a brief online survey that we recently conducted of librarians who support impact metrics at their universities (see Chapter 8 for more details), 76% of the librarians who said they support impact also said that they support altmetrics (25 out of 34 question respondents). While this percentage was admittedly less than the percentage of librarians who reported in the survey that they support bibliometrics, it's still a significant enough percentage to indicate that altmetrics support is becoming common among impact-aware librarians. Consequently, to conclude this In Practice chapter, we take a look at some of the ways motivated librarians are helping to incorporate altmetrics into their institutions.

Just as we saw with bibliometrics, one of the most popular ways that libraries are providing altmetrics information to researchers is via

Activity #3: Exploring and Harvesting Data Using Altmetric

Now that we better understand the function and structure of the so-called Altmetric donut, it's time to start searching for Altmetric data on our own, using resources that have partnered with the company, like Scopus. Imagine for a moment that you are a specific researcher preparing an impact statement for a file for tenure or promotion (you can use Heather Piwowar again, if you can't think of another name). Using Scopus (or, in a pinch, the Altmetric bookmarklet) look up several articles that you have written or that you know have been influenced by your work.[9] How many of these articles have Altmetric data available for them? How similar are the donuts for these articles according to the Altmetric color legend? How do the articles' Altmetric scores compare to the number of citations that they have generated to date? What, if any, surprises did you find when browsing within the metrics (e.g., individual tweets, posts, etc.) that make up your Altmetric score(s)?

Taking a moment to think carefully again about your interests and priorities as this researcher, consider these questions: What information from this exercise would you want to add to your file's impact statement? Would you include the same information for all of the articles in your portfolio or change it from article to article? Would you use this data to demonstrate some impact for articles without citations or to bolster the impact of the articles that already have high bibliometrics attached to them? How might these decisions change based not only on the altmetrics themselves but also on the citation culture of the academic discipline or opinion of your eventual evaluators? Finally, once these decisions have been made, how will you present all of this information (e.g., with a chart, graph, or paragraph explaining your metrics)? Will you report the data as raw numbers, take screenshots of sections of the Altmetric donut, or create an original visualization using Excel or other data visualization program?

As a librarian, the more you can think about these scenarios and walk through some of the questions that they generate, the better positioned you will be to offer suggestions or advice to researchers.

the creation of online research guides. Of the guides available at the time of writing, we particularly like "Measure Your Impact," published by the University of North Carolina's (UNC) Health Sciences Library.[10] Its friendly, practical title helps clarify for users both the guide's audience (those interested in their research impact, i.e., researchers) and its approach to metrics (outcome-based rather than theoretical). Another feature we like is that UNC's health sciences librarians have chosen to include information about altmetrics as a page within the guide. Built using the content management system LibGuides, the guide's altmetrics home page uses a smattering of boxes to promote a mixture of information, images, and links to other authoritative sources related to altmetrics. In a box titled "Learn More about Altmetrics" in the bottom-left corner of the guide, one can find information about the online April 2013 issue of the *ASIS&T Bulletin* that focused on altmetrics as well as a link to the NISO Altmetrics Standards Project White Paper (see Chapter 5). The main column of the page presents a short overview of altmetrics and lists some potential benefits of its adoption. Practical details about how to obtain altmetrics using tools like Altmetric and Impactstory are also given a little lower down. Overall, the UNC Health Sciences Library guide delivers what it promises by showing researchers ways to retrieve the most popular altmetrics for measuring their research impact while at the same time encouraging interested users to pursue more information about the altmetrics movement. What's more, the guide is kept up to date—no small feat when it comes to the fast-changing world of altmetrics—and succeeds in being informative without being overly lengthy.

One of the more unique ways that librarians are getting involved with altmetrics is by giving dedicated presentations on the subject to members of their universities or even just to members of the their own university libraries. An excellent documented example of this is the presentation, "Altmetrics and Librarians: How Changes in Scholarly Communication Will Affect Our Profession," given by two librarians, Stacy Konkiel and Robert E. Noel, at the University of Indiana Bloomington in 2012.[11] This PowerPoint-based presentation, available to view in UI's DSpace institutional repository, addresses the university's librarians and library staff with the goal of introducing them to the overlap between altmetrics and scholarly communication. The presentation starts with a wide-ranging look at the state of scholarly communication and digital scholarship in academia, and then turns to the effect new technology has had on the measurement of impact. From here, the presenters introduce a number of altmetrics tools (as they existed at the time), examine the university guidelines for promotion and tenure, and close with a look at the role librarians will play in preparation for further discussion. Konkiel and Noel's slides provide a great example of how librarians can and are making important inroads for altmetrics by raising it as a topic within their local units. As more librarians are taking the time to discuss of altmetrics in combination with larger LIS issues, the more we are seeing the spread of practical, enriching comments about the purpose, place, and role of altmetrics across libraries and academia in general.

Moving Forward

Much like bibliometrics, gaining comfort and knowledge with altmetrics takes a certain amount of dedication and practice. These next steps, based on the exercises and discussions in this chapter, can help anchor your limited time and resources by focusing your training in productive and meaningful ways.

▼ **Practice creating a total "statement of impact."** Starting with the bibliometric statement of impact discussed in Chapter 4, try to expand your personal statement of impact by collecting and incorporating your understanding of altmetrics. Be sure to give careful consideration as to which metrics best highlight the impact of individual works and of researchers in different disciplines. Doing this may help you better articulate the varying role that altmetrics plays in the measurement of impact.

▼ **Explore different altmetrics categories.** Each altmetrics tool categorizes its metrics differently. As you take the time explore the different ways that tools group and discuss altmetrics categories, try and identify the one that speaks best to you or to the researchers you work with most. If necessary, you may consider creating your own unique categories to describe altmetrics indicators. Later, this understanding of altmetrics categories may help organize a research guide or assist users who are confused about altmetrics options.

▼ **Talk to researchers about their impressions, needs, and concerns regarding altmetrics.** Conversations with researchers about altmetrics can vary wildly as awareness and attitudes regarding altmetrics are highly variable. Not every researcher will want to hear more about the topic, or want to hear about it in the same way. By taking the time to listen carefully, you can start to create a fuller picture for yourself regarding the local challenges and opportunities surrounding altmetrics.

▼ **Pursue trials and explore tools.** While several key altmetrics tools are publicly available, a few require paid subscriptions, particularly at the institutional level. By seeking out temporary access to for-cost tools that may have value to you or your researchers, you give yourself the opportunity to evaluate the strengths and weaknesses of all altmetrics tools—and you may even help others with access to the trial discover the value of higher-level analytic products.

Additional Resources

Plum Analytics' Blog
While more squarely focused on PlumX news and tips, this blog is nonetheless a one-stop shop for staying current with the resource, including helpful links to presentations and walk-throughs of specific PlumX features. *http://blog.plumanalytics.com*

Impactstory's Blog
Impactstory's blog is one of the most comprehensive blogs for altmetrics news and discussion. Contributors Heather Piwowar, Jason Priem, and Stacy Konkiel understand the importance of educating librarians and involving them in altmetrics and have written several posts aimed squarely at a librarian audience. One post, "4 Things Every Librarian Should Do with Altmetrics," is of particular value to librarians looking to further their practical understanding of altmetrics. *http://blog.impactstory.org*

Altmetric's Knowledge Base
Chock full of information regarding Altmetric's products, troubleshooting tips, and advanced details, including an overview of Altmetric for Scopus. *http://support.altmetric.com/knowledgebase*

Swets' Blog Series on Altmetrics for Librarians
Fin Galligan, formerly associated with Swets, wrote a wonderful series of blog posts aimed at the application of altmetrics for librarians, including plenty of additional resources. Due to Swets' bankruptcy in 2014, these posts must now be accessed through the Internet Archive Wayback Machine at *http://web.archive.org*. See *http://web.archive.org/web/20140927150150/http:/www.swets.com/blog/altmetrics-for-libraries-3-themes*

"Analyze This: Altmetrics and Your Collection—Statistics and Collection Development"
Andrea Michalek and Mike Buschman, both of Plum Analytics, presented at the April 2014 Charleston Conference and wrote these excellent conference proceedings, expanding on the role altmetrics can play in library functions, particularly as they relate to COUNTER statistics. *http://www.plumanalytics.com/downloads/v26-2_AnalyzeThis.pdf*

Notes

1. We hope catalogers and reference librarians agree with this!
2. Heather Piwowar and Jason Priem, "The Power of Altmetrics on a CV," *ASIS&T Bulletin* 39, no. 4 (2013): 10, *http://asis.org/Bulletin/Apr-13/AprMay13_Piwowar_Priem.html*; Heather Piwowar and Jason Priem, "The Altmetrics CV" (presentation, PLOS ALM Workshop, San Francisco, CA, October 2013), *http://article-level-metrics.plos.org/files/2013/10/Piwowar-Priem.pdf.*
3. "Carl Boettiger," Impactstory, accessed January 8, 2015, *https://impact story.org/CarlBoettiger.*
4. *Adventures in Library Instruction* (podcast) (*http://adlibinstruction.blogspot.com*) went on hiatus in 2012. Concerns about measuring its impact on the library community led to Rachel's interest in metrics.

5. This feature from Google Analytics shows you the website where users clicked on a URL to bring them to your website. This allowed Rachel to find some nonobvious sources, such as a link to a course management system that a podcast episode had been linked to for a class.
6. Similar to Google Analytics, Rachel often used Impactstory to find out who had mentioned the podcast, which sometimes linked back to a source and sometimes offered the opportunity to further interact with listeners.
7. "About Us," Altmetric, accessed January 8, 2015, **https://www.altmetric.com/about.php**.
8. This may seem like a forward suggestion, but studying the relationship between citations and altmetrics for researchers at your institution can go a long way in evaluating the relative value of altmetrics for those researchers.
9. "The Altmetric Bookmarklet," Altmetric, accessed January 8, 2015, **www.altmetric.com/bookmarklet.php**.
10. "Measure Your Research Impact: Introduction," UNC Health Sciences Library, accessed January 8, 2015, **http://guides.lib.unc.edu/measure impact**.
11. Stacy Konkiel and Robert E. Noel, "Altmetrics and Librarians: How Changes in Scholarly Communication Will Affect Our Profession" (presentation, Indiana University Bloomington Libraries In-House Institute, Bloomington, IN, May 7, 2012), **https://scholarworks.iu.edu/dspace/handle/2022/14471**.

Section 4
SPECIAL TOPICS

Chapter Seven

Disciplinary Impact

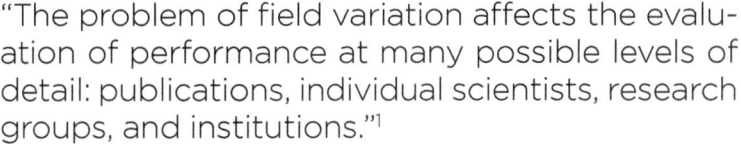

"The problem of field variation affects the evaluation of performance at many possible levels of detail: publications, individual scientists, research groups, and institutions."[1]

—Filippo Radicchi, Santo Fortunato, and Claudio Castellano, "Universality of Citation Distributions: Toward an Objective Measure of Scientific Impact"

So far in this book, we have largely looked at impact as a topic approachable from two unique perspectives: the print-based perspective of bibliometrics and the web-based perspective of altmetrics. Yet impact is by no means a field of neat binaries, and for many researchers, the process of measuring impact is not only a mix of altmetrics and bibliometrics, but also a mix of qualitative and quantitative information, scholarly output and creative output, and issues from one field and methods from another. This problem of complexity (or perhaps we should say *complexities*) is especially visible when we compare common practices for measuring impact across the disciplines. In this chapter, we seek to do exactly that, as well as identify the strengths and weaknesses of popular tools and metrics relative to different disciplines.

The Three Disciplines

According to the Oxford English Dictionary, the word *discipline* can be defined as "a particular school or method of instruction." A discipline, in other words, is a specialty area of training or research, where *disciples* (better known as researchers) share a particular set of values, methods, and assumptions about the world around them. In modern terms, a discipline is usually interpreted to mean one of the three major academic subject groupings: sciences, social sciences, or arts and humanities. Occasionally one of these groupings is further broken down into more specific disciplines (e.g., medicine and the biological sciences, engineering, fine arts)—although this largely depends on local universities' culture and organization or the academy at a given moment in time.

Disciplines can also be broken into more practical academic units such as subjects or departments, which require even more specific applications of disciplinary methods and values. Certain subjects, however, can complicate this breakdown because their methods and values come from multiple disciplines, making them to some extent multidisciplinary. Multidisciplinary subjects are typically concentrated in the social sciences (e.g., global studies, environmental policy), although they exist in every major discipline. The existence of such subjects also points to another recent trend within higher education: whole departments or research centers founded to study a broad research topic that requires researchers from multiple disciplines to work together in deeply entwined collaboration. Such interdisciplinary units are a natural extension of multidisciplinary subject research, and they afford many researchers in traditional disciplines a unique opportunity to work closely with and exert influence on experts in wholly different fields.

For purposes of this chapter, we will continue to use "discipline" to refer to the three major academic groupings of the sciences, social sciences, and arts and humanities. Additionally, we will continue look at issues of impact measurement related to multidisciplinarity and interdisciplinarity.

> "Performance metrics based on values such as citation rates are heavily biased by field, so most measurement experts shy away from interdisciplinary comparisons. The average biochemist, for example, will always score more highly than the average mathematician, because biochemistry attracts more citations."[2]
>
> —Richard Van Noorden, "Who Is the Best Scientist of Them All?"

Impact Across the Disciplines

If comparing research in different disciplines is like comparing apples and oranges, then comparing researchers' impacts in different disciplines is sort of like trying to explain why the best way to pick out an apple isn't to look for bright orange color and a fresh, citrusy scent. Research across the disciplines can certainly be related, but it's a huge mistake to overlook the inherent differences between the output and expectations of a humanities researcher and a social sciences one—especially when checking for impact. To help elucidate these differences, we will now look at each of the major disciplines and some of their shared and unique practices surrounding output and impact.

> "Blinding me with science—science!"
> "Science!"
> "Science!"
>
> —Thomas Dolby, "She Blinded Me with Science"

The Sciences

We begin our disciplinary tour with the one that started it all: the sciences. (And yes, feel free to channel your best Thomas Dolby here.) Ever since the 19th-century reorganization of university curriculum into the modern disciplines, the sciences has stood out as the primary driver of publication culture in higher education—hence, its close relationship to bibliometrics.

Today, the sciences—now often grouped as science, technology, engineering, and medicine (STEM)—is deeply invested in the use of bibliometrics for purposes of personal and institutional benchmarking. It continues to expect its researchers to produce most of their output in the form of scholarly articles, journal impact factor remains, by and large, the "king" of science metrics. It's used to determine the strength of many individual researchers' portfolios and judge the relative success of scientific departments across research-focused institutions.

However, years of dissent over impact factor's value and its dominance across the sciences has recently led to increased diversity in the sciences' adherence to the impact factor metric. In 2009, for example, the American Mathematical Society, the major mathematical society in the US issued a statement denouncing the use of impact factor for evaluating mathematical scholarship, calling it inappropriate in light of the nature of publications in the field.[3] By contrast, most biomedical sciences rely almost exclusively on impact factor for their impact calculations and evaluations. Thus, while the general rule about the dominance of impact factor in the sciences remains, the actual practice of using impact factor may vary quite dramatically, depending on the scientific subject's citation culture and the extent to which a scientific researcher's area of focus can be translated into a Journal Citation Reports (JCR) subject category.

Let's now take a brief look at some notable subjects within the sciences that represent areas of development or exception when it comes to the traditional bibliometrics paradigm.

Biomedical Sciences
Earlier, we mentioned that bibliometrics continues to dominate biomedical researchers' approach to measuring impact—a fact supported by the extensive citation culture of the biomedical field and the comprehensive coverage of biomedical subfields within Thomson Reuters' JCR tool. However, despite this dominance, it's worth pointing out that several attempts have been made over the last three years to get biomedical researchers to expand their use of bibliometrics by embracing what Impactstory cofounder Jason Priem has called the "spectrum" of impact.[4] In early 2013, the American

Society for Cell Biology released the "San Francisco Declaration on Research Assessment" (DORA), a public document that openly disputes the idea that impact factor can be used as an accurate measure of research or researcher quality.[5] Originally signed by 155 individuals and 82 organizations, DORA has since been endorsed by over 12,000 individuals and nearly 550 organizations, including many representatives from the biomedical sciences.

Other recent examples of successful outreach to the biomedical community on the subject of impact come from libraries. Of these, the most well known is probably the Becker Model, a freely available online project created by librarians at the Bernard Becker Medical Library, which is affiliated with Washington University in St. Louis' School of Medicine. According to the project site, the Becker Model is a framework for "tracking diffusion of research outputs and activities to locate indicators that demonstrate evidence of biomedical research impact."[6] Accordingly, the model identifies five types of impact tailored to the needs of practices of biomedical researchers: Advancement of Knowledge, Clinical Implementation, Community Benefit, Legislation and Policy, and Economic Benefit. By allowing for an unusually broad spectrum of impact, the Becker Model is able to recognize a wide variety of scholarly contributions, including gray literature, data, outreach efforts, and social media applications. Additionally, within each impact category, the model gives impact measurements to match specific types of scholarly contributions. These secondary matching features, on top of the five diverse impact areas, are what makes the Becker Model such a well organized and comprehensive impact tool for scholars seeking to discover new ways of demonstrating their impact beyond journal articles and impact factor. Furthermore, the Becker Model is an example of how more biomedical researchers are recognizing that traditional bibliometrics may not always be sufficient to tell the story of impact and that other metrics may in fact be more appropriate when tracking various scholarly contributions or the influence of research on a various situations.

Mathematics
The field of mathematics is a trendsetter when it comes to reevaluating how to measure impact and evaluate researchers within the sciences. As explained by the 2009 statement by the American Mathematical Society (AMS), referenced at the beginning of this chapter, math is not a field like other sciences: It's not as sensitive to new discoveries or singularly concerned with recent publications. It's not uncommon for a mathematics journal article to receive no citations for several years, only to become suddenly cited two or three decades later due to changes in the direction of the research. Monographs, specialized works on a single subject of a field, are still widely used in mathematics, unlike many of the more technology-dependent sciences, resulting in an unusual diversity in math's citation culture compared to other sciences. For these and other reasons, the AMS statement singles out peer evaluations—yes, qualitative metrics!—as the best primary tool for evaluating mathematicians and their portfolios. Personally, we find it interesting that one of the disciplines that arguably understands more about metrics than any other has largely decided to discard them. But again, the decision comes down in part to citation culture, and in the case of mathematics, the culture does not merit the primary use of bibliometrics or altmetrics.

Physics
Physics, like math, is a field within the sciences that can also be considered something of a trendsetter within the metrics and evaluation discussion, though in its case, the reason is less a rejection of citation culture and more the embrace of new methods of web-based scholarly publication. With the help of initiatives like SCOAP³ (Sponsoring Consortium for Open Access Publishing in Particle Physics) and arXiv, two open access models for distributing scholarly output, physics has largely escaped the traditional publishing paradigm that otherwise defines most of the discipline.[7] With this move away from the monopoly of print-based journals and proprietary models of publication, physics has naturally begun to turn to alternative methods of citation as well, such as citing prepublication articles in arXiv (where they may be easily discovered and referenced). Because the

sole metric available for arXiv articles is times cited, collected via Google Scholar, its use by physicists isn't a giant leap away from the use of traditional metrics. At the same time, the popularity of arXiv does show an important shift: The prepublication versions of articles uploaded to open access repositories are being deemed sufficiently valid to be citation-worthy. Not surprisingly, we are also starting to see more white papers (i.e., papers with no journal or editing body attached—a research essay, essentially) uploaded to and cited within arXiv as well. It is also worth mentioning that physics, like math, relies more heavily on monograph publications than most science disciplines and that the qualitative reputation of a monograph publisher is still one of the most popular ways that researchers "track" the impact of their publications.

Computer Science
One feature of computer science researchers that sets them apart from other groups of scientists is their output of traditional scientific publications, like journal articles and conference proceedings, and of original computer code. Code is a relatively new scholarly output from the perspective of higher education, and its culture of citation is very different from that of other text-based formats—in part because of its ability to quickly bridge the gap between the academy and professional (or even popular) audiences. Many computer scientists have turned to designated online repositories to make their code or research data freely available to users, including other researchers in the field. These sites, which include GitHub (code-focused), Figshare (data-focused), and Dryad (data-focused), help researchers track interactions with their submissions and produce on-demand reports of recent metrics.[8] With these resources now well known and used across the field, computer scientists can now track how their code is being used in ways never before possible. Should this trend continue, these repositories and their alternative metrics have the power to reshape the ways researchers share their ideas and tangible products, like code, with one another. In the meantime, however, they at least strongly argue for the use of both bibliometrics and altmetrics in computer science researchers' portfolios.

> "In the social sciences, the level of specialization, measured by the proportion of intraspeciality references, remains stable between 1935 and 1965... and then increases until the mid-1990s to about 50%, to drop again to just below 40% in the face of growing interdisciplinarity.... This means that after the mid-1990s, a paper in a given [social science] speciality is more open to other disciplines than specialities within its own discipline."[9]
>
> —Vincent Larivière and Yves Gingras, "Measuring Interdisciplinarity" in *Beyond Bibliometrics: Harnessing Multidimensional Indicators of Scholarly Impact*

The Social Sciences

Next up on our excursion through the disciplines is the social sciences, a group of academic subjects focused on humans and human society. Due to the looseness of this definition—an artifact of the genre's split from the sciences in the 18th century—the social sciences is probably the most diverse of all the major disciplines. Both methodologically and in terms of research output, the social sciences is difficult to generalize. Some of the more quantitative subjects, such as psychology and anthropology, require researchers to possess in-depth knowledge of scientific methods and facts, while others, such as history and communication, require researchers to be trained in more qualitative methods and theories, which might equally be suitable to researchers in the arts and humanities. As a consequence, certain subjects within the social sciences are occasionally grouped with other disciplines, and often share faculty with other departments on college campuses (e.g., sociology and statistics; gender studies and English literature; neuroscience and education). This tendency toward multidisciplinarity and interdisciplinarity also makes expectations for researcher output more difficult to identify than in the sciences or arts and humanities. Most social scientists have some culture of journal publication and citation—particularly those whose methods are closer to that of the sciences—yet monographs are also common benchmarks for productivity among the more senior and tenure-track social science researchers.

On top of this split between journal article output and monographs, which we saw to some extent in the sciences, social scientists also must contend with demand within their subjects for more specialized forms of research output, ranging from large original datasets to more creative works that draw on or build connections to society outside of academe. For these outputs, bibliometrics does not often provide a sufficient strategy for tracking impact, leaving many researchers heavily reliant on qualitative information or personal narratives of intent. In recent years, however, growing awareness of altmetrics and web-based tools for providing metrics has provided these researchers with some relief. Still, knowledge about altmetrics is still not widespread in the discipline, and many social scientists continue to look for reassurance from colleagues, administrators, librarians, and grantmaking agencies regarding the proper use of such metrics and how to combine them with ongoing citation benchmarks.

We will now look at a few specific subjects within the social sciences that illustrate and extend the issue of research output and impact measurement for the discipline.

Communication
Communication is, in many ways, the quintessential social science. Its scholars almost inevitably span the spectrum in terms of training, methods, outputs, and expectations for productivity. For example, the International Communication Association (ICA), the largest and most prestigious scholarly organization within the field, currently recognizes 21 divisions within its membership, including information systems, mass communication, health communication, public relations, visual studies, journalism studies, and ethnicity and race in communication. Within a given college or university, however, these divisions are often by necessity flattened into either a single communication department or a smaller set of departmental divisions, each of which must conform to a set of internally uniform guidelines as to what it means to achieve productivity. For communication researchers whose areas of focus favor more quantitative or theoretical methods, this often means journal article publications—although monographs are also common over time. By contrast, researchers who focus more on public areas of communication, such as journalism and public relations, are

often expected to produce a mixture of traditional print-based scholarship and public-facing outputs, such as press releases, speeches, newspaper articles, fictional works, videos, investigative reports, blog posts, handbooks, and more. In either case, the result is a highly varied culture of citation, depending on the exact nature of one's research as well as the overlap with other social science, science, or arts and humanities subjects. One just needs to look at the list of top communication journals in JCR (2013) to see this split play out: Out of 74 journals, less than six communication journals earned an impact factor of over 2.0 (8.1%) and only 33 earned above 1.0. By contrast, cell biology, which has a strong citation culture, has 139 journals with impact factors above 2.0, just over 75% of those listed in the JCR 2013 edition.

In the end, communication researchers often find themselves using broad bibliometric tools, like Google Scholar Citations, to discover their outputs' impact on their peers and colleagues and online tools, like Google Search, Twitter, Facebook, and website analytics, to discover the impact of their outputs on society in general. In this sense, communication researchers are already attuned to the value and potential of altmetrics, although their awareness of altmetrics as a movement and as a set of tools is still developing across most institutions.

Political Science

Political science is another field within the social sciences that provides an interesting case when it comes to standards for output and the measurement of impact. Like communication, political science encompasses a highly diverse set of research interests, ranging from theoretical analyses of historical intersections between power and culture to studies of contemporary political events and campaigns. As a public-facing field, it also is known for generating output that is frequently consumed by a mixed audience of scholars and members of the general public (albeit sometimes packaged in drastically different ways). Consequently, many political science researchers are expected to produce single-author journal articles and conference proceedings and track their engagement with the public in the form of television and radio interviews, social media engagement, blog posts, and articles or opinion pieces written for popular publications.

What's more, because of the range of interests in the field, there are over 150 journals with citation records significant enough to appear in JCR under the mantle of "Political Science"—nearly double that of communication.[10] To mitigate this host of options, some political science departments have taken to encouraging faculty to publish their research in a shortlist of highly regarded journals, which may or may not reflect the impact factors reflected by JCR. According to a 2009 study that surveyed 304 US colleges and universities, 21% of PhD-granting political science departments required scholars to publish at least one article in *American Political Science Review, American Journal of Political Science*, or *Journal of Politics*, despite the fact that none of these publications had the top impact factor in 2009.[11] Thus, while the use of shortlists within the social sciences ostensibly makes it easier for faculty to understand how to meet the requirements for tenure and promotion, the practice can actually discourage pre-tenured faculty from pursuing research venues that better fit their areas of expertise or that generate more citations on average over time. In the case of political science, the effect is also a general stunting of the use of bibliometrics and altmetrics when calculating impact, with the exceptions of times cited and easily collected metrics for web-based usage. For researchers with the desire (or need!) to produce scholarship outside of pre-vetted venues, both bibliometrics and altmetrics may come in handy.

History
History is an academic field that toes the line between disciplines, particularly the social sciences and the humanities. As an area concerned with the relationship between individuals and society, history fits within the definition of the social sciences—yet it is a field primarily concerned with the in-depth study of human culture, which is indisputably the domain of the humanities. Additionally, historians frequently borrow methods from sciences, particularly large sets of data derived from studies that relate to human society. This mutability leads to interesting discussions about the measurement of historians' impact, which most departments resolve by relying heavily on qualitative indicators of researcher quality, combined with some quantitative indicators of researcher productivity and, to a certain extent, public outreach. At the same time, the expectation

persists within most history departments that researchers with faculty positions will focus not on journal articles as their primary method of dissemination, but on the publication of monographs, like scholars in the humanities. For example, within criteria for tenure and promotion used by American University's Department of History, it states that "the norm in the Department, before tenure is recommended, is publication of one book… or, in rare cases, publication of a large number of articles in important, refereed, scholarly journals." However, it continues, "the Department recognizes that changes in the academic publishing industry have made it increasingly difficult to publish a traditional bound monograph in some fields."[12] Thus, the practices for measuring impact in history are centered on the "fuzzy metrics" of the book publishing industry and strangely inseparable from the use of metrics related to journals, journal articles, and other diverse forms of scholarly output. The use of metrics is especially noticeable for history researchers who work with methods or subjects that overlap strongly with the sciences or the more quantitative social sciences. Having noticed this trend, librarians at some universities have made attempts to specifically push history students and researchers to use at least citation-based metrics as shown by training sessions recently offered to history affiliates at the Bodleian Library.[13]

Altmetrics has also begun to feature as a discussion within the field of history—although less as a means of measuring historian's scholarly output than as a rich resource for future historians and social scientists who may eventually be interested in the studying early 21st-century society through the patterns in the information gathered by online networks.[14] The decision by the Library of Congress to archive public Twitter tweets, over 170 billion generated between 2006 and 2010, has opened a doorway for historians today to consider social media's value as a means of capturing trends and influences within the public imagination.[15] While this is admittedly a small step toward the adoption of altmetrics by history scholars, the existence of such discussions makes it considerably easier for historians with an interest in documenting the public impact of their monographs or other scholarly outputs to submit altmetrics to colleagues and administrators for consideration along with familiar markers of quality and impact.

> "The prospects of altmetrics are especially encouraging for research fields in the humanities that currently are difficult to study using established bibliometric methods. Yet, little is known about the altmetric impact of research fields in the humanities."[16]
>
> —Björn Hammarfelt, "Using Altmetrics for Assessing Research Impact in the Humanities"

Arts and Humanities

Last but not least, we come to the arts and humanities—the disciplinary pairing that presents by far the greatest challenge when it comes to the systematic measurement of scholarly impact. This is because both the arts and humanities place a high value on creative forms of expression, from written works and paintings to films and live performances. In the case of the humanities, this expression is an integral part of the discipline's overall interest in the ongoing production of human culture. In the case of the arts, creative expression is the discipline's overriding focus, with many faculty actively working to produce, perform, or curate creative works to achieve their own forms of critical expression. Still, while it is easy to dismiss the arts and humanities as "too different" from the sciences and social sciences to be part of discussions of impact measurement, to do so ignores the amazing diversity of scholarship produced by arts and humanities researchers as well as the real-world pressures that such researchers are increasingly facing when it comes to demonstrating impact for purposes of reappointment, promotion, and funding. As we will discuss later in this chapter, the arts and humanities are also disciplines that have a strong record of participation in interdisciplinary research, rivaling the social sciences, which makes their need to converse with other scholars about issues of measurement all the more relevant to their future growth.

Let's take a moment to look at two in-depth examples of fields from the arts and humanities that demonstrate some of the key ways that faculty and scholars measure impact in these disciplines.

English and the Humanities

English is a subject that is often used as an exemplar of the humanities, a fact that hearkens to its longstanding position as part of modern university curriculum (within English-speaking countries and universities, at least) as well as the fact that it appears, on its face, to be concerned with a totally different set of methods and materials than the fields that one associates with the sciences or social sciences. This reputation is based on a good deal of truth. English as a field is very much interested in the knowledge that can be gleaned from the analysis of unique written texts such as fiction, lyrics, and poetry, which appear rarely as part of research in the sciences and social sciences. However, like its sister fields of American Studies and Cultural Studies, English is also a specialty that has come to look quite broadly at the relationship between creative forms of human expression and human culture and thought. As a result, it often becomes difficult to separate English's texts from the texts found in non-humanities fields like history, communication, and even computer science. English's textual expansion has also inevitably meant a change in the methods employed by at least some researchers within the field. A core example of this has been the number of English graduate students and scholars who are active in "digital humanities," a recently identified disciplinary subfield that focuses on the intersection between computing technology and humanities research.

At this point, you might well be asking "What have all these changes in the scope of the field got to do with how English scholars measure and track their impact?" The answer to this lies again in the reputation that English has made for itself, this time in terms of the seemingly limited scope of its scholarly output. According to a 2005 Modern Language Association (MLA) survey of departments at nearly 750 four-year institutions, English faculty seeking tenure are required to produce at least one single-author monograph (88.9% of respondents at doctoral granting institutions), and nearly a third of faculty are also expected to have made "progress toward completion of a second book" (32.9% of all respondents).[17] This considerable pressure on tenure-track researchers to produce one to two single-author monographs in a relatively short period of time implies that there is no diversity in English faculty's portfolios and that other forms of scholarship, such as journal articles, are simply not influential enough to be considered relevant to evaluation.

However, in practice, such implications could not be further from the truth. English researchers frequently engage in multiple forms of scholarship, from journal articles and conference papers to massive digital projects and data-driven works that nod to the aforementioned expansion of the humanities into new disciplinary domains. Early career English scholars are especially apt to produce works that are less than full book length as part of the process of building up their professional reputations. Nevertheless, as of present, few English scholars, early career or otherwise, make the attempt to quantify their reputations through the use of bibliometrics or altmetrics. This gap will likely continue unless the availability of impact metrics specific to humanities' subjects improves—at which point, the humanities adoption of both bibliometrics and altmetrics might begin to more closely mirror the social sciences.

The Humanities Metrics Gap

One factor that helps explain the metrics gap within English and similar humanities fields is the seeming lack of support for arts and humanities scholars from within the larger impact measurement community. Indeed, the fact that Thomson Reuters, widely seen as the main bibliometrics provider for academia, does not offer an "Arts & Humanities" edition of Journal Citation Reports can be interpreted by some researchers as a snub (although the company would doubtless disagree). That said, it's worth noting that newer bibliometrics providers like SCImago have begun offering arts and humanities focused metrics, including rankings of journals within English's relevant subject categories like "Literature & Literary Theory."[18] Likewise, the 2011 release of Thomson Reuters' Book Citation Index can be seen as an acknowledgment of the need for better citation-based metrics for fields that are heavily reliant on monographs and edited volumes, yet researchers are still in need of quantifiable ways to prove their influence for promotion and funding.

continued on next page

> *continued from previous page*
>
> Altmetrics use within the humanities continues to be another area of potential growth, but it's not common practice, even though altmetrics offers numerous advantages for fields like English, such as the ability to gauge the immediate impact of books, journal articles, and conference papers through activity-based metrics like saves and downloads. By embracing these short-term measures of interest from across the scholarly community (or, in some cases, the public community), English scholars could help provide a counterpoint to the field's relatively weak citation culture—a weakness that has discouraged bibliometrics providers from creating or expanding their humanities metrics. At the same time, it is also fair to say that altmetrics providers have also struggled to promote the use of quantitative impact tools to an audience of scholars and administrators largely interested in qualitative assessment. Even the successful scholarly peer network Mendeley—probably the most humanities-friendly of the peer networks offered at the time of this book's publication—only includes internal records for a fraction of the articles published in English-focused journals.[19] Altmetrics harvesters similarly lack significant participation by English and humanities scholars, which has led to a dearth of development of metrics or benchmarks appropriate to the field and discipline. To quote Björn Hammarfelt, a Swedish bibliometrician who has authored of numerous works on the subject of metrics for the humanities, "The possibilities that altmetric methods offer to the humanities cannot be denied but… there are several issues that must be addressed in order to realize their potential."[20]

Dance and the Arts

When examining artistic fields' output, it's important to recognize that academia values the production of scholarship *and* the production of creative works, including performances, objects, exhibitions, designs, inventions, recordings, and compositions. Consequently, "the arts" is a phrase that describes a unique set of areas within higher education, in which both scholars and practitioners may cultivate substantial reputations and impacts.

Within the field of dance—one of the core performing arts—faculty are generally expected to devote their time to both scholarly and creative outputs. Within the scholarly category, one can see print-based outputs that are very similar to other humanities fields: monographs published with respected university presses, book chapters in edited works, and articles and reviews from peer-reviewed performing arts journals like *Dance Research Journal*. However, within the latter creative category, one would also expect to see outputs that are unique to dance such as choreography performed at national, peer-reviewed dance festivals; recordings of dance works distributed to the public online or as films; and faculty projects that have received grant funding from significant groups and organizations. Thus, while many researchers based in other disciplines may also be capable of producing and submitting creative work, it's fair to say that the arts is the only academic realm in which a mixed portfolio of scholarly and creative work is expected, if not explicitly required.

Another unique and important characteristic of dance and the arts is how academic members interpret the idea of impact and impact measurement. As a field with a weak citation culture (even more so than most of the humanities), dance is typically less concerned with bibliometrics than it is with qualitative evidence of scholarly impact, such as book reviews and peer evaluations of published work. At the same time, to suggest that dance is uninterested in quantitative evidence of impact is to overlook the many ways that dance practitioners have long been deeply engaged with what some call "fuzzy" metrics (see the "Fuzzy" Metrics—Non Citation-Based Metrics sidebar in Chapter 3). These non citation-based metrics are well known in performance-based circles for their ability to capture elusive qualities of creative works, such as the exclusivity of a festival (e.g., acceptance rate) or the comparative popularity of a performance's run (e.g., ticket sales or number of shows). What's more, fuzzy metrics provide faculty in dance departments with an easy entrée into the world of altmetrics as both function based on a broad definition of impact, including numbers generated by activities that go beyond the strict walls of academia. In this sense, it seems only a matter of time before dance, the performing arts, and other fields that toe the line between scholarship and practice begin acknowledging that activity-based metrics are relevant to measuring impact.

What about Library and Information Science?

So far in this chapter, we have looked at impact measurement through the lens of disciplines that librarians might be familiar with based on their teaching, liaison, and collections work. But what about the field that unites us all as professionals and researchers in our own right? How do our own outputs and practices as members of the library and information science (LIS) community measure up to those of the sciences, social sciences, and humanities?

Reflecting on this question is a great way for readers to see the subtle difficulties that all researchers face in localizing conversations about impact, which is an important topic of consideration for LIS scholars and professionals who must eventually face an evaluation for purposes of reappointment, promotion, or funding. One problem that most LIS members face early on in their careers is the sandwiching of "library science" and "information science" into a single subject category. Although these two subjects share a similar general area of interest (e.g., information and information behavior), they nevertheless possess remarkably different traits when it comes to output and audience, such as highly divergent citation cultures and different perspectives on the value of professional literature. This is in part because most information science researchers possess PhDs while the vast majority of library science researchers are practicing librarians who possess a terminal master's degree. While such differences are widely recognized within the LIS field, they have yet to be reflected in major bibliometrics resources like JCR, SJR, and Google Scholar—all of which offer users only a single consolidated subject option: "Library and Information Science." The result is an inconsistent set of "top journal" lists for LIS, which favors the interests and practices of information science researchers and largely undermines the impact of researchers who publish in library-focused professional or scholarly venues.[21] This oversight can have far-reaching consequences for librarians in faculty or tenure-track positions, just as it does for scholars in other complex fields that are not well parsed by bibliometrics providers.[22] What's more, because the vast majority of practicing librarians also produce and consume scholarly and creative output in the form of conference presentations, blog posts, unconferences, book reviews, and other forms not always well covered by citation-based metrics, it's hard not to argue that the solution to LIS's impact problem likely lies with getting more library science researchers and librarians to embrace alternative, activity-based impact metrics that can better measure our "profession of practice." We will return to this idea again later in Chapter 8.

Current Topics and Conversations about Disciplinary Impact

Quantitative vs. Qualitative Impact

In this book, we have talked a lot about quantitative methods for measuring the impact of print-based scholarly literature. But what about all the qualitative methods for measuring such outputs? Does the inclusion of bibliometrics in a CV, application, or portfolio distract from other methods of measuring of quality? Worse still, what if citation-based metrics paint a bleak picture of the impact of one's work relative to others' in the field? These are many researchers' anxieties, and it's important not to neglect them when broaching the topic of impact.

As we have seen in our jaunt through the disciplines, many fields reject the use of quantitative metrics like impact factor in researcher evaluations just as others demand their use. By contrast, we have yet to see an academic subject that doesn't to some extent recognize the value of qualitative indicators of research quality, such as external reviews of a work or portfolio by peers or equivalent experts in a field. This is because qualitative information is by far the best way of capturing detailed information about the quality of a scholarly or creative work, at least as it can be judged by a given audience. Quality and impact are related attributes of a researcher's output, but they're not the same thing—hence the need across the disciplines for both forms of research assessment. Thus, quantitative information in the form of metrics tells us as librarians and researchers something important about the *ways* that a work or other entity is being used as well as the *extent* it has been used within a given context. However, as we have established throughout this book, quantitative information is always open to interpretation, a critical lens that must be supplied through qualitative sources like comments, reviews, and researcher narratives. For this reason, the real trick is to find the appropriate balance between quantitative metrics and qualitative support to fulfill the discipline's demands while at the same time highlighting the particular ways an output has been impactful. This is why it is still important for scholars in fields with weak citation cultures to seek out metrics for their output. When properly understood, an output's bibliometrics may suggest relatively high levels of impact or may help reveal instances of impact that, in and of themselves, hold special value from a qualitative perspective. Altmetrics offers a similar advantage to researchers in qualitative fields, but it may additionally help support researchers in established quantitative disciplines simply by providing a different perspective on impact and scholarly communication. This is not to say that bibliometrics and altmetrics never paint a negative picture of a scholar's impact—no more than one could say that there are never scholars who do not produce impactful work. However, as librarians, it's our responsibility to remind faculty that the absence of a metric does not necessarily indicate a lack of impact and that to keep track of one's impact through both qualitative and quantitative methods can significantly increase one's understanding of how impact works and is cultivated in a field and discipline.

> "The changing relations between disciplines and specialties are obviously complex and can be affected as much by the internal developments of new concepts or instruments as by monetary pressures."[23]
>
> —Vincent Larivière and Yves Gingras, "Measuring Interdisciplinarity" in *Beyond Bibliometrics*

Interdisciplinarity and Comparing Impact Across the Disciplines

Interdisciplinarity—the combining of two or more distinct academic specialities around a larger problem or research area—has been a growing trend within the academy for well over a decade now. During this time, interdisciplinary projects have revealed opportunities for researchers looking to increase their impact beyond the confines of their disciplines as well as serious complexities for those seeking to measure that impact once it has been achieved. For instance, many major federal grant providers have made explicit their support for interdisciplinary research by creating funding opportunities that are specific to such endeavors. In 2007, the National Institutes of Health (NIH) spent $210 million to launch a five-year

Interdisciplinary Research program, which eventually produced nine separate research consortia, each of which developed integrated research projects, core services, training programs, and administrative structures.[24] Likewise, the National Science Foundation (NSF) has set up its own subsite dedicated to interdisciplinary research with the primary goal of assisting researchers interested in "submitting an unsolicited interdisciplinary proposal for which there may not be a natural 'home' in one of the existing NSF programs."[25]

With many researchers in the sciences dependent on grant dollars for their continued appointments and promotions, the emphasis placed on interdisciplinary projects by funders has proved to be successful motivation. As for researchers outside the sciences, collaboration with other fields and disciplines has afforded scholars in the social sciences, arts, and humanities with opportunities to distinguish themselves from their peers, while at the same time generating interest in their research from an untapped population of readers and publishers. However, where scholars from fields with weak citation cultures may naturally see an advantage working with those outside their domain, those in fields with strong citation cultures are more likely to see it as a disadvantage. Do you measure the impact of interdisciplinary research outputs by the standards of the contributing field with the stronger citation culture or by the standards of the field with the weaker culture? Are other scholars in a given discipline more or less likely to cite or read articles published by a team of interdisciplinary authors? Dealing with these concerns adds an edge to measuring interdisciplinary research impact, particularly within the sciences.

Luckily, several advances in both research and impact promise better near-term solutions to the interdisciplinary research conundrum. On the research front, numerous studies have been published about the strategies that different researchers have used to measure disciplinary impact, from bibliometrics sourced outside of Thomson Reuters' products to methods that look more closely at the disciplinary diversity of resulting citations and co-citations.[26] Within the world of impact, the development of network theory-based models like Eigenfactor (see Chapter 3) have also helped raise the possibility of creating percentage-based metrics that could effectively compare impact across a range of disciplines, at least for interdisciplinary articles. And lest we forget, altmetrics has promised from its very beginning to be a path to more discipline-agnostic metrics—metrics that apply not only to published interdisciplinary outputs but also to data sets, presentations, websites, and other forms that interdisciplinary research often manifests in (see Chapter 4). These broader altmetrics can help interdisciplinary scholars demonstrate impact to faculty peers and administrators seeking to evaluate their research, and they can also help such scholars effectively apply for new funding as federal grant applications increasingly ask principal investigators for information about their previous "research products," not just their previous publications.[27]

Although better opportunities and techniques for measuring interdisciplinary impact are an important part of the continued success of interdisciplinary research across academia, another requirement of equal, if not greater importance, is clear communication within interdisciplinary collaborations about the different definitions of impact. In the same way that assessment best practices recommend an up-front discussion between participants about methods and outcomes, researchers collaborating across disciplines are best served when they reveal the diversity within their cohort at the start rather than the end. As librarians and interdisciplinary researchers in our own right, we can help encourage these conversations as part of early phase project planning and help introduce new methods for satisfying the impact requirements of each stakeholder to the best possible extent. Frequently, the result still leaves open a small degree of risk, but it is a risk that is accepted as a form of enrichment, much in the same way that all creative endeavors require a degree of uncertainty in order to innovate.

Moving Forward

At the beginning of this book, we talked about impact as a word with multiple meanings, defined as much by disciplinary context as by different sets of methods and tools. In this chapter, we have dived deeper, discussing some of the ways that different disciplines approach the idea of impact, even within themselves.

As academic librarians, we are often asked by faculty and students to tell them what it means to have a "good" impact factor. While we know from experience that the answer to this question is highly dependent on a researcher's field of study, too often we neglect to go the extra mile and educate our users proactively about the factors that may affect their approach to measuring impact. Impact factor is an excellent way of broaching these conversations with faculty and students, but it is really only a small part of the larger issue of disciplinary impact. By encouraging researchers at all levels to think more critically about the type of metrics that may be most appropriate given both the norms of their discipline and the outputs of their specific research field, librarians have an opportunity to help scholars better prepare their projects and advocate for their eventual portfolios. Administrators, too, may see a benefit in having these discussions with librarians, especially if the library is seen as a center of support for faculty seeking reappointment, promotion, and funding. However, when speaking on behalf of any field or population, it's essential for librarians to do their homework by reading the research, keeping up with local definitions and expectations, and being sensitive to the diversity of scholarship our institutions are built on.

Further Reading

"San Francisco Declaration on Research Assessment" (DORA)
> An initiative authored during the 2012 American Society for Cell Biology (ASCB) Annual Meeting in San Francisco, DORA serves as a combined declaration and petition for better methods for assessing scientific research. It's supported by over 500 separate organizations and includes general recommendations for funders, publishers, research institutions, and researchers. *http://am.ascb.org/dora/*

Ehsan Mohammadi and Michael Thelwall, "Mendeley Readership Altmetrics for the Social Sciences and Humanities: Research Evaluation and Knowledge Flows," *Journal of the Association for Information Science and Technology* 65, no. 8 (2014): 1627–1638, doi:10.1002/asi.23071.
> In this 2014 article published in *JASIST*, Mohammadi and Thelwall take a much-needed look at the representation of humanities and social sciences in Mendeley. While the authors show significant correlations between Mendeley records and Web of Science citations, they conclude that overall representation of nonscience disciplines in Mendeley remains relatively low.

Björn Hammarfelt, "Using Altmetrics for Assessing Research Impact in the Humanities," *Scientometrics* 101, no. 2 (2014): 1419, doi:10.1007/s11192-014-1261-3.

> In this *Scientometrics* article, longtime advocate of humanities metrics Björn Hammarfelt takes a look at how well humanities publications, including both journal articles and books, are covered by altmetrics tools. Though the results are mixed, Hammarfelt concludes that the future holds much promise for adoption of altmetrics within the humanities.

Caroline Wagner et al., "Approaches to Understanding and Measuring Interdisciplinary Scientific Research (IDR): A Review of the Literature," *Journal of Informetrics* 5, no. 1 (2011): 11–26.

> In this rich article, a team of authors led by Caroline Wagner review research in order to highlight the many difficulties associated with the accurate evaluation of interdisciplinary researchers, including disagreement over definitions and issues of proper attribution.

Additional Resources
BLOGS AND ARTICLES
Mads Bomholt, "Altmetrics in the Humanities and Social Sciences," *Altmetric* (blog), June 4, 2014, *http://www.altmetric.com/blog/humanities/*.

> This special post on the Altmetric blog is guest-authored by Mads Bomholt, an Altmetric support specialist and PhD candidate in history. In it, Bomholt takes a look at the current and potential role altmetrics can play and how the difference between "attention" captured by altmetrics does not necessarily reflect impact in the field.

The Citation Culture Blog

> The Humanities and Social Sciences tag within *The Citation Culture* blog brings up a number of blog posts relevant to discussions of impact across the disciplines. These include several thoughtful opinions and in-depth recaps of ways the humanities and social science fields are being impacted by the development of metrics. ***https://citationculture.wordpress.com/category/humanities-and-social-sciences/***

ORGANIZATIONS AND GROUPS

The following sites represent past, present, and future opportunities for interdisciplinary researchers interested in seeking federal funding. Note that while this list is not exhaustive, it can be used to help educate others about the research opportunities specific to research across academic silos.

▼ **National Science Foundation (NSF):** Interdisciplinary Research *http:// www.nsf.gov/od/iia/additional_resources/ interdisciplinary_research/*

▼ **National Institutes of Health (NIH):** Interdisciplinary Common Fund *http://commonfund.nih.gov/Interdisciplinary*

▼ **National Endowment for the Humanities (NEH):** Digital Humanities Implementation Grants *http://www.neh.gov/grants/ odh/digital-humanities-start-grants*

Notes

1. Filippo Radicchi, Santo Fortunato, and Claudio Castellano, "Universality of Citation Distributions: Toward an Objective Measure of Scientific Impact," *Proceedings of the National Academy of Sciences of the United States of America* 105, no. 45 (2008): 17268, doi:10.1073/pnas.0806977105.
2. Richard Van Noorden, "Who Is the Best Scientist of Them All? Online Ranking Compares H-Index Metrics across Disciplines," *Nature*, November 6, 2013, *http://www.nature.com/news/ who-is-the-best-scientist-of-them-all-1.14108*.
3. "The Culture of Research and Scholarship in Mathematics: Citation and Impact in Mathematical Publications," American Mathematical Society, accessed January 8, 2015, *http://www.ams.org/profession/ leaders/culture/CultureStatement09.pdf*.
4. Examples of this can be found not only in Priem's in-person talks about altmetrics but also in his early published and copublished articles such as Jason Priem et al., "Uncovering Impacts: CitedIn and Total-Impact, Two New Tools for Gathering Altmetrics," *http:// jasonpriem.org/self-archived/two-altmetrics-tools.pdf*.

5. See "San Francisco Declaration on Research Assessment," American Society for Cell Biology, accessed January 5, 2015, *http://am.ascb.org/dora/*.
6. "Assessing the Impact of Research," Bernard Becker Medical Library, Washington University School of Medicine, accessed January 9, 2014, *https://becker.wustl.edu/impact-assessment*.
7. "SCOAP3—Sponsoring Consortium for Open Access Publishing in Particle Physics," SCOAP3, accessed January 9, 2015, *http://scoap3.org/*.
8. Impactstory has a handy chart showing which metrics are tracked by which repository: *http://blog.Impactstory.org/ultimate-guide-everything-else/*.
9. Vincent Larivière and Yves Gingras, "Measuring Interdisciplinarity," in *Beyond Bibliometrics: Harnessing Multidimensional Indicators of Scholarly Impact* (Cambridge, MA: MIT Press, 2014), 196.
10. As of the 2013 edition of JCR, 156 journals were listed under the subject heading of "Political Science."
11. John M. Rothgeb Jr. and Betsy Burger, "Tenure Standards in Political Science Departments: Results from a Survey of Department Chairs," *Political Science and Politics* 42, no. 3 (2009): 516, doi:10.1017/S1049 096509090829. In 2009, the top journal for political science according to JCR's impact factor was *Political Analysis* with a score of 3.756 followed by *American Political Science Review* with a score of 3.207.
12. "Developmental Criteria to Be Applied in Personnel Action Involving Reappointment, Promotion, and Tenure," American University, last modified February 2011, accessed January 9, 2015, *https://www.american.edu/provost/academicaffairs/upload/History-Tenure-and-Promotion-Guidelines-FINAL-2-5-2011.pdf*.
13. "Training Sessions for Historians," *Bodleian History Faculty Library at Oxford* (blog), February 1, 2013, *http://blogs.bodleian.ox.ac.uk/history/2013/02/01/training-sessions-for-historians/*.
14. For example, see Heather Piwowar, "Citation Data and Altmetrics for Historians and Social Scientists" (presentation, ScienceOnline 2013, Raleigh, NC, February 2, 2013), *http://scienceonline2013.sched.org/event/7b271b51cb628bb85699ad3e0c35ed6d#.VEGDUrywLuU*.

15. Erin Allen, "Update on the Twitter Archive at the Library of Congress," *Library of Congress Blog*, January 4, 2013, *http://blogs. loc.gov/loc/2013/01/ update-on-the-twitter-archive-at-the-library-of-congress/*.
16. Björn Hammarfelt, "Using Altmetrics for Assessing Research Impact in the Humanities," *Scientometrics* 101, no. 2 (2014): 1419, doi:10.1007/ s11192-014-1261-3, *http://uu.diva-portal.org/smash/ record.jsf?pid=diva2%3A703046&dswid=7195*.
17. MLA, *Report of the MLA Task Force on Evaluating Scholarship for Tenure and Promotion*, December 2006, *http://www.mla.org/pdf/ taskforcereport0608.pdf*.
18. "Journal Rankings," SCImago, accessed January 9, 2015, *http:// www.scimagojr.com/journalrank.php*.
19. According to a study conducted by Ehsan Mohammadi and Mike Thelwall, only 14% of the Web of Science articles tagged as "Literature" in 2008 were covered by Mendeley and only 4% included Mendeley readership statistics. By contrast, social science subjects averaged 58% coverage in the network and 44% of these had readership statistics. See Ehsan Mohammadi and Mike Thelwall, "Mendeley Readership Altmetrics for the Social Sciences and Humanities: Research Evaluation and Knowledge Flows," *Journal of the American Society for Information Science and Technology* 65, no. 8 (2014): 1630, doi:10.1002/asi.23071.
20. Hammarfelt, "Using Altmetrics."
21. For an interesting study of the inconsistencies that result from the consolidation of complex subject fields like LIS in bibliometric journal rankings tools, see Péter Jacsó, "The Need for End-User Customization of the Journal-Sets of the Subject Categories in the SCImago Journal Ranking Database for More Appropriate League Lists: A Case Study for the Library & Information Science Field," *El Profesional de la Información* 22, no. 5 (2013): 459–73, *http://dx.doi. org/10.3145/epi.2013.sep.12*.
22. As many readers know, the division between tenure-track and non-tenure track librarians and faculty and non-faculty library positions can be a highly charged topic of conversation, to the extent that even objective differences between institutions can turn into professional minefields. For instance, according to a 2014 study,

only 44% of academic librarians among members of the Association of Research Libraries (ARL) have both faculty status and tenure, while some librarians have neither tenure nor faculty status. Our goal for now is not to dive into such matters; however, we believe it is both fair and practical to point out that for a variety of reasons, some academic librarians primarily produce outputs that target the scholarly portion of the LIS community, while other librarians primarily produce outputs that are most heavily consumed by members of the LIS community and even the general public. For more information about the 2014 study, see Shin Freedman, "Faculty Status, Tenure, and Professional Identity: A Pilot Study of Academic Librarians in New England," *Portal: Libraries and the Academy* 14, no. 4 (2014): 533–65, doi:10.1353/pla.2014.0023.

23. Larivière and Gingras, "Measuring Interdisciplinarity,"198.
24. "NIH Launches Interdisciplinary Research Consortia," NIH News, September 6, 2007, ***http://www.nih.gov/news/pr/sep2007/od-06.htm***; "Interdisciplinary Research," NIH Office of Strategic Coordination—The Common Fund, last modified June 25, 2014, accessed January 9, 2015, ***http://commonfund.nih.gov/Interdisciplinary/overview***.
25. "Introduction to Interdisciplinary Research," National Science Foundation, accessed January 9, 2015, ***http://www.nsf.gov/od/iia/additional_resources/interdisciplinary_research/index.jsp***.
26. For an excellent overview of research on methods for measuring the impact of interdisciplinary research, see Caroline Wagner et al., "Approaches to Understanding and Measuring Interdisciplinary Scientific Research (IDR): A Review of the Literature," *Journal of Informetrics* 5, no. 1 (2011): 11–26.
27. The change in terminology from *publications* to *products* started in January 2014 with the National Science Foundation. For a short article about the significance of this change, see the highly cited and discussed Heather Piwowar, "Altmetrics: Value All Research Products," *Nature* 493, no. 159 (2013): doi:10.1038/493159a.

Chapter Eight

Impact and the Role of Librarians

"I ...am a librarian."

—Rachel Weisz as Evelyn Carnahan, *The Mummy*

And so we come at last to what is perhaps the biggest question of this book—what do libraries offer the world of impact? And how are we as librarians implicated in the making of meaningful metrics?

One of this book's central premises is that librarians play an important role in bringing tools and methods for measuring scholarly impact to the arena of scholarly practice. In the same way that librarians use their knowledge of research tools and skills to enhance the interests of users, librarians today have the potential to shepherd researchers toward the metrics, methods, and tools that best suit their short- and long-term goals. This is why the aim of this book (as referenced in its title) is to help librarians not only gain a foundational understanding of the variety of metrics at play across academic institutions in the 21st century, but also to encourage librarians to apply this knowledge to their interactions with constituents at their institution, all the time, at every level.

Now we know what some of you are thinking, and we want to assure you that "*Yes*, you are indeed ready to start meaningfully using your knowledge about scholarly metrics today." The fact is, most librarians already have the know-how and environmental awareness required to start applying new information about impact measurement to their academic environments immediately, regardless of whether they feel they have mastered the subject personally. Thus, in this final chapter, we review some ways that academic librarians can make a difference in larger conversations around scholarly impact, and we highlight a few practical ideas for effectively applying your current knowledge.

Librarians as Central Stakeholders

Throughout this book, we have hinted at the fact that many librarians are already engaged in the spread and discussion of scholarly impact. From consulting one on one with faculty to creating original online guides and workshops, motivated LIS professionals around the world are showing themselves to be serious movers and shakers when it comes to bringing impact measurement to academic researchers' attention. However, as we pause to consider the ongoing roles that librarians can play with regard to scholarly impact, it is worth considering some of the more fundamental ways that librarians, as a group, have positioned themselves to become major players in the development of the field.

Library Collections

Collections have long represented one of the best opportunities that librarians have for affecting the direction of scholarly impact. As we saw in the first section of this book (Chapters 1 and 2), the earliest citation-based scientometrics were created by researchers to help librarians make better decisions about their collections, such as which serials to purchase and which ones to cancel. The application of journal metrics to collection development decisions continues to be one of its touted uses as evidenced by the promotional materials published by Thomson Reuters.[1] As collection development specialists work to ensure that their library holdings are well suited to their users' needs, they may find it appropriate to consider metrics such as journal rankings, impact factor, SJR, and SNIP. Some scholars even argue that altmetric data like social bookmarking metrics have a role to play in evaluating journals.[2] However, as any good collection manager knows, metrics alone can never tell the complete story of an item's value within the context of the entire collection. In this way, the approach that librarians already take to the use of metrics in collections decisions has the potential to provide a valuable model for how researchers can use impact metrics to shape their research decisions.

> "By reporting altmetrics... for their content, institutional repositories can add value to existing metrics—and prove their relevance and importance in an age of growing cutbacks to library services."[3]
>
> —Stacy Konkiel and Dave Scherer, "New Opportunities for Repositories in the Age of Altmetrics"

Institutional Repositories

In addition to their core collections of research materials, many libraries have set themselves up to shape the world of impact through the development of institutional repositories (IRs). IRs are digital spaces that allow libraries to support researchers while simultaneously promoting open access. From a metrics perspective, they also provide the opportunity for institutions to capture unique information about how online users interact with locally produced researcher content (after it has been grouped under a unified, university brand). However, beyond the common mandates for graduate students to provide digital versions of their theses and dissertations to these repositories, many IRs suffer from low adoption and use among their own campus researchers. While there may be many explanations for this, one of the most likely is a simple lack of understanding amongst faculty about the benefits of placing research materials into an IR in the first place. In this sense, IR-based altmetrics can play an important role in incentivizing repository adoption as they can provide faculty and administrators with new information about the institution-level impact of works, individuals, or even whole departments. Analyzing IR metrics can also provide institutions with valuable insights regarding things like social media presence and "hot" papers (e.g., those most frequently downloaded or viewed). One IR platform, Bepress, has even partnered with Altmetric to embed Altmetric badges within its platform. All of these changes show how powerful libraries with IRs can be in shaping the future of impact measurement.[4]

> "University faculty, administration, librarians, and publishers alike are beginning to discuss how and where altmetrics can be useful towards evaluating a researcher's academic contribution."[5]
>
> —Scott Lapinski, Heather Piwowar, and Jason Priem, "Riding the Crest of the Altmetrics Wave"

Relationships with Academic Populations

Another way librarians are well poised to affect the future of scholarly impact is in their set of relationships with researchers, administrators, students, and publishers. At most academic institutions, librarians represent a unique population of academic personnel, in that their primary purpose is to support the needs of other academic groups, even when such groups may be in partial conflict with one another over the priorities of the institution or the definition of impactful research. Such support requires a degree of organizational neutrality that frequently makes the library a safe space for researchers, students, and administrators to engage in sensitive campus discussions. Publishers, too, are known to seek out librarians as partners in their endeavor to bring products to academic institutions, understanding that librarians prioritize the needs and concerns of the larger campus community, even though they may offer publishers personal feedback and critical suggestions. For these reasons, librarians tend to enjoy a trusted status within academic culture. This trust can be leveraged via outreach to highlight complex topics that require the input of disparate populations, putting most academic librarians in an excellent position to bring together their faculty, administrators, students, and publishers to help tackle issues of impact and emerging research metrics.[6] Furthermore, as more librarians have stepped into roles that take advantage of relationships with core scholarly impact stakeholders, developers of new metrics have become increasingly interested in hearing directly from librarians and in partnering with them to create new metrics tools and categories. Institutional altmetrics providers like PlumX (which, not coincidentally, was cofounded by a former librarian), Altmetric, and Impactstory have led the way in this respect as well as various sources of altmetrics data, such as PLOS, Figshare, and Mendeley, which have all been effective in their efforts to connect with librarians as partners and collaborators.[7]

Scholarly and Professional Knowledge

Last but not least, we believe that librarians are in an excellent position to be players in the future field of impact because of their own basic meta-responsibilities when it comes to engaging with information. As referenced briefly in Chapter 7, academic librarians are typically required to contribute in some way to the LIS field, whether that contribution is in the form of a peer-reviewed journal article or a poster presentation at a well-respected professional conference. The expectation to engage with information on its scholarly and professional levels has already paved the way for librarians to declare their interest in scholarly impact and to act on that interest in ways that will be openly recognized by their peers and evaluators. From this perspective, it can be argued that librarians have a significant head start on scholars who are situated in fields that have yet to acknowledge the relevance of impact metrics—or even fields that just have yet to recognize the relevance of newer impact topics like altmetrics. The freedom to adopt metrics as a research focus gives librarians the chance to move the development of metrics forward in directions that comport with the LIS field's rich understanding of researchers' information behaviors, needs, skills, and anxieties.

Moving Forward

Now that we accept the general notion that librarians can be catalysts in the field of scholarly impact, the next logical step is to look more closely at *how* librarians are actually doing this—asking the question, What strategies are librarians adopting to move forward the development and acceptance of research metrics in all of its varieties?

Identifying Areas of Support

Having a clear and comprehensive plan of support is one of the best ways librarians are preparing scholars for new advances in the world of metrics. As we have established, many academic libraries are already involved in supporting bibliometrics, whether it be through the purchase and maintenance of relevant tools such as Web of Science, JCR, and Scopus or through ongoing education in the use of these metrics-yielding tools. By adding more recent altmetrics tools and concepts to this support plan, librarians can help ensure that users will learn about the full range of tools and metrics that can meet their needs, empowering users to make choices that are ultimately best for them. Identifying areas of impact support also encourages libraries to prepare internally for metrics-related requests from diverse populations of patrons, from faculty members going up for tenure to researchers wanting to show the impact of their grant-supported research to scholars simply wondering if their research affects audiences outside of academia.

Here, however, we must keep in mind that offering support to library users is never as simple as putting up a list of links or publishing a few paragraphs of text online that can be left unattended for months on end. Implied in the step of declaring areas of impact support is the promise that librarians will keep up with the latest discussions within bibliometrics and altmetrics alike. Reading this book is a great start for those looking to get up to speed, but given how quickly the landscape shifts in this area, librarians supporting metrics must also make the time to regularly check new developments and update their internal service plans accordingly. At the end of this chapter, you will find our suggestions for avenues that will help you stay current, particularly with regard to the still-buzzing field of altmetrics.

Applying Scholarly Metrics to Your Daily Life

Theoretical knowledge is all well and good when it comes to scholarly impact, but applied knowledge is ideal for moving forward with the newest crop of metrics and tools. Librarians who truly want to get involved in the development of more meaningful, reliable metrics must make the leap from being researchers of scholarly metrics to being regular users of such metrics, at least as part of their professional activities. With this in mind, it becomes easier to see how the information covered in this book can be used to support the work of *other* researchers and librarians and support *your* work as a researcher or a librarian or both. We especially believe this is true when it comes to altmetrics because altmetrics tools and measurements cover works and audiences that are highly relevant for librarianship but basically unaccounted for within the scope of traditional citation-based metrics. If a librarian hopes to become skilled in the art of contextualizing research impact, he or she must put into practice metrics that can account for the majority of library science, including web-based formats and real-time professional opportunities. Once we embrace this principle, we discover that the search for meaningful metrics is not about questions like "How can I publish in a journal with a high impact factor?," but rather about the question "How can I demonstrate the impact of *this* work as it appears in *these* contexts?" For example, if the work is a librarian's presentation at a professional conference, the answer to this question might involve distributing an evaluative survey to audience members in addition to counting the number of attendees and related comments in online spaces like Twitter or the conference website. The collection of both quantitative and qualitative information can help librarians more accurately measure the impact their works have on a given audience. Uploading the presentation to SlideShare can also give presenters more metrics over time in the form of views, downloads, and favorites by SlideShare users. When combined, these diverse metrics can tell a powerful story about a librarian's research to a group of external viewers.

In the end, using both bibliometrics and altmetrics to support our scholarly output can add new and powerful evaluative measures to the field of librarianship *and* serve as an example within academia, showing evaluators that they must gain a basic familiarity with multiple metrics as a matter of course. Remember, the use of web-based metrics can demonstrate the impact of a librarian's work in new and exciting ways![8] As individuals, we can each serve as action leaders in this area, gradually leading other librarians to adopt many types of metrics to the advantage of the profession as a whole.

Becoming an Advocate

Librarians are natural leaders when it comes to issues like metrics as we offer a "neutral" perspective within academia as well as expertise when it comes to academic sources like databases. Accordingly, when we talk about becoming advocates, we don't mean that librarians should serve as uncritical promoters of bibliometrics or altmetrics for every institution or across every research area. Rather, we encourage librarians interested in furthering the development of meaningful metrics to become advocates by championing the *idea* of scholarly impact, both locally and remotely.

Advocacy for scholarly impact can take many forms and can be as simple as a five-minute discussion with a departmental colleague or as complex as a formal suggestion to reword an institution's criteria for evaluation at the administrative level. It can also manifest externally—a general call for the development of better metrics standards within academia or for a specific disciplinary subgroup. Moreover, while librarians can become effective advocates as individuals, the most powerful forms of librarian advocacy requires other campus and outside partners to be successful. Grassroots efforts in the form of "hallway chats" with colleagues is a good example of engaging campus partners as these chats can frequently build into bigger conversations and actions down the line. Outside partners can also bring a fresh perspective and increased validity to advocacy efforts. For example, at coauthor Rachel Borchardt's institution, American University, an effort by the library to host a series of expert-led "scholarly communication" workshops is helping to shape the conversation regarding the evolution of metrics while also reinforcing other library-driven advocacy efforts. Likewise, recent librarian efforts to partner together with altmetrics tool providers and organizations like NISO can effectively increase advocacy efforts at higher and broader levels.

Overall, there is no one right way for librarians to approach advocacy. After all, there are only a few things that we as a profession can consistently agree to advocate for! That said, metrics advocacy has the potential to be an incredible gateway for game-changing discussions of traditional and emerging metrics at the group, departmental, school, college, and university levels and beyond. This is because advocacy takes place not only within academic institutions but within the entire higher education community. Part of the reason we have written this book is to stimulate thoughts and opinions that will someday lead to better informed discussions about the future of metrics across multi-institutional groups and organizations. However, librarians first need to add to the discussions that are currently taking place, whether that's "at home" or at a national or international level. So don't delay, join today! You, too, can make a difference.

Surveying Support for Metrics

In Fall 2013, we conducted a six-question survey to learn more about the people who provide academic institutions with support related to bibliometrics, altmetrics, and research impact. In the survey, we asked participants to identify their positions, the types of metrics they support, and what they do to support these different metrics categories. We received responses from 38 individuals, most of whom identified as librarians or library employees (see Figures 8.4–8.6 for the results of this survey). While the results are not a definitive statement of library involvement with scholarly metrics, they do provide a valuable snapshot of what many respondents are doing to make impact a part of their respective institutions' cultures.

Figure 8.4. Survey Results

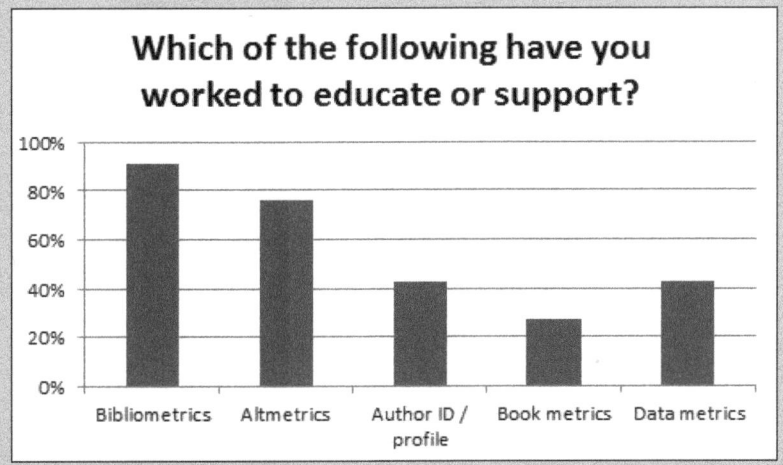

continued on next page

continued from previous page

Figure 8.5. Survey Results

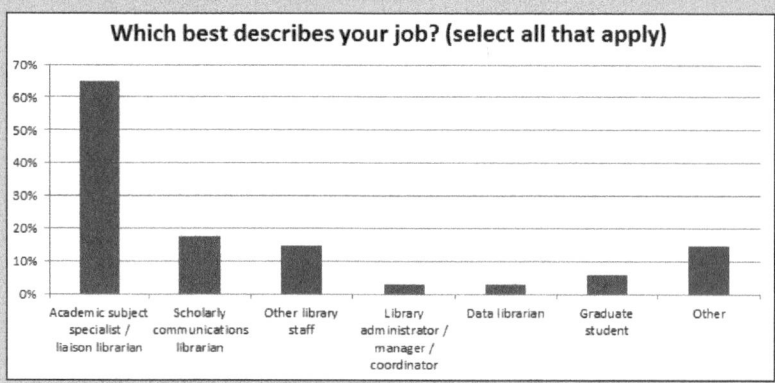

Figure 8.6. Survey Results

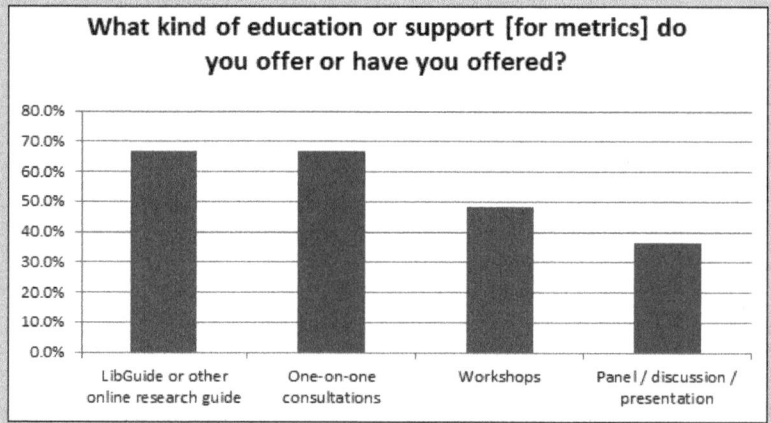

Readers will note that within the population of respondents, support for altmetrics was by no means universal. Instead, the breakdown of librarians who reported that they currently support both bibliometrics and altmetrics more or less mirrors the penetration of altmetrics within the rest of academia. Do these results mean that altmetrics usage would increase if more librarians supported it? One can only speculate. However, the demographics of survey participants do demonstrate that, at least for now, responsibility for metrics at institutions still falls mostly to subject specialists and library liaisons. If the present trend continues, it will be critical for librarians to strengthen their collective understanding of how metrics are applied to different subject specialities as discussed in Chapter 7.

Librarians in the Wild

The adoption of a strategic stance toward scholarly impact is a great goal for any academic library. However, as librarians and LIS professionals, we also know that sometimes it can be difficult to be the first voice—or a single voice—to push for impact investment within an academic organization. Thus, before we move to conclude this chapter, let's look at four practical tips that individual readers can use to prepare themselves to become leaders and motivators for impact at any level.

Tip #1: Stay Current

Staying current is an essential part of building both the confidence and critical awareness required to be an effective discussant of scholarly metrics. By reading this book, you have already taken a big step in getting up to speed on meaningful metrics. But reading a book—any book—is not enough to stay on top of impact for long. The cutting edge of metrics always moves faster than the world of print, and librarians must ensure that they remain on top of the current conversations through frequent online research. Blogs, for instance, including those listed at the end of our chapters, are often used as forums where scholars from varying disciplines can summarize recent developments, offer opinions, and debate various topics. Peer networks provide another forum where information sharing about metrics occurs; ResearchGate's Q&A and Mendeley groups, for example, are two very active spaces that fit this resource category. Following metrics leaders and toolmakers on Twitter can also be a way to discover recent developments, conversations, and updates from conferences that discuss metrics.

While online resources help readers stay on top of the latest changes in the metrics community, it is still incredibly important for librarians interested in the academic side of metrics development to keep abreast of its presence within the LIS literature. As more research about impact is produced, many questions surrounding the applicability of altmetrics and its relationship to bibliometrics will be settled, or at least more clearly defined. This is why that throughout this book we have tried to highlight quotes from recent works published by librarians and bibliometricians that collectively push the field of impact into the future. For readers seeking newer articles, we recommend browsing Google Scholar, arXiv, and the popular LISTA and LISA databases to discover relevant LIS literature. Some of the resulting articles may be peer-reviewed and published in journals like *Scientometrics* while others may be prepublications or white papers that represent research in progress. As always, articles released without peer review will require more scrutiny than those that have passed through a process of vetting. At the same time, as we have already seen examples of unpublished papers that have garnered significant impact in the field, it's equally important not to discount these unvetted resources out of hand.[9]

Conferences offer another excellent opportunity for librarians to stay abreast of new developments in scholarly metrics. Conferences dedicated to metrics do exist and can offer incredible opportunities for librarians to hear bibliometricians share research from across the field. A good example of this is the Altmetrics Conference, a two-day event that was held for the first time in London in 2014, featuring representatives from key groups such as Thomson Reuters, PLOS, Altmetric, Springer, and Elsevier.[10] However, library conferences also have much to offer librarians wishing to stay current about impact. The ALA, ACRL, Charleston Conference, and Internet Librarian International, all annual or biannual conferences, have recently featured one or more events focused on altmetrics and libraries or speakers from the world of altmetrics. But of course, the need to stay current with impact is not strictly limited to keeping up the subfields of altmetrics and bibliometrics, important as they may be. On the contrary, it's important here to note that there are many issues within academia and librarianship that have the potential to affect the future of scholarly impact, including, but not limited to, open access, data management, and institutional/government funding for academic libraries. To achieve a true understanding of what is happening with metrics, it's important to be aware of these related trends in research and to add them as factors in the makeup of the scholarly environment.

Altmetrics and Open Access

Although this book's purpose is primarily to familiarize librarians with the research impact landscape, we realize that impact affects and is affected by related higher education issues, such as scholarly communication.

As mentioned in Chapter 1, the methods that researchers use to communicate with each other about their work has rapidly evolved, thanks largely to online technologies such as peer networks, blogs, repositories, and even media hosting sites. As a result, some people in higher education have questioned whether print-based, peer-reviewed publications (with their ever-increasing costs and access restrictions) are still integral to the advancement of scholarly research. Is there a way to make more research freely available rather than force users to go through a paywall? Such questions closely mirror the development of altmetrics and open access, both demonstrating value in pursuing scholarship beyond traditional models of publication.

As we've seen, one of the primary ways research impact is measured is at the scholarly journal level, which is often accessed only at a cost that must be paid by users or academic libraries. If open access advocates attempt to dissolve the monopoly of these subscription journals through online publication, how can we continue to judge the quality of the resulting scholarly works? This is where discussions of both article-level metrics (see Chapter 3) and post-review practices come into play. For instance, while many open access journals do still offer peer-review as part of their publication model, networks such as Faculty of 1000, PubPeer, and Peerage of Science offer an alternative review service for those that do not, based on after-the-fact user ratings.[11] Some of these services also offer a kind of altmetrics by providing users with an indication of internally judged article quality, similar to peer review. Although these options are largely offered by independent sites that aren't integrated into altmetrics harvester tools, they will continue to impact scholarly publications and research metrics as open access options are refined.

Another similarity between open access and altmetrics is the concern they both generate over the "legitimacy" of their results. In the case of open access, the concern is over the possible proliferation of open access "scam" journals—something that is an unfortunate reality and can give

continued on next page

continued from previous page

some researchers pause when considering whether to publish in an unfamiliar open access journal. The fear of illegitimate open access publications is not unlike the "gaming" concern that has been raised by some critics against altmetrics adoption. However, just as safeguards are now in place within the internal monitoring of altmetrics providers to catch and eliminate attempts at gaming, a number tools have been developed to combat the creation of sham open access journals, such as the Beall's List, which identifies open access publishers and publications that seem to exist primarily to extract publication costs from authors rather than freely contribute to available scholarly knowledge.[12]

In the long run, open access and altmetrics have excellent chances of continuing to thrive, based on their reflection of the practical needs, desires, and interests of motivated researchers, librarians, and other passionate populations. Keeping up to speed on developments in both areas can give advocates in both spaces a much-needed boost. For this reason, we strongly recommend that readers continue to watch open access and consider its place in their libraries.

Voices from the Field

"Graduate students might be familiar with how *they* do research, but most have not thought about the science of science beyond seeking out tips from peers and mentors about professionalism in their fields. Including a few minutes to explain terminology such as 'research life cycle,' 'research products,' and 'scholarly communication' will avoid confusion during teaching."

—Kayleigh Ayn Bohémier, Science Research Support Librarian, Yale Center for Science and Social Science Information

Tip #2: Get Networked

Once a librarian becomes comfortable with the process of staying up to date with changes in impact, the next step he or she can take is to become more active in discussing those changes with others. Networking with other metrics stakeholders happens through many of the same channels as staying current, but instead of merely consuming information, the librarian is also actively reaching out to stakeholders and engaging them in conversation. This engagement may include asking stakeholders questions or starting a new discussion on Twitter, in peer networks, at conferences, or on blogs. Getting networked is also about developing new connections between the people in your existing network that may have an interest in metrics in one form or another. Such people may include researchers, librarians, and technology developers as well as evaluators and administrators (who are often, but not always, the same people!). Whenever possible, engage these parties in impact conversations and introduce people that do not ordinarily interact to each other.

Ultimately, there is no magic formula for creating a successful network. While there are designated online tools for establishing connections outside of your institution, creating links between yourself and other individuals within an institution ultimately depends on many factors, including the institution's size, culture, disciplinary strengths, and the opinions of its influential members. That said, by studying how librarians at similar institutions have successfully established networks, one may identify strategies that will work in a local situation. For this reason, we have included in this chapter two cases studies submitted by actual librarians who are already engaging with impact at their universities. To learn more about these cases, we suggest contacting their authors or getting in touch with other librarians in active roles related to impact.

Tip #3: Facilitate Conversations and Share Knowledge

Once a robust network of local impact stakeholders has been established, the next step is to leverage these networks to create opportunities for outreach, communication, and productive face-to-face discussion. Like getting networked, these opportunities don't need to be strictly limited a single academic institution—they can instead involve members of multiple

Voices from the Field: Jennifer Elder, Social Sciences Librarian, Emory University

Case Study: Collaborating with Colleagues to Develop Citation Analysis Services

Recently, a group of subject librarians at my university formed a citation analysis group so that we could effectively respond to requests for citation analysis assistance from faculty and students, and also so that we could begin developing workshops on citation analysis for faculty, students, and librarians. The group was led by a research psychologist from the university's Council on Library and Information Resources and included two science librarians and two social science librarians.

Our group met a half dozen times in the spring and early summer to discuss our experiences with offering citation services, such as requests to provide citation analyses for faculty members who were applying for tenure or promotion, requests to perform departmental comparisons of faculty based on their h-indices, and requests for help with tracking citations while in the process of applying for a grant or journal editorial position.

With all of these requests, we recognized some challenges. Common threads in our group discussion included realizing the need for the librarian to establish a realistic timeline for completing a citation analysis project as well as the need for him or her to emphasize that each citation analysis tool, whether conventional or altmetric, has biases and will produce unique results and impact factors.

We decided that these challenges should be major considerations in the development of our citation analysis services. We also believed that creating citation analysis services templates and examples would help us communicate more clearly with faculty and students. To create templates, we pooled the analyses that we had previously done and used them to develop a standard protocol and timeline for citation service delivery as well as report templates for individuals, departments, and institutions. Our group also decided to post citation analysis information to our "Impact Factors and Citation Analysis" guide, providing researchers with information about our citation analysis services as well as an overview of key topics in research impact.[13]

In addition to creating tangible products for faculty in need of impact assistance, our citation analysis group was successful in creating a community of people who could support one another when difficulties arose and who could proofread each other's citation analyses for accuracy. Furthermore, the groundwork laid by the citation analysis group has enabled me to develop new citation analysis workshops for librarians and graduate students.

institutions who share a common goal. One way to facilitate conversations is to start a working group, task force, or other productive committee. These groups can have different purposes, such as the dissemination of knowledge coordinated among group members, advocacy of policies or positions, or the discovery of new information relevant to metrics. Hosting a workshop, discussion panel, or series of events at your institution or in professional organizations is one avenue for sharing and creating knowledge as is writing and publishing journal articles, white papers, blog posts, or tweets related to metrics. Bolder librarians can also contact toolmakers via e-mail, in person, or through Twitter, encouraging them to address specific needs of academic users or to grow their collections of innovative tools and metrics. Finally, creating a research guide, handout, or even a listserv for your institution can help increase the likelihood that local metrics knowledge will be disseminated broadly. Ultimately, having a network of individuals who are used to being contacted and called upon to voice opinions places librarians in an ideal position to create buy-in for larger institutional decisions. Getting the balance of outreach and facilitation right may take some trial and error—but remember, small failures can be completely valid! It took the effort of hosting several workshops before one of the authors of this book, Rachel Borchardt, hit on the idea of distributing informational flyers during an open meeting of American University's Committee for Faculty Actions, a body that reviews researchers for review, promotion, and tenure. By doing so, she ensured that scholars anxious about incorporating metrics into their files would have access to concrete resources, including contact information of librarians who could offer personal assistance.

For an additional example of how you can use professional networks to disseminate knowledge about impact, we encourage you to read this chapter's second case study: a librarian at Kansas University discusses how she successfully implemented a series of hosted workshops by partnering with faculty members from within her established network.

Voices from the Field: Ada Emmett, Head of the David Shulenburger Office of Scholarly Communication & Copyright, University of Kansas

Case Study: Leveraging connections to maximize success

At my university library, we are always experimenting with new ways to better engage faculty on scholarly communication topics like open access and research impact. One of the ways that we have done this is to identify open access "champions," who then serve as faculty liaisons to our program in the library. These faculty, in addition to having an understanding of open access, are willing to advocate and promote projects and services that advance campus discussions and efforts.

Recently, I worked with a long-standing University of Kansas faculty champion of open access, Marc L. Greenberg, who thought of offering a workshop aimed at educating humanities faculty about the intersection between open access, research visibility, and impact. Together we codesigned and copresented a series of three workshops.

We advertised the workshops through a variety of methods, including sending an e-mail to departments with humanities faculty (using Professor Greenberg's extensive contacts and networks on campus) and asking our Open Access Advisory Board faculty members and open access faculty liaisons to disseminate information about the workshops as they saw fit. Prior to each workshop, we sent a handout to all of our attendees asking them to do some "homework" in preparation for the session. This homework consisted of setting up accounts for sites like ORCID, Academia.edu, LinkedIn, and Google Scholar.

The actual workshop discussion then centered on ways that faculty can use free and open online tools to increase the visibility of their research and also how this research visibility leads to improved research visibility and impact. Over 50 faculty members attended the three workshops, with one of the three workshops having standing room only. We have since been able to adapt this workshop for different audiences, including graduate students.

In the end, we learned that when faculty lead the discussions, give presentations, and help with promotion, we get larger attendance at our library events. Leveraging our network helped get more faculty interested in our workshops and contributed to campus awareness about open access and methods to improve the visibility of their scholarship.

> **Voices from the Field**
> "Graduate students are great candidates for learning about metrics. Training them to take charge of their own metrics benefits them greatly and can help the whole field of metrics progress."
>
> —Jennifer Elder, Social Sciences Librarian, Emory University

Tip #4: Think Critically and Broadly

Our fourth and final tip for librarians looking to get involved with impact deviates slightly from the previous ones—it's more of a recommendation for personal practice than it is for taking action. As much as attending conferences, e-mailing key stakeholders, and getting involved in committees can help propel individuals forward in terms of their impact empowerment, the best and most essential thing that each of us can do to become a productive part of scholarly impact is, frankly, to exercise our minds with critical thinking and reflective practice.

As you gather information about impact and what various academic groups are doing to help shape it, take some time to examine your own ideas, beliefs, and actions about research and communication within the context of librarianship. You may find, over time, that some of your assumptions about what works best for you or your library's users will change or that the support services you have long offered research stakeholders no longer match up to the needs they are expressing via your networks. By training ourselves to be open to change, yet conscious of tradition, we allow ourselves to strengthen and grow as librarians and researchers alike. Similarly, it is essential for each of us to carefully assess existing impact support practices, thus uncovering areas within our libraries that could be improved upon, reinforced, or even abandoned. Is your research guide still an effective tool for delivering metrics concepts? Has the attitude, culture, or knowledge level regarding metrics at your institution changed since the implementation of a workshop, making it necessary to overhaul its contents? Is it time for your library-wide metrics implementation group to reach out and coordinate with outside partners? Learning and creating metrics knowledge is only half the battle. Without taking the time to reflect on our practice, our time and effort can easily be wasted.

Questions are another excellent practice to add to your approach to impact and all of its 21st-century variants. Get in the habit of asking questions of yourself, your practice, and of others to gain knowledge and refine strategies. The simple act of questioning one's assumptions is one of the best ways of making progress in any area of life as it may lead to unexpected ways of approaching a problem or finding a new solution. After all, altmetrics itself began as a movement when 21st-century researchers began asking whether there was a better way to measure impact, and then sought to test the principle. In that same vein, we encourage readers not to be afraid to answer questions posed by others about impact and to challenge themselves to follow up on such questions with their own research and reflection. Developing strategies and tools is great, but helping others to create their own metrics strategies and tools is even better. Use your successes to help others succeed and your failures to prevent others from failing.

Finally, whenever possible, do your best to keep an open mind when it comes to discussing meaningful metrics. Considering the pros and cons of different perspectives on impact allows each of us to cultivate a more nuanced understanding of complex research problems and offers us the freedom to make connections between seemingly unrelated topics. Indeed, sometimes, the best opportunities for innovation arise in the unlikeliest situations. Consequently, the individual combination of receptiveness and preparation ensures that these opportunities can be maximized to their full potential. And while it's perfectly natural—and recommended!—to develop personal opinions regarding metrics and tools, we each must recognize that imparting these opinions to others blindly, rather than providing information for others to develop their own opinions, will ultimately be a less productive path to discovering the best metrics solutions for the future. On the other hand, if we accept that others may have different value systems regarding metrics, we can avoid pitfalls such as introducing the right metrics at the wrong time or forcing metrics into situations when they are more or less unneeded.

Final Thoughts

At the beginning of this book, we talked about metrics as a collection of stories—some about bibliometrics, others about altmetrics, but all of them about the search for meaning in a world of academic relativity.

Now as we reach the conclusion, we hope that you have gained a greater understanding of the metrics and tools that are available and in use in this search for impact, allowing you to tell new stories on behalf of your scholarly communities as well as on behalf of yourselves. We also hope that in this chapter, you have received some concrete ideas for how to move forward with this understanding, and we hope you will join the greater discussion about what constitutes the future of research impact.

The field of scholarly impact is rapidly changing and, to some degree, highly subjective. There are very few universally agreed-upon practices when it comes to the application of research metrics, yet many individuals and institutions hold strong beliefs when it comes to metrics' use and practice. As we have surely seen in our own institutions, the process of measuring the quality and impact of scholarship can be confusing, frustrating, and even potentially harmful when misused or misunderstood. However, rather than see this challenge as a barrier to the success of new metrics, we encourage you to consider it an opportunity—one that each of us can actively contribute to, making a better system for researchers, evaluators, and, yes, librarians, too.

Thus, we end with a call for many more voices and many more stories, each of which we believe can teach us all something meaningful about what it is to make and to measure an impact.

Notes

1. Librarians are identified as a key audience throughout the Thomson Reuters website, explicitly on its product pages and implicitly in its online white papers. For a recent example, see Thomson Reuter's InCites page, which lists librarians first among its targeted users, followed by publishers, researchers, and bibliometricians: "About JCR," InCites, accessed January 9, 2015, **http://about.jcr.incites.thomsonreuters.com/**.

2. Stefanie Haustein, *Multidimensional Journal Evaluation: Analyzing Scientific Periodicals beyond the Impact Factor* (Hawthorne, NY: Walter de Gruyter, 2012).
3. Stacy Konkiel and Dave Scherer, "New Opportunities for Repositories in the Age of Altmetrics," *Bulletin of the Association for Information Science and Technology* 39, no.4 (2013): 22.
4. For more information on the relationship between institutional repositories and altmetrics, we recommend the work of Stacy Konkiel, a former science data management librarian at Indiana University Bloomington, who is now director of marketing and research at Impactstory. See Konkiel's Google Scholar profile for a comprehensive list of her articles: **http://scholar.google.com/citations?user= eslVzYQAAAAJ&hl=en&oi=ao**.
5. Scott Lapinski, Heather Piwowar, and Jason Priem, "Riding the Crest of the Altmetrics Wave: How Librarians Can Help Prepare Faculty for the Next Generation of Research Impact Metrics, *College & Research Libraries News* 74, no. 6 (2013): 292, **http://crln.acrl.org/content/74/6/292.long**.
6. And because, as one altmetrics tool provider said, "[Librarians] get it!"—an indication that our receptiveness and understanding of metrics also makes us great partners.
7. As proof of Figshare's dedication to librarian collaboration, one need look no further than the "God Save Librarians" t-shirt they give away to librarians: **https://twitter.com/figshare/status/461056401268551680**.
8. For more reasons to use altmetrics in your own work (and encourage others to use it), check out Heather Piwowar and Jason Priem's excellent article highlighting ten reasons to adopt altmetrics: "The Power of Altmetrics on the CV," *Bulletin of the Association for Information Science and Technology* 39, no. 4 (2013): 10–13, **http://www.asis.org/Bulletin/Apr-13/AprMay13_Piwowar_Priem.html**.
9. A good example is Jason Priem, Heather A. Piwowar, and Bradley M. Hemminger's 2012 white paper "Altmetrics in the Wild," which has been cited over 80 times in two years, despite not being a peer-reviewed publication: "Almetrics in the Wild: Using Social Media to Explore Scholarly Impact," arXiv.org, Cornell University Library, March 20, 2012, **http://arxiv.org/abs/1203.4745**.

10. For additional information on the Altmetrics Conference, including recordings from previous conferences, see *http://www.altmetrics conference.com/schedule/*.
11. "PubPeer: The Online Journal Club," PubPeer, accessed January 9, 2015, *https://pubpeer.com*; "Home" page, Peerage of Science, accessed January 9, 2015, *http://www.peerageofscience.org*.
12. "List of Standalone Journals," Scholarly Open Access, last modified January 7, 2015, accessed January 9, 2015, *http://scholarlyoa.com/individual-journals/*.
13. "Impact Factors and Citation Analysis: Introduction," Emory Libraries and Information and Technology, last modified January 9, 2015, accessed January 10, 2015, *http://guides.main.library.emory.edu/citationanalysis*.

Glossary

acceptance rate. The percentage of total submissions that a scholarly or creative venue accepts for publication or inclusion. See **fuzzy metrics**.

ALMs. Abbreviation for article-level metrics, a category of altmetrics popularized by online scholarly sites such as the Public Library of Science (PLOS).

altmetrics. A set of methods based in the social web used to measure, track, and analyze scholarly output. Originally "alt-metrics," altmetrics is one of the newest additions to the study of impact.

Article Influence Score. A journal-level bibliometric that measures a journal's articles' influence over the first five years after publication. It is calculated by dividing a journal's Eigenfactor Score by the number of articles in the journal. See Eigenfactor Score.

average. The sum of all values divided by the total number of values. Used interchangeably with "mean."

bibliometrician. A person who conducts research in the field of bibliometrics. Sometimes conflated with practitioners of related fields like scientometrics, informetrics, and altmetrics.

bibliometrics. A set of quantitative methods used to measure, track, and analyze print-based scholarly literature; a field of research concerning the application of mathematical and statistical analysis to print-based scholarly literature. Sometimes defined as a branch of library and information science. The term *bibliometrics* was invented in the late 1960s as an update of *statistical bibliography*.

citation. A formal reference that makes clear the influence of another work on a researcher's new output. A citation should provide readers with all crucial information for identifying and locating the influencing work, often following a style guide's conventions.

citation analysis. A research method that examines a set of citations for frequency and patterns. Most citation analyses are performed on journal article citations because of historical practices in the production and collection of citation information. Citation analysis is represented in much of the research published within the bibliometrics field.

cited half-life. A journal-level bibliometric that determines the median age of articles cited by a journal in the current JCR year. It is used to help researchers and librarians estimate how long a paper published by a specific journal will continue to be cited. See **JCR**.

data. A set of facts, statistics, or items of information collected based on the shared possession of one or more characteristics. Just as there are many types of data, there are many ways that data can be collected, stored, referenced, used, and analyzed. All quantitative research relies to some extent on the collection and use of data.

downloads. An online altmetric that refers to the number of times that an electronic item has been downloaded from a specific site. Most sites that provide download information do not provide identifying information about who has downloaded a work, although some sites limit downloads to affiliated users.

Eigenfactor score. A journal-level bibliometric that measures a scientific journal's total importance. It is calculated by the number of times articles from a journal published in the past five years have been cited in a JCR year.

favorites. An online altmetric that indicates the number of times that an online work, researcher, or entity has been marked as a "favorite" by users of a network, who are typically registered members. Like many altmetrics, favorites do not necessarily translate across different online networks due to differences in scope, categorization, and audience. See **readers**.

fuzzy metrics. An informal term sometimes used to describe metrics based on data that is not directly drawn from usage or that lacks some element of precision relative to what it purports to indicate. See acceptance rate as one example.

harvester. A scholarly tool or service that collects metrics data from multiple online sources (e.g., ImpactStory and PlumX).

h-index. An author-level bibliometric that measures a researcher's cumulative impact on his or her field based on the distribution of citations that he or she has received. It's formula considers both the number of articles a researcher has published to date and the number of citations received by each publication, and uses these to determine a citation threshold (h) that only a certain number of publications can be said to meet or pass over (also h). There are many variations of the h-index, each of which adjusts the citation count threshold in some way. Also known as the "Hirsch index."

h5-index. A journal-level bibliometric that measures a journal's impact using articles published by a journal within the last five years. See **h-index**.

i10-index. An author-level bibliometric developed by Google that is calculated based on the number of articles published by the author that have been cited at least ten times to date.

Immediacy Index. A journal-level bibliometric that measures the average number of times a journal's articles are cited during a single calendar. This index helps give a sense of whether a journal is more or less likely to yield article citations quickly by publishing research of immediate interest and value.

impact. The perceptible force or effect that one entity exerts on another. In scholarly circles, impact is the traceable influence that a scholarly entity has on other research in the discipline, although it may also include the influence exerted by individuals, institutions, publication venues, etc. and on entities beyond the immediate research community.

impact factor. A journal-level bibliometric calculated by dividing the number of citations that a journal has received in a given JCR year by the total number of citable items published by the journal in the two previous years. It is traditionally calculated based on the citations indexed by the Science Citation Index and Social Sciences Citation Index, both of which are part of Thomson Reuters' Web of Science. See **ISI** and **JCR**.

informetrics. The study of information from a quantitative perspective. An umbrella field that encompasses scientometrics, bibliometrics, and altmetrics. While the term is not commonly used, *informetrics* does appear in certain broad academic journals such as the *Journal of Informetrics*.

interdisciplinary. A way of describing any research that requires the deep entwining of two or more academic disciplines or traditionally disparate fields of study. It is sometimes conflated with multidisciplinary research, which likewise involves two or more disciplines but does not require the same level of disciplinary cooperation and interconnectedness.

IR. An abbreviation for institutional repository. An IR is an institutionally sponsored online space that facilitates the collection and preservation of digital objects, typically for purposes of research. In many cases, IRs are managed by academic librarians, and thus can play a role in the library's commitment to issues of open access and involvement in web-based metrics. See **open access**.

ISI. An abbreviation for the Institute for Science Information, a company that was the forerunner to Thomson Reuters. ISI helped pioneer the Science Citation Index, Social Science Citation Index, Journal Citation Reports, and impact factor. See **impact factor** and **JCR**.

JCR. An abbreviation for Journal Citation Reports, a citation-based journal ranking resource published annually by Thomson Reuters. See **impact factor** and **ISI**.

LIS. An abbreviation for library and information science, a field now recognized by many academic institutions. LIS combines traditional issues of librarianship (i.e., library science) with evolving topics and theories of information (i.e., information science).

mean. The sum of all values divided by the total number of values. Used interchangeably with "average."

median. The number that appears in the middle of a list of numbers when sorted according to value. Median can help provide helpful contrast to mean when analyzing data set that contains one or more significant outliers.

metric. A standard of measurement. Metrics can be used only when information is quantifiable and available.

open access. A movement within the scholarly communication field that believes scholarly information should be made free online for end users to access, distribute, and modify so long as it is properly attributed. Because of its emphasis on online information and alternative publication models, open access is frequently seen as overlapping with the interests of altmetrics developers and users.

readers. An online altmetric that indicated the number of users who have tagged an item as "read," "reading," or "to be read." Readers is a good example of the difference between altmetrics and bibliometrics: Bibliometrics presumes that until a work has been cited, one cannot presume it has made an impact, while altmetrics suggests that the act of reading can itself be a form of impact. Similar to the "saves" metric employed by some online networks. See also favorites.

scientometrics. The study of measuring and analyzing science using quantitative approaches. Because of the sciences' strong citation culture, scientometrics is often seen as overlapping with bibliometrics. More recently, some overlap has also been recognized between scientometrics and newer impact fields like altmetrics.

SJR. An abbreviation for ScImago Journal Ranking, a journal-level metric alternative to the more traditional impact factor. SJR is based on citation data provided by the database vendor Scopus.

SNIP. An abbreviation for Source Normalized Impact per Paper, a journal-metric that helps researchers compare impact metrics across different academic subjects. SNIP works by calculating the ratio between a journal's citation count per paper and the citation potential of a journal's subject field.

social web. (1) The collection of online spaces that help facilitate social relationships across the Internet; (2) the social relationships that drive the use of various online sites and tools. The social web is frequently used in connection with discussions of online interactive sites, including, but not limited to, social media, blog networks, and scholarly peer networks.

times cited. An article-level bibliometric that measures the number of times an entity has been cited according to a given data source or sources. Times cited is classically applied to individually scholarly entities, such as journal articles, but can also refer to the number of times an author or a venue like an academic institution has been cited. Because it's impossible to accurately trace all the ways, places, and methods an entity can be cited, times cited metrics must be considered, at best, minimal estimates.

usage. The way(s) that something is used or instances of something being used. Within the altmetrics community, there is disagreement over what constitutes the valid "use" of a scholarly entity and how to differentiate between different types of usage captured by certain online tools.

views. An online altmetric that counts the number of times users have viewed a specific entity's online record; it generally represents the minimal threshold for online interaction. Because viewing an entity takes little commitment on the part of users, particularly if viewed only briefly, the views metric is most useful as an indicator of interest within a certain population or by the general public if not limited in access to one population.

webometrics. The quantitative study of the construction and use of information resources on the World Wide Web. Today, webometrics has been largely overtaken by the more recent term *altmetrics*, although it still appears occasionally in the literature and in bibliometric circles. See **altmetrics**.

Acknowledgments

This work would not have been possible without the help and support of many wonderful, intelligent, incredible people. While we cannot possibly thank them all, we are grateful to be able to acknowledge at least a small number of them here.

First, we would like to acknowledge to the many authors, librarians, researchers, toolmakers, students, and practitioners who have contributed over the years to the fields of bibliometrics and altmetrics. Without your hard work and dedication, higher education would not be nearly as exciting, and there would really be no point to a book like this. Our special thanks go out to altmetrics innovators Jason Priem and Heather Piwowar, who were generous enough to write the foreword to this book. Thanks, too, to the outstanding academic librarians who directly contributed to this book by sending us their stories and case studies, and who participated in our online impact measurement support survey. Your voices are at the heart of these pages.

We are also extremely grateful to the University of Washington Libraries and American University Library, for granting us the time and resources to complete this book in addition to our normal librarian responsibilities. Sincere thanks to the co-workers and colleagues who supported us with kind words and good humor throughout the writing process, including Nancy Huling and Melissa Becher. We especially want to recognize Alex Hodges, who was the first brave soul to review our full book draft, and whose patience and kindness cannot be overestimated. Thanks as well to the lovely people at ACRL Press, including Kathryn Deiss and copy-editor Katie Palfreyman, whose positivity and excellent editorial work were instrumental in bringing this book to press.

Last but not least, we are so grateful to our loving families and friends, respective and overlapping, for keeping us balanced and occasionally pretending to be interested in scholarly metrics even when they really weren't. Thanks to Jason Puckett, for giving us the courage to start this project. Special thanks to Adam Smith and Ryan Roemer, who are the best partners each of us could ask for. And finally, thanks to you the readers, for having the interest and energy to jump into the crazy world of scholarly impact alongside us. These are interesting times, and we look forward to moving forward with them, together.

Author Bios

Robin Chin Roemer is the Instructional Design & Outreach Services Librarian at the University of Washington Libraries, and the former Communication Librarian at American University in Washington, DC. Robin's interests include educational technology, scholarly impact, long distance running, and the great outdoors. She currently lives in Seattle, Washington with her husband and their small dog, Rusty.

Rachel Borchardt is the Science Librarian at American University in Washington, DC. In addition to research metrics, her library passions include instruction, assessment, and marketing. In her spare time, she enjoys Ultimate Frisbee, running, and playing games of all kinds. Her dream is to one day own a pinball machine, preferably Medieval Madness. She currently lives in Arlington, Virginia with her husband, Dalmatian-mixed breed dog, Rorschach, and two cats, Sadie and Cole.

Saginaw Chippewa Tribal College
2274 Enterprise Drive
Mt. Pleasant, MI 48858